AUTOBIOGRAPHICAL MEMORY

AUTOBIOGRAPHICAL MEMORY
AN INTRODUCTION

Martin A. Conway

Open University Press
Milton Keynes · Philadelphia

Open University Press
Celtic Court
22 Ballmoor
Buckingham
MK18 1XW

and

1900 Frost Road, Suite 101
Bristol, PA 19007, USA

First Published 1990

British Library Cataloguing in Publication Data

Conway, Martin A.
    Autobiographical memory: an introduction.
    1. Man. Memory
    I. Title
    153.12

ISBN 0 335 09849 5
      0 335 09848 7(pbk)

Library of Congress Cataloging-in-Publication Data

Conway-Martin A., 1952–
    Autobiographical memory: an introduction / Martin A. Conway.
        p.   cm.
    Includes bibliographical references and index.
    ISBN 0–335–09849–5 (cased). — ISBN 0–335–09848–7 (paper)
    1. Autobiographical memory. I. Title.
BF378.A87C65 1990
153.1′3—dc20   90–40787 CIP

Typeset by Colset Private Limited, Singapore
Printed in Great Britain by Biddles Ltd, Guildford and Kings Lynn

This book is for my parents, Maurice and Teresa Conway

• CONTENTS

• LIST OF TABLES

• LIST OF FIGURES

• PREFACE

I started writing this book when I was undertaking postdoctoral research at the Medical Research Council's Applied Psychology Unit in Cambridge. I then moved to the Department of Psychology at the Hatfield Polytechnic and, a year later, to the Department of Psychology at the University of Lancaster. Many colleagues in these institutions helped, advised, and encouraged me to complete this book. In particular, Debra Bekerian at the Applied Psychology Unit made useful comments on some of the early chapters and always found time to talk about research into autobiographical memory. In addition to this, the general academic environment of the Applied Psychology Unit and the support of its director, Alan Baddeley, greatly influenced my thinking about autobiographical memory. Ben Fletcher at the Hatfield Polytechnic encouraged me to continue with the book when I might have given up and, more recently, colleagues at Lancaster University have supported and encouraged me. I would particularly like to thank Alan Collins who read and commented on all the draft chapters and who did not flag in his attempts to teach me the difference between 'principles' and 'principals' – he, of course, is not responsible for my learning disabilities.

A special thanks is also due to Peter Hall who, as a non-psychologist, read and commented on some of the chapters from the perspective of a 'naïve' reader. He was kind enough to reassure me that his interest in psychology had not been greatly diminished by this experience. Other colleagues who have helped by their support and encouragement are Peter Morris of the University of Lancaster and Gillian Cohen of the Open University. The students whom I have guided through experimental projects in this area have always made me rethink assumptions I felt to be 'safe' and generally supported my belief that, despite the problems of researching autobiographical memory, the subject matter is in itself sufficiently interesting to outweigh more mundane concerns. Thanks are also due to Open University Press, whose patience over endlessly extended deadlines helped keep my stress levels to within almost manageable limits.

I owe my greatest debt of thanks to my wife Dr Susan Gathercole who encouraged, directed, and gave a sceptical reception to my wilder ideas. More than anyone else she is responsible for ensuring that the book was an introduction to, rather than polemic tract upon, autobiographical memory. Finally, my sons Jim and Steve Conway reminded me – just when I needed reminding – that writing a book is, and should be, only a small part of one's life.

• OVERVIEW

Why write an introductory text on autobiographical memory? There seem to me to be two broad classes of reasons for this. The first class is purely pragmatic: Autobiographical memory is a comparatively new area of research for cognitive psychologists and there is now quite a wide range of research scattered across different journals and book chapters. As there is no other text which brings together this research and reviews it for the non-specialist reader, then the present book would seem to meet an obvious need. The second, and more important, class of reasons relates to the nature of the area. Autobiographical memory constitutes one of the areas where cognitive psychologists have no choice but to confront aspects of human cognition which are often set aside in mainstream cognitive research. These are aspects such as emotions, the self, and the role and nature of personal meanings in cognition. Many of these issues feature centrally in the research reviewed in the chapters in this book.

Introductions can be simple or complex. Although the present book is designed for the non-specialist, readers who have some knowledge of cognitive psychology and the psychology of memory should find the book useful. Professionals in other areas who have some grounding in the study of memory, e.g. clinicians, educationalists, neuro-psychologists, applied psychologists, etc., will also find the material in this book highly accessible.

The chapters have been written so that each is self-contained and can be read as a review of a sub-area of autobiographical memory. However, the reader who does not have a specific topic in mind will gain a fuller perspective by reading the chapters as they are ordered. Chapter 1 provides an outline of various features of autobiographical memory which distinguish it from other types of knowledge. Many of the major issues which have motivated research to be reviewed in later chapters are also introduced here. Chapter 2 presents a selective overview of some of the early, and original, research into autobiographical memory. Again important issues which inform later chapters are introduced in Chapter 2.

Chapters 1 and 2, then, set the agenda and Chapters 3 to 9 provide detailed accounts of autobiographical memory research. In Chapter 3 the role of temporal information in autobiographical memory is considered and the extensive literature on this topic is reviewed. As in all the chapters the aim here is to give fullest coverage to the major papers. No attempt is made to review all the literature which relates to an area. Rather, the aim is to highlight the major theoretical concerns, describe, and evaluate to some extent, the relevant findings. Chapter 4 reviews the research into memory vividness and the nature of 'flashbulb' memories. Related to this, Chapter 5 considers research and theory into the role of emotions and the self in determining the nature of auto-biographical memories. Chapters 6 and 7 review, respectively, research into the organization in memory of specific autobiographical memories and the process of memory retrieval. In these chapters the idea that memories might be organized in terms of a *thematic* structure is introduced, as is the notion of a cyclic retrieval process. Chapters 8 and 9 consider impairments and breakdowns of autobiographical memory in infancy, old age, brain damage, and in emotional disorders. The notions of thematic structure and cyclic retrieval are applied to findings in these areas and developed in response to these findings. Also the role of personal meaning in impairments of autobiographical memory is considered.

Chapter 10 is rather different from the preceding chapters. Here the purpose is to identify general properties of autobiographical memory which have emerged from the research reviewed in the earlier chapters. Recent research which has attempted to investigate the role of autobiographical memory in cognition more generally, especially in conceptual processing and problem solving, is then reviewed. Speculations as to a general model of the form of specific autobiographical memories are briefly considered. Finally, we return to personal meanings and consider what type of theory might be appropriate for modelling autobiographical memory. In this section it is argued that the computational approach to mind, as currently conceived, may not provide us with as adequate account of personal meanings and, consequently, with an effective way of modelling autobiographical memory.

1 • IDENTIFYING AUTOBIOGRAPHICAL MEMORY

What is autobiographical memory? The fact that we use the term 'autobiographical memory' might be taken to imply that autobiographical memory is some thing or object, for example, some special and distinct memory system. Some psychologists hold exactly this view (see Chapter 9) and argue that autobiographical memory is, indeed, a separate identifiable area of memory. Other psychologists are not convinced of this claim and point to problematic types of knowledge that are hard to classify. For example, I *know* how to ride a bicycle, but is this an autobiographical memory? Can I *remember* how to ride a bicycle in the same way that I remember what I had for breakfast this morning? Is remembering that I must write the first chapter of this book the same as remembering my name? We will see in this chapter that there are good reasons for supposing that different types of knowledge may be represented in memory in different ways. It does not follow, however, that autobiographical memory is a separate and distinct type of memory. Rather, the approach taken here will be that autobiographical memories have certain distinguishing characteristics which they share with other types of knowledge, and that it is the *pattern* of these characteristics rather than any single distinguishing feature which help us identify autobiographical memories.

A further problem is that autobiographical memories also appear to take different forms. For example, I know the address of the house in which I currently live but I also have a vivid memory of the day we moved into that house. Are both these types of knowledge autobiographical memories? I know that when I was a child I went to a nursery school but I have no images I can bring to mind of that time. In what sense is this knowledge equivalent, as a memory, to the many images which come to mind when I think of my primary school, grammar school, or university? In the present chapter we will touch upon these issues, and in Chapters 6, 7, and 9 we will consider them in much more detail.

Two further issues which will concern us here and, indeed, in later chapters are the veridicality (truth content) and attributes of autobiographical memories. It is clear that autobiographical memories do not literally represent the details of an event; they are not like a film recording, taken by the brain, of an experience (but see Chapter 9). If autobiographical memories are not veridical or true representations of events, then what sorts of representations are they? How wrong can an autobiographical memory be before we conclude that it is a fantasy? Related to this question are issues concerning what types of knowledge are typically contained in a memory. Do we remember the thoughts and feelings we had during an event? The sensory details of the event? The time of an event? Providing some preliminary answers to these questions will allow us to develop a more specific idea of what is meant by 'autobiographical memory'. The present chapter is, then, a 'first pass' at some of these questions, which directly underlie the research considered in detail in the chapters which follow.

Types of memory

Many different types of memory may emerge even when we consider only a single event. Read the following account of a person taking part in an experiment and, as you do so, try to think of what sorts of memories you might have if you had experienced this event:

> Pretend you have been asked to take part in a psychology experiment and, also, that this is your first experience of being a 'subject'. You arrive at the psychology department ten minutes before your appointment. A secretary shows you where to wait and offers to make you a coffee while you are waiting. After about ten minutes a man shows up who introduces himself as the experimenter and takes you to the laboratory.
>
> On the walk to the lab. the experimenter chats about the different sorts of research going on in that lab. It turns out that the first thing you have to do is not an experiment at all, but simply involves looking at a video which shows single words one after the other at a rate of a few seconds per word. Each word is preceded by an instruction which is either 'read aloud', 'write' or 'read and listen'. The experimenter explains that you are 'testing' stimuli to be used with brain-damaged patients and that it is important that he establish that normal people can in fact carry out each instruction in the few seconds allowed for each word. The video lasts about two minutes and you have no problems saying the words aloud, writing them, or reading them silently in the time allowed. The experimenter, however, then reveals the true purpose of the video and asks you to remember all the words on the tape and what you did with them (i.e. said, wrote, or read). After you have attempted to remember all you can, the experimenter explains the purpose of the experiment and repeatedly apologizes for not revealing that it was a memory experiment – he claims that he did not want you to 'rehearse' the words while you were seeing them. You are then paid and the experimenter takes you back to reception. (See Gathercole and Conway 1988 for an account of this experiment from the experimenter's point of view.)
>
> Some days later, a friend – who is also about to take part in their first psychology experiment – nervously asks you what happened. You provide a

short description of the event, perhaps emphasizing how friendly people were and how undemanding the actual experiment was (possibly you can even remember one or two of the words from the video). You conclude that the whole thing was 'money for old rope'!

Consider now three features of memory involved in this experiment. First, in order to say the words aloud you had to be able to read each word and convert the visual input into sound. Second, in order to perform the experimenter's and your friend's remembering tasks you had to understand what they meant by 'remember', i.e. that you refer back to some previously experienced episode. Third, you had actually to recall the episode and provide your examiners with certain explicit information (the words on the video) or implicitly specified information (what happened). These three types of memory have been characterized by Tulving (1985) as procedural, semantic, and episodic memory.

Procedural memories are usually thought to represent information which is employed in fairly automatic behaviours. Tulving (1985: 387) characterizes procedural memory as the retention of 'learned connections between stimuli and responses including those involving complex stimulus patterns and response chains'. Procedural memories are not thought to be accessible to consciousness – although as these memories are learnt the information must have been accessible to consciousness at some point – and, once acquired, are thought to be difficult to modify. For instance, whistling, riding a bicycle and, in the example above, converting visual input to sound are behaviours which may be mediated by well-established, and difficult to modify, procedural memories.

In contrast, semantic memory contains information about states of the world and this information is in the form of declarations (see Tulving 1972, 1983, 1985). A much used example of a semantic memory is the proposition 'canaries have wings'; other types of relations also comprise semantic knowledge, e.g. a canary is a bird, restaurants have waiters, Budapest is the capital of Hungary, 'remember the words' means 'recall the words I previously showed you'. The important point about semantic memories is that they are consciously accessible and can be manipulated and modified. There is, however, one important similarity between semantic and procedural memories: we would not want to say that, when we say aloud a written word or when we understand an instruction, that we *remembered* how to speak or what the words mean. Thus a person whistling a tune might say that s/he remembered the tune but not that s/he remembered how to whistle. Similarly, a person responding 'true' to the statement 'a canary has wings' would not claim that s/he had the *experience* of remembering this fact about canaries when making her/his response.

The experience of remembering appears to be limited to the recall of events or episodes. In fact Tulving (1972) coined the term 'episodic memory' to refer to situations in which a person remembers an experienced event which contains spatio-temporal knowledge (i.e. details of time and place). Episodic memory is similar to semantic memory in that it represents information about (past) states of the world and this information is open to conscious inspection and, perhaps, to conscious manipulation. The two types of memory differ in that episodic memories are context bound, refer to times and places, and are closely associated with the experience of remembering. Semantic memories, on the other hand, are context free, the knowledge is not typically linked to times and places, and access of semantic memories does not usually involve the experience of remembering. It seems then that our study of autobiographical memory may simply be limited to the study of episodic memory. Indeed, Tulving (1983) states that the terms 'episodic memory' and 'autobiographical memory' are equivalent. Moreover, as episodic memory has been extensively researched by psychologists, we should be in a position to provide a fairly full account of autobiographical memory. Such, however, is not the case and there are a number of reasons for this.

One of the principal problems is that the term 'episodic memory' has come to refer to a particular way of studying memory. In the example experiment above, the experimenter (after a delay of a few minutes) asks the 'subject' to remember the words in the video. This is a paradigm case of episodic memory and contains a number of features which will help us characterize episodic memory. To begin with, the study of episodic memory often – but by no means always – features memory-for-words lists. Memory is assessed either immediately or after some, usually short, delay – say a few minutes or hours. Most importantly, the aspect of the episode which the experimenter selects for study is carefully controlled so that the experimenter can be fairly sure how each subject processed the stimuli. In fact, the usual way this is achieved is by ensuring that it is immensely difficult for the subject to carry out any elaborate or meaningful processing of the stimuli. Similarly, the memory test removes any possible interpretation the subject might want to place on the episode – i.e. that it was easy. Thus episodic memory, as this had been studied by psychologists, might be thought of as a part of autobiographical memory: as the study of special events which have been carefully designed to minimize the degrees of freedom the person has in responding to details of the event. Moreover, the experimenter only ever examines memory for a very delimited set of event features. As useful as the study of episodic memory has been in exploring aspects of memory, the fact remains that in autobiographical memory many other aspects of events – which are not usually studied in the laboratory, indeed in many cases *cannot* be studied in the laboratory – are critical to remembering.

An additional problem is that, although it might be maintained that episodic memory is distinct from other types of memory, i.e. semantic memory, this strict division of knowledge cannot be maintained for autobiographical memory. For instance, it may be that a person owns a car and can respond very rapidly to the query 'Do you own a car?'. We would clearly want to claim that the person was drawing upon autobiographical knowledge but we would not want to argue that a specific memory was accessed in the process of question answering. Perhaps a person in answering this question was drawing upon factual autobiographical knowledge (Conway 1987). Thus autobiographical memory includes memories for specific experiences and memory for the personal facts of one's life.

A further difference is that autobiographical memories for specific experiences represent interpretations of complex events which are extended in time and may feature multiple actors and locations (e.g. a memory of one's wedding day, first day in a new job, etc.). Remembering these events may take place soon after the event but usually takes place days, months and years later and the constraints upon the act of remembering may be rather nebulous (i.e. What happened? What was it like?). In the example experiment, above, fairly recent or immediate memory for explicitly specified micro-details of the event, characterize the episodic memory of the experiment. Long-term recollection of general features of the event, interpretations, and some recall of a few specific details characterize the autobiographical memory of the experiment. Obviously both types of memory are 'autobiographical' in the sense that they both involve context-bound information and conscious recollection – the experience of remembering – but it is the latter type which psychologists have singled out as being autobiographical memories. These distinctions between episodic, and autobiographical memories, suggest that autobiographical, but not episodic, memory may be subdivided further.

Types of autobiographical memory

Curiously, few psychologists have attempted to subdivide autobiographical memories into types. Possibly this is because simply not enough is known about autobiographical memory to make this a worthwhile exercise or the task, to be feasible, requires the application of an abstract or general model of memory which does not yet exist. In this section two classificatory schemes are considered. The first, proposed by Brewer (1986), assumes that autobiographical memories are distinct from other types of memories because of their self-reference. Within this class of memories with direct self-reference Brewer distinguishes between image and non-image based memories of repeated and single events. The second scheme is derived from Johnson's (1983, 1985) multiple-entry modular memory system (MEM). The MEM model proposes that the memory system as a whole has evolved as a set of separate sub-systems. Experienced events are encoded to varying degrees in all sub-systems and the extent and nature of these multiple encodings can lead to memories of different types and, in particular, to different types of autobiographical memories. We shall see that both these approaches help sharpen our thinking about the nature of autobiographical memory and draw attention to important properties of different types of memories.

Brewer (1986: 29) identifies four classes of autobiographical memory and a number of other classes of non-autobiographical memory, some of which will be described below. The essential underlying theme of Brewer's classification is that autobiographical memories are autobiographical to the extent that they entail information related to the self. As Brewer goes on to point out, this characterization is not particularly useful unless one has at least some idea of what the term 'self' means (we shall see in Chapter 5 that this is in fact something of a problem).

Brewer offers the following preliminary sketch of the self, 'the self is composed of an experiencing ego, a self-schema, and an associated set of personal memories and autobiographical facts' (1986: 27). The ego is characterized as a conscious experiencing entity and it is memory of the ego's experience which we designate by the term autobiographical memory. The self-schema is described as a generic cognitive structure containing information about one's self. Just as we may have semantic knowledge, say, about capital cities, so we have generic (semantic) knowledge about ourselves, e.g. personal goals, attitudes, preferences, etc.

The classification of autobiographical memory which follows from this is based in part on the degree of ego-self involvement, in part on the means of acquisition, that is whether an event is repeatedly experienced or not, and in part on whether the memory is image based or not. A *personal memory* is an imaged-based representation of a single unrepeated event, for example, a memory of having taken part in an experiment. An *autobiographical fact* is formally identical to a personal memory with the exception that the memory is not image based. An autobiographical fact, then, would allow a person to answer 'Yes' to the question 'Did you take part in an experiment this morning?' *without* that person's having to retrieve images of the event (although, of course, this might occur anyway). A *generic personal memory* is also formally similar to a personal memory but differs in that the repeated event or series of similar events is represented in a more abstract form that that corresponding to personal memories. For example, if a person had taken part in many experiments, then his or her memory of any particular experiment might be difficult to date exactly, might not contain any distinguishing features, but may include general features of all experiments and some general details of the specific experiment the person was trying to remember. Non-imaginal generic memories are classified as part of the self-schema and presumably represent highly abstracted personal knowledge taken from repeated experiences, e.g. 'I'm the sort of person who volunteers to take part in scientific research.'

One of the advantages of this approach is that it allows some gradation of auto-biographical memories in terms of self-reference. Thus, by this approach, it might be argued that the principal difference between recall of a word list (an episodic memory) and recall of the experimental episode as a whole (an autobiographical memory) is that the former entails less ego-self involvement than the latter. In this way then elaborate knowledge structures relating to the self and ego experiences are brought to bear more fully on the experience of the experiment as a whole. In fact, given that the word list in the example experiment was constructed to minimize the amount of meaningful processing a person could bring to bear on these stimuli, then complex knowledge structures would probably have struggled to impose any deep processing on this aspect of the experiment – this was, of course, exactly what the experiment was designed to do!

But how far does this classification of autobiographical memories in terms of degree of self-reference get us? The answer is 'some way . . . but not any great distance'. The reason for this is that the self-reference approach merely rewords the problem of what makes autobiographical memories autobiographical into 'what do we mean by ego-self involvement?' We shall see in Chapter 5 that some notion of the self is critical to under-standing autobiographical memory but also that the status of the 'self' as an explanatory concept is highly dubious. It is simply not clear what this term means and it is of little help to state that the self is an elaborate knowledge structure. Nevertheless, the self-reference approach provides us with one further characteristic of autobiographical memories, namely that, in comparison to other memories, personal memories will entail a greater degree of self-reference. Just how this characteristic might be further specified will be considered in Chapter 5.

What of the other aspects of autobiographical memory singled out by Brewer? Consider the notions of single-versus-repeated experiences and imaginal-versus-non-imaginal memories. It seems unlikely that a single experience which is memorable would ever be represented non-imaginally. In fact, Brewer's own example of a non-imaginal autobiographical fact (having breakfast this morning) is of a repeated experience. Yet there may be a number of issues involved here. Undoubtedly auto-biographical memories are complex representations containing many different sorts of information, and information in these memories may be accessible in different ways. For example, if you ask me did I have breakfast this morning, maybe I can answer by inferring that, as I always have breakfast, the answer must be 'Yes' and so no autobiographical memory need be accessed. Alternatively, I might do a fast memory check which simply verifies that I have some memory of having eaten early in the day and so answer 'Yes'. But if you ask me 'What happened at breakfast this morning?', then perhaps I would access the same memory, only this time I would generate images of the event and base my answer on these. Thus memories of single experiences may be accessed in different ways and it is the access process which determines imaginal or non-imaginal instantiation of the memory. Indeed, in Chapter 9 we will see that there is some clinical evidence demonstrating that 'forgotten' memories may come to mind after brain injury. Prior to the 'return' of these memories, it seems possible that patients had only autobiographical factual knowledge relating to the events subsequently remembered. In short, image and non-image-based representations of experienced events may entail complex process-ing sequences which are highly sensitive to task demands and have little to do with the underlying nature of autobiographical memories.

So far, we have seen that autobiographical memories may be identified by their self-reference and by virtue of being interpretations of complex events. Johnson's (1983, 1985) approach to autobiographical memory adds a number of other features to our putative classification of these memories. One of the central concerns of Johnson's (1983) multiple-entry MEM is to specify the types of information which a memory might contain. According to the MEM model there are (at least) three basic memory sub-systems – the sensory, perceptual and reflective. The sensory memory sub-system contains information about elementary aspects of perception such as object brightness, direction of movement, size, shape and so on. Johnson (1985) suggests that this sub-system may represent information which supports the operation of various motor skills (procedural memory). The perceptual memory sub-system represents high-level per-ceptual information such as the conscious experience of an array of objects. The reflec-tion sub-system represents information about internally generated events such as think-ing, imagining and planning. According to Johnson (1985: 17) the reflection sub-system records 'our attempts to control what happens to us and our commentary on the events that do happen to us'.

The MEM model proposes that all memories are represented in the various sub-systems but that the extent of representation of any single memory in any single sub-system varies with the nature of the precipitating event. To illustrate this let's try an experiment:

First of all, form an image of the following event: The marriage ceremony of Henry VIII to Anne Boleyn. As soon as you have your image forget it! The best way to do this is to engage in some other activity so, given that A = 1 and Z = 26, work out the value of the last four words in this sentence.

Now bring to mind – in the form of an image – a scene you remember from a wedding ceremony which you personally attended. After you've done this recall your image of Henry and Anne's wedding.

According to the MEM model, your memories – one of the imagined wedding and one of the wedding you actually attended – should differ in a number of interesting ways. The representation of the imagined wedding is primarily in the reflection sub-system, although, as the image involved some perceptual information, the memory will also be represented, but to a lesser extent, in the perceptual and sensory sub-systems. In contrast, your memory of the wedding you actually attended will be extensively represented in the perceptual and sensory sub-systems and will also have some representation in the reflection system.

Given this classification then, we might expect that the two memories would contain different sorts of features and Johnson (1985) conducted an experiment to examine this issue. In Johnson's experiment subjects were asked to remember perceived events (i.e. ones they had actually experienced) and events they had only imagined (e.g. dreams, fantasies, unfulfilled intentions). Subjects were then asked to say how they knew that the perceived events had in fact happened and how they knew that the imagined events had not in fact happened. What sorts of information would you use to answer these questions if they were asked about the 'wedding' experiment above?

Johnson's subjects showed a very clear pattern in their answers: perceived events were described in terms of properties of the event such as when the event happened and sensory details such as the colour of a person's clothes. A further large class of responses to perceived memories was in terms of the relation of the remembered event to other memories, e.g. other events occurring close to the target event. Thus autobiographical memories of perceived events were found to contain features which indicated extensive representation of the memory in the perceptual and sensory sub-systems and in the reflection sub-system (i.e. how the memory related to other memories). The features of memories of imagined events were, however, quite different and the predominant feature of these memories was that of extended reasoning. For example, a subject might argue that a remembered event violated the laws of physics, and therefore could not have happened, or that the memory violated some aspect of general knowledge (see Johnson 1985: 11). Thus memories of events which did not occur may be principally represented in the reflection sub-system and have few representations in the sensory and perceptual sub-systems (see also Johnson, Foley, Suengas, and Raye 1988).

The ideas of Brewer (1986) and Johnson (1985), in conjunction with the earlier distinctions between different classes of memories, suggest a growing list of features which may help us identify autobiographical memories. To begin with, autobiographical memories will typically be of complex events (e.g. a wedding), will contain high self-reference, will usually feature sensory, perceptual and reflective information fairly equally, and will be closely related to other memories. Any of these features taken on their own could apply to many different (non-autobiographical) classes of memory but the whole set of features would closely apply to autobiographical memories only. The next two sections examine two further aspects of autobiographical memories and we will then be in a position to consider a full list of features which will aid us in identifying autobiographical memories generally.

Are autobiographical memories 'true'?

In the last section we touched upon the topic of how people might distinguish between memories for events which have actually occurred and memories for events which did not occur (e.g. imagined events – see Johnson and Raye 1981 and Johnson *et al.* 1988 for further discussions of this issue). In autobiographical memory, however, it is not usually the case that a memory is completely false but rather that a memory relates to an event which did occur but not exactly as remembered. The present section is, then, concerned with the veridicality or truth content of autobiographical memories. As we shall see, however, it may be an important feature of autobiographical memories that they are never true in the sense that they are literal representations of events, and in this respect it makes little sense to ask whether an autobiographical memory is true or false. Nevertheless, autobiographical memories may be accurate without being literal and may represent the personal meaning of an event at the expense of accuracy.

In fact there has been little research into the issue of the veridicality of autobiographical memories, although it is a topic which has preoccupied philosophers for many centuries (cf. Brewer 1986 for further comments). Nevertheless there are some notable examples of erroneous autobiographical memories and these suggest a rather interesting aspect of autobiographical memory. Consider the following memory related by Johnson (1985):

> My family was driving through the San Joaquin Valley in California when we had a flat tire. We didn't have a spare, so my father took the tire off the car and hitchhiked up the road to a gas station to get the tire patched. My mother, brother, sister, and I waited in the car. The temperature was over 100 degrees, extremely uncomfortable, and we got very thirsty. Finally, my sister took a couple of empty pop bottles and walked up the road to a farmhouse. The woman who lived there explained to her that the valley was suffering from a drought and she only had a little bottled-water left. She set aside a glass of water for her little boy, who would be home from school soon, and filled up my sister's pop bottles with the rest. My sister brought the water back to the car and we drank it all. I also remembered feeling guilty that we didn't save any for my father, who would probably be thirsty when he got back with the repaired tire.
>
> (Johnson 1985: 1)

The point of this particular example is that, although the car trip and breakdown all actually happened, nobody went for water and the family remained in the hot car. Johnson argues that the water sequence may reflect a solution to the thirst problem which she imagined at the time and this became integrated with her memory of the event. Presumably, as the integrated memory did not violate general knowledge or physical laws and was associated with both sensory and perceptual details, the veridicality of the memory could not be established by Johnson herself (Johnson's memory was falsified by her parents who claimed that the latter half of the memory was false). It seems likely that many autobiographical memories may be like this: that is they consist of interpretations of events and include sensory and perceptual features as well as information about current thoughts, wishes, motivations and so on.

For some memories the false information may be inferred on the basis of other knowledge – this does not mean, however, that the memory is any less a memory! The film director Bunuel describes a 'false' memory of Paul Nizan's wedding which took place in the 1930s – a memory which, so Bunuel states, he had often related.

> The church of St-Germain-des-Prés, where he was married, is crystal clear in my mind's eye. I can see the congregation, myself among them, the altar, the priest – even Jean-Paul Sartre, the best man. And then suddenly, one day last year, I said to myself – but that's impossible! Nizan, a militant Marxist, and his wife, who came from a family of agnostics, would never have been married in a church! It was categorically unthinkable. Did I make it up? Confuse it with other weddings? Did I graft a church I know well onto a story that someone told me? Even today I've no idea what the truth is . . .
>
> (Bunuel 1985: 5)

On the basis of earlier distinctions we would not want to say that Bunuel does not remember the wedding of his friend simply because the recall is incorrect in certain details. From Bunuel's account it seems clear that he has the experience of remembering the wedding, the event is self-relevant, and contains sensory, perceptual, and reflective features. Unfortunately we will never know the reason for the erroneous location of Nizan's wedding in a church. But, as we shall see in the next example, it is occasionally possible to verify details of an autobiographical memory.

It seems then that the truth content of autobiographical memories is not a particularly significant attribute of this sort of knowledge and memories which are clearly false are still recalled as memories. Yet it cannot be the case that, in general, most people's memories of events are complete fantasies. If it were, then there could be little communication between people about experienced events. So it should be the case that distortions in autobiographical memories follow some sort of pattern and that this is the case for most memories and for most people. Bunuel's insertion of a church setting into his memory of Nizan's wedding is congruent with the actual event – it would have been surreal indeed (but not out of character!), had Bunuel's memory located the wedding in, say, a factory or grocery shop. The last example in this section indicates one way in which autobiographical memory distortions might be rule governed.

A particularly well-documented autobiographical memory was provided by Neisser (1982) in which he recalled hearing in a newsflash, which interrupted a radio broadcast of a baseball game, about the Japanese attack on Pearl Harbor (see Chapter 4 for further details). Many years later Neisser realized that this memory could not be veridical because baseball games are not played in December which is when the fateful attack took place. On the face of it Neisser's memory is rather similar to Bunuel's erroneous church-wedding recall as details – but not the main theme – of the memory proved to be incorrect. In the case of Neisser's memory, however, it appears that the memory is not as erroneous or absurd as the author originally thought. Thompson and Cowan (1986) were able to establish that, in all probability, Neisser had been listening to a sports commentary but that this was a commentary on an Army–Navy football game, not a baseball game. It is perhaps unsurprising that two professional sports should become confused in memory and this would especially be the case if, in this instance, the listener had little knowledge of or interest in football. Thus the error might simply be construed as a relatively minor reconstructive error in recall.

Errors in autobiographical memories, at least in the above examples, are comparatively minor if not trivial. They do not violate the meaning of the recalled episode; in fact, if anything they seem to emphasize the meaning. This, however, is not always the case. Following certain types of brain damage patients' accounts of past occurrences may be wildly incorrect and are usually referred to as 'confabulations'. Baddeley and Wilson (1986) report a series of studies with patients who were confabulators (see Chapter 9 for a more extended discussion). One patient, R.J., showed quite remarkable and bizarre confabulations. Consider the following example from Baddeley and Wilson (1986: 241):

> One weekend while at home with his family he sat up in bed and turned to his wife, asking her, 'Why do you keep telling people we are married?' His wife explained that they were married and had children, to which he replied that children did not necessarily imply marriage. She then took out the wedding photographs and showed them to him. At this point he admitted that the person marrying her looked like him but denied that it was he.

Such confabulations are rare even among severely brain-damaged patients but they are, none the less, striking in contrast to the 'erroneous' recall of healthy people. Essentially, confabulations show that the incorrect memories of normal people are really rather minor in nature. And if the view is taken that autobiographical memories do not constitute veridical records of experienced events but rather are interpretations of events which are partly based on actual occurrences and partly on some form of cognitive integration of events, then minor errors are only to be expected. Indeed by this view, a feature of autobiographical memories is that they will never be wholly veridical but rather will (usually) be compatible with the beliefs and understanding of the rememberer and preserve only some of the main details of experienced events. As Bunuel (1985: 6) says of his own autobiographical memory it is 'wholly mine – with my affirmations, my hesitations, my repetitions and lapses, my truth and my lies'.

What do autobiographical memories represent?

If autobiographical memories are not veridical or literal representations of experienced events, then what sort of information do they represent? In some respects this is an empirical question and is probably best answered by studies of autobiographical memory content (see Chapters 6 and 7). Yet certain general features have already been identified, for example, information about the location of an event and temporal information about the date of occurrence of an event, appear to be ubiquitous features of autobiographical memories. Of course, we can all recall memories of events that we find difficult to isolate definitely to specific locations. Similarly temporal information is typically very coarse-grained so a person recalling an event may be able to date the event only as occurring 'when at school' (see Chapter 3) and be unable to provide a more exact date. Moreover, location and temporal information may not be specifically represented as part of a memory but may be inferred in some way (i.e. this must have happened when I was at school because I can't have been more than 10 years old). So although location and temporal information may be general features of autobiographical memories, it is by no means clear that this type of information is a criterial feature or that it is always represented along with specific memories.

In a particularly interesting study Neisser (1981) compared the testimony given by John Dean, the former aide to President Richard Nixon, during the Watergate trials with tape recordings of conversations between Dean and the president. The inconsistencies between the testimony and the tape recordings, in Dean's recall of details – spatial, temporal, and linguistic – showed that this was an impossible task, but the basic accuracy of his recall of the *meaning* of his conversations with Nixon showed that his memory of this period of his life had accurately preserved a basically correct *interpretation* of the events (see Chapter 5 for an extended account of this study). Thus a critical feature of autobiographical memories is that they represent interpretations or meanings of experienced events.

Although autobiographical memories may primarily represent interpretations and not facts, it is clear that at least some factual information is preserved. This factual information tends to take the form of actors, actions, locations and (some) temporal information. Factual information in autobiographical memories is, however, coarse-grained and open to distortions – as we shall see in Chapter 7. Neisser (1986a) has recently argued for a 'nested' view of autobiographical memory. According to this view there are (at least potentially) multiple levels of descriptions of any event and these multiple levels are reflected in the structure and content of autobiographical memory.

For instance, in the case of a conversation between John Dean and Richard Nixon there are many levels of description which might be employed in giving an account of the event. One type of description might focus on the actors present, their positions in the room relative to one another, the types of clothing worn and general presentation of self. Another type of description might focus on features of the actual conversation such as voice intonations, non-verbal gestures, eye contact, the choice of specific wordings, speaker–listener turn-taking and so on. Yet another type of description might take into account potential meaning aspects of the interaction, such as the extent of Nixon's knowledge of the break-in and cover-up, the nature of Dean's knowledge both of Watergate and of Nixon, and the type of task Dean was attempting to achieve as a presidential aide. Clearly there are many levels of descriptions of any event and it is evident that some levels of description are better preserved in autobiographical memory than others, although all levels may receive some representation. Neisser's (1986b) point is that these different levels of description are nested within one another and that 'Recalling an experienced event is a matter not of reviving a single record but of moving appropriately among nested levels of structure' (Neisser 1986a: 71).

Conway (1988a) reports a study which illustrates this process of moving appropriately among levels of description. In this study subjects provided descriptions of what came to mind as they attempted to recall a complex event. Consider the following account provided by a 35-year-old subject when asked to recall her wedding day:

Well the first thing which comes to mind is the registry office. I can clearly see (closes her eyes) Paul who was wearing a green velvet suit, my parents and my in-laws, also Susan and Dee who were my bridesmaids and Paul's friend Ian – he was best man – standing in a semi-circle around a big mahogany desk upon which the registrar was organising some papers. This was just before the ceremony started.

This subject went on to recall further images of the event and some of these were closely related to information in the initial image (i.e. the best man's speech at the reception, how one of the two bridesmaids drank too much and wept loudly, only to experience intense remorse and retrospective embarrassment some days after the wedding). For present purposes the important point is that the images clearly contain some detailed perceptual and temporal information. Perhaps images then are one way in which specific details of an event are preserved.

An image, however, can represent only a small fraction of the information and levels of description present in events such as wedding days and conversations with American presidents. And although images may help a person move appropriately through the structure of an autobiographical memory of a complex event, their ability to represent many details of any event is severely limited (cf. Conway 1988a for further discussion of this point). Thus autobiographical memories may be structured (feature different levels of description of the same event), contain information about the meaning of experiences, and contain some specific details about an event (perhaps typically represented in the form of images). In subsequent chapters we will see how this view of autobiographical memories has guided research.

Summary: characteristics of autobiographical memories

The purpose of this chapter has been to narrow the range of the phenomena we wish to study under the rubric 'autobiographical' memory. We have seen that autobiographical memories may have a number of identifying characteristics. Any one of these characteristics on its own is not sufficient to differentiate autobiographical memories from other types of memories. Moreover the characteristics are not all or none; that is, other classes of memory may also have an autobiographical-memory characteristic but to a different degree. Table 1.1 attempts to show how different characteristics may be associated – to varying degrees – with different classes of memories.

The rows in Table 1.1 depict the characteristics which the earlier discussion focused upon. The columns in Table 1.1 specify classes of memories. Note that procedural memories have not been included in the table, even though these were discussed above. The reason for this is that so little is known about these sorts of memories that it is not possible to classify them, at least in terms of the characteristics in Table 1.1. Semantic memories share the least number of characteristics with autobiographical memories; there are, however, many features of semantic memories which have not been included in Table 1.1 and the reader can refer to Tulving (1983: 35) for a more extended list of semantic memory features. Tulving also lists a number of features of episodic memories which are not included in Table 1.1.

The main point of Table 1.1 is to provide us with some idea – albeit a crude one – of just what sorts of characteristics we might expect of an autobiographical memory but which we would not expect of other types of memories. The characteristics and entries in Table 1.1 should not, however, be regarded as absolute or indeed fixed properties of autobiographical memories. As research in this area develops, other identifying features will emerge and it may be that the characteristics in Table 1.1 will turn out not to be the critical identifying features of autobiographical memory.

For present purposes, Table 1.1 provides us with some features which may be more closely linked to autobiographical than other types of memories. The main type of autobiographical memory which psychologists have studied is described by the entries in the first column of Table 1.1. Autobiographical-memory researchers have rarely attempted *explicitly* to identify just what it is they are studying but rather have *implicitly* assumed the features shown in the first column of Table 1.1. Autobio-

Table 1.1 Characteristics of autobiographical memory

Characteristic	Memory type			
	Autobio-graphical memory	Autobio-graphical fact	Episodic memory	Semantic memory
Self-reference	High	High	Low	Low and rare
Experience of remembering	Always present	May be present but rare	Usually but not always present	Rarely present
Interpretation (personal)	Frequently present	Rare	Rare	Rare
Veridicality	Variable	High	High	Social consensus more important
Duration of memory	Years	Years	Days	Years
Context-specific sensory and perceptual attributes	Always present	May be present but rare	Always present	Never present
Imagery	Frequently present	May be present but rare	Frequently present	May be present but rare

graphical facts, shown in the second column of Table 1.1, have received little research attention and the few studies which have attempted to investigate factual aspects of autobiographical memory are considered in Chapters 9 and 10. Episodic and semantic memory will not be considered in detail but, from time to time, these two classes of memory will be contrasted with autobiographical memory, especially in Chapters 6 and 9. As can be seen from Table 1.1, however, the characteristics of self-reference, interpretation, lengthy memory duration, and context specific features, are more closely associated with autobiographical rather than other types of memories. And we shall see, in later chapters, that it is these characteristics which have been the main focus of much of the research into autobiographical memory.

2 • THE EARLY THEORISTS

The purpose of the present chapter is to outline some of the original thinking about and investigations of autobiographical memory and later chapters take up many of the issues introduced here. There is, however, one peculiarity in the history of the study of autobiographical memory which should be noted: Although much original research was performed in the late 1800s and early 1900s, there is a gap in the research record between the 1900s and the early 1970s in which only a handful of studies were reported. This is what Cohen (1986) refers to as the 'hundred years of silence'. During this century psychologists concerned themselves with human behaviour and, later, with information-processing models of cognition. Both these traditions showed little interest in long-term memory in general and no interest whatsoever in autobiographical memory. In fact, the re-emergence of interest in autobiographical memory can be loosely dated to seminal papers by Crovitz and Schiffman (1974) and Robinson (1976) (see Chapters 3 and 6).

Although the study of autobiographical memory did not progress in the first half of this century, psychology itself changed rapidly and dramatically, moving from behavioural psychology through information-processing psychology and on to 'cognitive' models of mind. The re-emergence of interest in autobiographical memory can, perhaps, be linked to the emphasis within cognitive psychology upon the nature of the representation of knowledge. Another factor in the reawakened interest is the recent concern among cognitive psychologists to understand cognition as this naturally occurs in everyday life rather than just in laboratory settings (see, for example, Neisser 1976, 1982). It will, however, become apparent in later chapters that, although the style of psychological theorizing has changed, many of the principal insights and the research agenda set by the early researchers continue to inform the study of autobiographical memory. With this in mind let us first of all consider the writings of Ribot, Galton, Bartlett and Freud.

Ribot: a vision in time

Ribot in his book *Diseases of Memory* (1882) formulated a theory of memory, part of which dealt directly with autobiographical memory. In order to understand Ribot's account of autobiographical memory, it is first necessary to consider some aspects of his general theory of memory. Ribot's starting point for theorizing about memory is a firm commitment to the principle that memory is a biological fact. Thus he argues that 'recollection completes the act of memory but does not constitute it' (p. 10). For Ribot 'recollection' was the conscious experience of remembering and critically involved localization of some conscious state to the past.

Two other properties of memory proposed by Ribot are the conservation of certain conditions and their reproduction. These properties do not necessarily entail recollection (the third element in Ribot's general account of memory): 'This third element, which is purely psychological, would appear, then, to be superadded to the others: they are stable; it is unstable; it appears and disappears; it represents the extent of consciousness in the act of remembering . . .' (p. 10). Ribot cites the following case as an illustration of the secondary role of recollection in remembering: 'A musician, who played the violin in an orchestra, was frequently seized with the momentary loss of consciousness' but 'continued to play . . . although remaining in absolute ignorance of his surroundings' and 'he followed the measure'. For Ribot this is an example of 'organic' memory as opposed to 'psychical' or recollective memory – see Schacter (1987) for a review of contemporary research into 'implicit' and 'explicit' memory which closely parallels Ribot's distinction between organic and psychical memory. The two principal properties of organic memory stated above are formulated more exactly by Ribot when he writes that the two psychological conditions for memory are '1. A particular modification impressed upon the neural elements, 2. An association, a specific connection established between a given number of elements'.

It might be thought that Ribot at this point is proposing some form of 'trace' theory of memory (see Tulving 1983) in which memories are encoded in a unitary fashion (say in a single neuron) and connected to other memories or traces. This, however, is not the case and Ribot's position is much more sophisticated and surprisingly contemporary (compare what follows with recent writings by McClelland and Rumelhart and their colleagues (1986)). Ribot considers a memory for an Apple and argues that the memory is a 'weaker' form of the perception of an Apple. The perception of an Apple is, however, a complex neurological event involving processing in many different areas of the brain. Thus a memory of an Apple is similarly neurologically complex. For Ribot, then, a memory is 'composed of numerous and heterogeneous elements; that it is an association, a group, a fusion, a complexus or *multiplicity*' (p. 25). What is important in Ribot's general view of memory is not the representation of isolated elements but the connections between elements and he concludes that 'A rich and extensive memory is not a collection of impressions but an accumulation of dynamical associations, very stable and very responsive to proper stimuli' (p. 31).

In summary then, Ribot's general view of memory is that memory is composed of 'a great number of nervous elements, each modified in a special manner, each forming part of a distinct association and probably ready to enter into others; and each of these associations containing within itself the conditions essential to the existence of states of consciousness' (p. 45). Of course, memory need not involve conscious experience – as in the case of the epileptic violinist.

The metaphor that drives Ribot's theory of autobiographical memory is that of visual perception. In particular, Ribot asks 'How do we locate ourselves in space?' and his answer is that we do so by referring to a point, the distance and orientation of which we already know. In the case of recollective memory the same principle applies and we localize a memory in time by employing reference-points, the (relative) date of which we know. For Ribot then autobiographical memory is indeed a vision in time (p. 47) – see Neisser (1988, discussed in Chapters 6 and 7) for a modern parallel of this view.

The principal reference-point is, of course, the present. Ribot argues that each state of consciousness partly overlaps with the immediately preceding state. Again this is analogous with vision and Ribot proposes that each state of consciousness might be considered to leave a short-lived after-image and hence the connection with an immediately preceding state of consciousness. In order to retrieve a particular memory the whole chain of previous states of consciousness would have to be traversed until the sought-for memory is located. But, as Ribot points out, such a retrieval process would be cumbersome and time consuming and it seems that people rarely, if ever, retrieve memories in this way.

Nevertheless, the notions of a reference-point and states of consciousness can lead to a model that does more accurately characterize the retrieval process and Ribot comments: 'I understand by reference-point an event, a state of consciousness, whose position in time we know – that is to say, its distance from the present moment, and by which we can measure other distances. These reference-points are states of consciousness which, through their intensity, are able to survive oblivion, or, through their complexity, are of a nature to sustain many relations . . .' (p. 51). For Ribot then there are certain outstanding reference-points which might be in the form of particularly vivid memories (see Chapter 4) or perhaps connect to vast numbers of other memories (see Chapter 6).

One issue which arises from this is: how are reference-points chosen? Ribot's answer to this question forms the central part of his account of autobiographical memory:

> Reference-points 'are not arbitrarily chosen; they obtrude upon us. Their value is entirely relative. They are for an hour, a day, week, a month; then, no longer used, they are forgotten. They have as a general thing, a distinct individuality; some of them, however, are common to a family, a society, or a nation. These reference-points form for each of us different series corresponding to the events that make up our life: daily occupations, domestic incidents, professional work, scientific investigations, etc., the series becoming more numerous as the life of the individual is more varied. These reference-points are like the mile-stones or guide-posts placed along the route, which, starting from a central place, diverge in different directions. There is always this peculiarity: that the series may, so to speak, be placed in juxtaposition and compared one with another (pp. 51–2).

Ribot goes on to argue that reference-point memories are recalled very many times and 'By repetition . . . localisation becomes immediate, instantaneous, automatic' (p. 52). Such rehearsals, or 'secondary states of consciousness' as Ribot refers to them, are essential if a memory is to become a reference-point. In Ribot's model, then, it is possible to have images which cannot be localized in time, perhaps because these have not been frequently rehearsed or perhaps because they have been experienced with great frequency and each memory has become associated, leaving only a set of undatable common features. Ribot gives the following example:

> I have made the journey from Paris to Brest a hundred times. All the images are superimposed, forming an indistinct mass; they are all, properly speaking, in the same vague state. Only those journeys marked by an important event appear as recollections; those alone which awaken secondary states of consciousness are localised in time, or remembered (p. 58).

One further point in Ribot's model of autobiographical memory relates to how memories fail to preserve the length of duration of events. Ribot illustrates this with the following memory:

> I recall at this moment very vividly a visit which I made a year ago to an old Chateau in Bohemia. The visit lasted two hours. Today I go over it again readily in imagination. I enter by the great door, I traverse in order courts, corridors, halls, and chapels; I see again the frescoes and decorations; I find my way with ease through the labyrinth of the old castle to the moment of departure. But it is impossible for me to conceive of this imaginary visit as lasting two hours. It seems much more brief (pp. 58–9).

Ribot proposes that it is a general principle of memory that lengthy events will be contracted and brief events expanded. He also considers that the more that is known about an event the longer that event is likely to seem when retrieved from memory. We shall see later (Chapter 3) that recent research lends some support to this proposal. Before summarizing the main aspects of Ribot's model of autobiographical memory we might consider one last illustration provided by Ribot in order to demonstrate the dysfunctionality of literal recall.

> The late Dr Leyden was remarkable for his memory. I am informed, through a gentleman who was intimately acquainted with him, that he could repeat correctly a long act of Parliament, or any similar document, after having once read it. When he was, on one occasion, congratulated by a friend for his remarkable power in this respect, he replied that, instead of an advantage, it was often a source of great inconvenience. This he explained by saying that, when he wished to recollect a particular point in anything which he had read, he could do it only by repeating to himself the whole *from the commencement* till he reached the point he wished to recall. (Ribot, p. 61, quoting a case described by Abercrombie)

Ribot comments 'We arrive, then, at this paradoxical conclusion: that one condition of memory is forgetfulness' (p. 61).

The principal components of Ribot's model of autobiographical memory are:

1 Memories are organized in terms of reference-points.
2 Reference-point memories are maintained by rehearsal and may be highly vivid and have multiple connections to other memories.

3 Events which become reference-point memories may be specified by personal concerns, by some form of group consensus, or by society.
4 Other, non-reference-point autobiographical memories, are localized in time by use of reference-point memories and are not so well organized in memory.

(See James 1890/1950, Chapter 16, for a review of other nineteenth-century research which also supports Ribot's conclusions.)

Ribot also argues that other forms of organization may come to supplant reference-point organization and, when this occurs, it is no longer possible to localize memories in time. For example, the organization inherent in a language may come to supplant the reference-point organization originally used to represent memories of experiences of words in the language. In such cases memory becomes decontextualized and organized in alternative ways – in other words it becomes semantic (see Chapter 1). Finally, Ribot developed a principle of memory which arose out of his studies of brain-damaged amnesic patients – the law of regression. Ribot noted that many amnesics cannot remember events from the recent past but can remember events from the more remote past, from their early adulthood and youth. In order to account for this he proposed the law of regression which states that more recent memories are less stable and therefore more vulnerable to damage than more remote memories which are well established in memory. In Chapter 9 this 'law' will be examined in more detail.

In later chapters we will see that many of Ribot's proposals concerning auto-biographical memory have been confirmed by recent research. Next, however, we consider another nineteenth-century scientist who is credited with the first use of the currently most popular methodology for studying autobiographical memory: the cue-word technique.

Galton: cueing autobiographical memory

In his book *Inquiries into Human Faculty and its Development* (1883) Galton reports a fascinating series of studies of his own memory. The principal method he employed was to pick some object or word and count how many 'ideas' came to mind in a certain time period. The 'ideas' which occurred to Galton were largely recollections of childhood events and events from adulthood. However, Galton also mentions corroborating evidence he obtained from other people. For example, one of Galton's subjects reported remembering the left hand 'by a mental reference to the rocking-horse which always stood by the side of the nursery wall with its head in the same direction, and had to be mounted from the side next to the wall' (p. 183). Galton argues that abstract ideas may be represented by memories of events from a person's individual history.

The term 'abstract ideas' does not capture quite what Galton has in mind here and he goes on to suggest that the memories may be more like 'cumulative ideas' or 'generic images'. For Galton a generic image is something like a composite portrait – that is the face resulting when a number of photographic negatives of many different faces are superimposed on one another (a technique invented by Galton). We might note here the parallel with Ribot's example of his memory of a frequently repeated journey from

Paris to Brest. However, Galton also points out that just as in the composite portrait a highly distinctive face may remain distinctive so a highly distinctive event will remain in memory along with the generic image. For Galton, then, stimuli such as objects and concepts mainly evoked generic and specific images of experienced events. Although this is interesting in itself Galton's concern was with the variety and nature of the entire range of his thoughts evoked by such stimuli and, accordingly, he attempted to study these more directly.

Let us first consider Galton's general method in his 'psychometric experiments'.

> My method consists in allowing the mind to play freely for a very brief period, until a couple or so of ideas have passed through it, and then, while the traces or echoes of those ideas are still lingering in the brain, to turn the attention upon them with a complete and sudden awakening; to arrest, to scrutinise them, and to record their exact appearance. Afterwards I collate the records at leisure, and discuss them, and draw conclusions. It must be understood that the second of the two ideas was never derived from the first, but was always directly from the original object. This was ensured by absolutely withstanding all temptation to reverie (p. 185).

Galton first applies this method when taking a walk along Pall Mall 'during which time I scrutinised with attention every successive object that caught my eyes' (p. 187) and allowed a couple of thoughts to pass through his mind. Galton estimates that he performed this procedure on some 300 items during the course of his walk. The experiment was 'imperfect' because no record was kept of the ideas (or stimuli), nevertheless some interesting findings arose: 'samples of my whole life had passed before me . . . many bygone incidents, which I had never suspected to have formed part of my stock of thoughts' (p. 187). Galton was amazed by the variety of his thoughts and remembrances and particularly by the diversity of his memories, many of which had not been recollected for many years. In order to examine this further, Galton decided to repeat the experiment. This time, however, the results were not so remarkable and Galton found that many of his previous thoughts were repeated. Indeed he concluded that his memories and thoughts were like a great procession of actors filing across a stage, only to walk round the back of the stage to reappear in the procession in slightly different guise: On first viewing this procession one is amazed at the diversity, whereas second and subsequent viewings are less surprising because of the repetition of the actors.

In order to investigate this in more detail Galton then subjected himself to an experiment. In this experiment he carefully selected a list of 75 words. He then exposed himself to each word and timed how long he took to bring to mind two separate ideas to each word (with a maximum time limit of four seconds) and made a note of the time taken and of what the ideas were. He repeated this experiment four times at intervals of a month, each time in a different location. He found that, across all trials, he brought to mind ideas at about the rate of one every 1.4 seconds. This may seem rather slow but Galton indicates that some of the words led to much longer times than others. He comments: 'it is very difficult to get a quick conception of the word "carriage" because there are so many different kinds . . . that the mind possibly hesitates amidst an obscure

sense of many alternatives . . . But limit the idea to say a landau and the mental association declares itself more quickly' (p. 190). We shall see in later chapters that such
variability in retrieval times is a hallmark of autobiographical memory.

But what of the variety of 'ideas' Galton brought to mind? Only 57 per cent of
Galton's 'ideas' were unique, that is they occurred on just one occasion. In contrast
some words always gave rise to the same ideas and he comments that he had not
expected to find that 'out of every hundred words twenty-three would give rise to
exactly the same association in every one of the four trials' (p. 192). The remaining
words were associated with the same idea on two or three trials. Galton concludes
that his initial impression of the great diversity and richness of his thoughts and memories was incorrect: about half his thoughts were in fact unique and not repeated, the
remainder were, however, frequently repeated.

This was depressing news for a man who had originally been amazed by the richness
of his own thinking, but worse was to follow. Of the memories which Galton had
recalled, his initial impressions had led him to believe that these were of long 'forgotten' events arising spontaneously to mind as he meditated in Pall Mall. In the
experiments it turned out that this was not the case. Virtually all the autobiographical memories he recalled were ones that had been rehearsed in the past, of
which he had on occasion thought about and pondered over. He comments that 'As
I understand it the subject must have a continued living interest in order to retain an
abiding place in memory' (p. 192). Even on the very few instances when a 'forgotten'
memory came to mind, Galton was unimpressed by the detail of his recall:

> The instances, according to my personal experience, are very rare, and even
> those are not very satisfactory, in which some event recalls a memory that had
> lain *absolutely* dormant for many years. In this very series of experiments a
> recollection which I thought had entirely lapsed appeared under no less that
> three different aspects on different occasions. It was this: When I was a boy, my
> father, who was anxious that I should learn something of physical science, which
> was then never taught at school, arranged with the owner of a large chemist's
> shop to let me dabble at chemistry for a few days in his laboratory. I had not
> thought of this fact, so far as I was aware, for many years; but in scrutinising the
> fleeting associations called up by the various words, I traced two mental visual
> images (an alembic and a particular arrangement of tables and light), and one
> mental sense of smell (chlorine gas) to that very laboratory.
>
> (Galton 1883: 193)

But such vague recollections were rare and Galton concludes:

> Forgetfulness appears to be absolute in the vast majority of cases, and our
> supposed recollections of a past life are, I believe, no more than that of a large
> number of episodes in it, to be reckoned perhaps in the hundreds of thousands,
> but certainly not in tens of hundreds of thousands, that have escaped oblivion
> (p. 194).

It cannot be said that Galton had a specific view of autobiographical memory as such.
Indeed, he was principally concerned with the diversity of his own thoughts. His
studies, however, clearly suggest certain aspects of autobiographical memory, namely

that only a comparatively small number of events can be remembered and these are nearly always events which have been well rehearsed. In addition, he clearly considered memories and concepts to be closely interrelated and argued that personal experiences formed part of the meanings of concepts for an individual (see Chapter 10 for some recent corroborating evidence). Finally, Galton also felt that autobiographical memories revealed in a strikingly distinct way the self of the rememberer and he concludes his psychometric experiments with the following comment on his own memories:

> They lay bare the foundations of a man's thoughts with curious distinctiveness, and exhibit his mental anatomy with more vividness and truth than he would probably care to publish to the world (p. 202).

Freud: the past as dictator

Freud and Breuer (1893/1974) in their famous book *Studies on Hysteria* gave a central role to autobiographical memories in the genesis, maintenance, and treatment of neuroses. Freud's proposal was that emotionally traumatic experiences, the memories of which, for various reasons (see Chapter 8), have been repressed, directly underlie neuroses. The repression of such memories prevents their being recalled into consciousness, yet the emotions associated with those experiences continue to affect the person. Freud suggests that it is as though the pain arising from the wound of a psychic injury continues to afflict the sufferer, even though the actual injury is no longer recalled. Treatment of neuroses was chiefly concerned with leading the patient to recollect the moment of psychic injury so that the pain was eased and the network of psychological defences, arising from the incident, was undone. In Freud's later work this process of the repression of painful experiences with consequent psychological dysfunction is linked to his psychosexual theory of development and his theory of mind. This link allowed Freud to put forward an account of the fascinating phenomenon of childhood amnesia and this is discussed in detail in Chapter 8.

Let us return to the studies of Freud and Breuer and consider an example case reported in full in the *Studies on Hysteria* and described more briefly by Freud (1909/1962). Fräulein Anna O. suffered from a range of hysterical symptoms including paralysis of the arm, disordered visual perception, and paraphasia. She was a very intelligent but frustrated person in that she had never had any outlet for her intelligence other than her own day-dreams. She had nursed her father, to whom she was very close, through a painful and ultimately terminal illness. The full nature and treatment of her case will not be outlined in further detail here, but in order to illustrate the role of autobiographical memory in neurosis (as proposed by Freud) consider the following account of one of Anna O.'s experiences:

> She once woke up during the night in great anxiety about the patient (her father), who was in high fever; and she was under the strain of expecting the arrival of a surgeon from Vienna who was to operate. Her mother had gone away for a short time and Anna was sitting at the bedside with her right arm over the back of her chair. She fell into a waking dream and saw a black snake coming towards the

sick man from the wall to bite him. . . . She tried to keep the snake off, but it was as though she was paralysed. Her right arm over the back of the chair, had gone to sleep, and had become anaesthetic and paretic; and when she looked at it the fingers turned into little snakes with death's heads (the nails). . . . When the snake vanished, in her terror she tried to pray. But language failed her: she could find no tongue in which to speak, till at last she thought of some children's verses in English and then found herself able to think and pray in that language. When the patient had recollected this scene in hypnosis, the rigid paralysis of her right arm, which had persisted since the beginning of her illness, disappeared and treatment was brought to an end.

(Freud 1909/1962: 38)

Cases such as these, and Freud and Breuer describe many more, led Freud to conclude that '*our hysterical patients suffer from reminiscences*. Their symptoms are residues and mnemic symbols of particular (traumatic) experiences' (my italics) (1962: 39). Freud, however, was not directly concerned with developing a theory of memory but rather with a theory of mind. Yet his legacy, which remains largely ignored in the contemporary study of autobiographical memory, was to emphasize the role of emotion and the effects of memories upon subsequent personality and behaviour. In Chapters 5 and 8 we will return to some of the questions raised by Freud's work.

Bartlett: reconstructing the past

Bartlett in his seminal book *Remembering: A Study in Experimental and Social Psychology* (1932) proposed that memory was fundamentally reconstructive. He argued that 'In a world of constantly changing environment, literal recall is extraordinarily unimportant' (p. 204). For Bartlett memories were always reconstructions of past events to meet the needs of current concerns. Moreover, he proposed that representations in memory are in the form of *schemata*. Schemata for autobiographical memories represent general impressions or attitudes to an event. Memories are interpretations both at encoding and retrieval. According to Bartlett memories 'live with our interests and with them they change' (p. 212).

Under this view then, what exactly happens when a person 'remembers' a past event compared to, say, when that same person simply entertains a train of thought? Bartlett comments:

> in remembering a man constructs on the basis of one 'schema', whereas in what is commonly called imagining he more or less freely builds together events, incidents and experiences, that have gone to the making of several different 'schemata' which, for the purposes of automatic reaction, are not normally in connection with one and other (p. 205).

Bartlett does not deny that there may be memory 'traces', some fragments of more or less literal knowledge of a past event. His main point is that these are incorporated into the construction of a memory. He did, however, consider such fragments or images to be peculiarly autobiographical and, somewhat like Galton, comments:

> Images are, in fact, so much a concern of the individual that, as everybody

knows, whenever, in psychological circles, a discussion about images begins, it very soon tends to become a series of autobiographical confessions (p. 217).

Yet in Bartlett's view, such autobiographical images were of little account and only provided a source of knowledge for other types of cognitions:

> By the aid of the image, and particularly the visual image . . . a man can take out of its setting something that happened a year ago, reinstate it with much if not all of its individuality unimpaired, combine it with something that happened yesterday, and use them both to help him solve a problem with which he is confronted today (p. 219).

Bartlett, then, lays heavy emphasis on the reconstructed nature of remembering and upon the encoding of interpretations of events rather than the literal representation of such events. It will become apparent in later chapters that this challenge to students of autobiographical memory has not been taken up. And questions about the reconstructive nature of autobiographical memories have yet to be seriously addressed by appropriate investigations. Nevertheless, Bartlett's view is in keeping with the general view of autobiographical memory outlined in Chapter 1, that autobiographical memories represent meanings and interpretations rather than literal accounts of events. Similarly Bartlett's proposal that autobiographical memories are a 'resource' (see Robinson 1986a) for other types of cognition has yet to be seriously explored, although some research relating to this will be described in Chapter 10. Finally it is worth pointing out that many contemporary psychologists argue that Bartlett placed too much emphasis on the reconstructive aspect of memory. Certainly memory is reconstructive but there must be something with which to construct. It seems likely that reconstruction occurs only some of the time and that in many cases remembering is accurate, a fact which, surprisingly, is difficult to explain by 'schema' theory. More recently, Brewer (1986) has proposed that autobiographical memory is only 'partly' reconstructive, by which he seems to mean that specific details are often recalled and that reconstruction occurs less frequently than Bartlett suggested. This view implies that reconstruction may be of only minor importance in the recall of most autobiographical memories.

The early experimentalists

Ribot and Freud were essentially theorists and not experimentalists, at least in respect to autobiographical memory. Moreover their theories were not theories of autobiographical memory and, as such, did not immediately generate research traditions into autobiographical memory. Nevertheless their ideas, especially Freud's, exerted a strong influence over autobiographical-memory research in the late nineteenth century and we will consider some of this research shortly. The work of Bartlett came later than that of the other theorists discussed in this chapter and occurred at a time when the dominant paradigm in psychology was barely concerned with memory and wholly unconcerned with autobiographical memory. Bartlett's unfluence upon memory research in general was not to be felt until the 1970s. Galton, in contrast to Ribot, Freud, and Bartlett, was much less of a theorist (though not so poor as his detractors sometimes claim) and much more of an experimentalist, and his work greatly influenced technical aspects of early studies of autobiographical memory. It should also be emphasized that some ninety years later Galton's cue-word technique was to become one of the main techniques used by cognitive psychologists in their studies of autobiographical memory (see Chapters 3, 6, 7, and 9).

A very early large-scale survey of autobiographical memory and memory function in everyday situations was undertaken by Colegrove (1899). Colegrove constructed a questionnaire which covered, amongst other things, earliest memories, recall from different time periods in a person's life, and ease of recall of pleasant and unpleasant memories. In his study Colegrove sampled 1,658 people, mostly college students. In the days before computers, this led to a vast pool of data requiring herculean labours just to tabulate it. To give some idea of the difficulties facing early researchers into autobiographical memory, consider the following comment by Colegrove on his own data:

> The tabulation required almost incessant labor for five months. The results were first tabulated upon two rolls of paper whose combined length was fifty-two feet by one foot eight inches in breadth.
>
> (Colegrove 1899: 230)

One can well imagine why this type of research was not to the taste of many nineteenth-century psychologists. In his detailed examination of the types of memories recalled for different chronological periods in a person's life Colegrove noted some interesting changes. First of all, there were few memories from the earliest years of life (childhood amnesia) and these memories were dominated by the recall of novel experiences and repeated occurrences (see Chapter 8). Memory for novel experiences gradually decreased for older groups of children, although memory for repeated experiences was maintained at fairly high levels. The ages 10 to 14 years were marked by memories of 'mischievousness and destructiveness' which would seem to typify that age of childhood. At puberty and shortly after, ages 14 to 19 years, Colegrove noted a marked change in the content of memories. He comments 'Now, too, the memories of high ideals, self sacrifice and self forgetfulness are cherished'. Wider interests than self and immediate friends become the objects of reflection and recollection. The third decade of life, 20 to 29 years, was marked by memories of novel and repeated experiences, and the fourth decade, 30 to 39 years, is marked by more thoughtful and reflective recollections. Later decades, particularly over the age of 60 years, were marked by a decline in auditory and tactile memories which had been common in other periods. It is not clear what these findings might mean but the emergence of a reflective period in recall after the age of 30 years has recently gained some support from more contemporary work and we shall consider this in Chapters 3 and 8.

One overall observation made by Colegrove, that might have pleased Bartlett, is that memories are recalled which are in harmony with the 'psychical life' of the period through which the rememberer is living. He concludes that 'These facts suggest that what is remembered does not primarily constitute definite memories, but a memory complex' (p. 236). In other words, memories are constructed in terms of current interests rather than simply retrieved. Finally, Colegrove found that pleasant memories were retrieved more frequently than unpleasant memories and that this difference gradually narrowed as the rememberer became older so that his eldest respondents recalled pleasant and unpleasant memories almost equally easily, although there was still a slight advantage to pleasant memories.

Colegrove's study was a questionnaire study and it is unclear just how reliable his findings are. For example, did his respondents claim to find recall of pleasant memories easier than recall of unpleasant memories because they *believed* they should recall pleasant memories well? If so then their judgements might reflect a belief about memory rather than the actual performance of memory. Despite these problems Colegrove's study is important and we shall see that later work has produced findings which support and extend at least some of his original findings (see Chapters 3 and 8).

Arguably the most heroic study of autobiographical memory was performed by Smith (1952) who systematically attempted to recall all memories from all periods in her life. She succeeded in recalling 6,263 memories of events occurring between the ages of 2 to 61 years. She was able to verify the dates and accuracy of her memories against diary records kept by her mother and by herself. The findings of Smith are complex and, as Brewer (1986) points out, it is difficult – but not impossible – to comprehend her report of the data from her study. Here we will consider only a few of her findings but the paper is to be recommended for the serious student of autobiographical memory. First, Smith examined the distribution of memories correctly recalled across her life span and found that most memories were from recent time periods, that is the last ten years or so. Although recall rates gradually declined as the periods sampled became more remote, Smith also noted slight increases in the recall rates for the periods 30 to 15 years of age followed by a sharp decline into the period of childhood amnesia (6 years old to birth). We shall see in Chapter 3 that recent research generally supports this pattern of distribution of memories across the life span (see Smith 1952: Table 1, p. 154).

Other findings by Smith were that by far the most dominant form of autobiographical recall was that of visual imagery. Novelty of remembered events and the distinctiveness of an event within a series of events were also powerful determinants of recall. Smith also noted a tendency for some memories to 'fuse' giving rise to composite memories. One particularly interesting case reported by Smith is of a subject's very early verbal memory (Smith studied a small sample of other diarists in order to compare their performance for the early years of life against her own). The example is as follows:

> *B* says he was 'watching the *ma-fu* unhitch the horse from a carriage in which we have just arrived at home. The *ma-fu* leads the horse down a covered passage with a high threshold. As the horse comes to the sill, the *ma-fu* commands "*joh*" for the first front foot and first hind. My first realisation that animals understand words for the horse obediently stepped high each time to miss the sill.'
>
> (Smith 1952: 158)

What is interesting about this, as Smith points out, is that the rememberer, *B*, recalls as part of his memory Chinese words which he had not heard for over 50 years. In Chapter 10 we will briefly review recent research which has suggested that memories for (unused) languages may persist in memory, in some form, for very long time periods indeed.

The studies of Colegrove and Smith are similar in style to the early work of Galton, that is they are essentially empirical, data-collecting exercises. Other work undertaken in the early years of this century was more theoretically driven in that it was more or less directly based on Freud and in particular on Freud's theory of repression. Extensive critical overviews of this work can be found in Meltzer (1937) and Dudycha and Dudycha (1941). The Meltzer review examines investigations of the effects of feeling or emotion on memory. Reviewing 26 separate studies, some of which directly examined rates of recall of pleasant and unpleasant autobiographical memories, he concluded that there was little consistent evidence in favour of the view that unpleasant memories are remembered less frequently than pleasant memories. Instead the data support the rather more general conclusion that affectively toned stimuli (regardless of valence of the affect) influence remembering more markedly than emotionally neutral stimuli. The Dudycha and Dudycha review examines studies of childhood amnesia and essentially concludes that the few studies which had been conducted at that time supported the view that recall from the earliest years of life was extremely impoverished for specifically emotional events. Freudian and other types of explanation for childhood amnesia received at best contradictory support from these studies.

Perhaps the best of the early studies of childhood amnesia was reported shortly after the Dudycha and Dudycha review, by Waldfogel (1948). In Waldfogel's study 124 college students recorded as many of their childhood memories as they could recall in an 85-minute period. Later, subjects were retested in the same way, making it possible to compare consistency of recall across the two sampling periods. Various other measures of personality and intelligence were also taken and memories were scored for pleasant, unpleasant, and neutral emotion. Waldfogel's principal finding, however, related to the distribution of memories from the age of 0 to 8 years. This distribution was initially flat, rising slowly up to the age of about 2 to 3 years and then accelerating dramatically up to the ages of 6 to 8 years where it gradually levelled out. Waldfogel argues that this mirrors the type of distribution seen in the development of language and intellect when this is plotted over the first years of life. As he found no consistent relations between personality factors and recall rates, and because the distribution of pleasant and unpleasant memories was essentially the same in all the years sampled, he concluded that his findings lend no clear support to Freud's notion that emotional memories of childhood are repressed. Instead, he argues that the ability to encode and retrieve memories parallels intellectual development and is dependent upon cognitive development. We will see in Chapter 8 how this proposal of Waldfogel's has been developed by subsequent research.

The modern agenda

The theorizing and research of the early investigators of autobiographical memory raised many issues, some of which have been pursued in later research and others which have received no subsequent attention. Issues which remain of abiding interest are: the temporal properties of autobiographical memory, organization of memories, memory vividness, self and memory, emotion and memory, childhood amnesia, and neurological impairments of autobiographical memories. Other topics, such as the use of autobiographical memories (Bartlett) have yet to be taken up in any serious way by cognitive psychologists. We shall see in the following chapters just how modern research has qualified and developed the thinking of the early researchers.

3 • THE TIME OF YOUR LIFE

Imagine you have been commissioned to write your autobiography. In order to do this you decide to take stock of your life in the following way: you will set aside some time each day for one month and write down *all* the events you can recall experiencing and their corresponding dates – few people it appears have attempted this but see Smith (1952: discussed in Chapter 2) for a noble attempt. Which periods of your life would contain the most memories? For instance, would the distribution of memories across different ages show some distinct pattern – perhaps most memories would be recalled from early adulthood and fewer memories from other periods? Would the distribution of memories across your life-span be the same or similar to the distribution for other people? For example, would all people of your age show the same distribution? Would older and younger people show a different distribution? How could we explain peaks and troughs in the number of memories recalled across the life-span? Might the obtained distribution reflect a particular way of searching autobiographical memory rather than the underlying organization? In this chapter we examine various types of research which have tried to answer these questions.

Before considering specific studies let us make some simple assumptions that we can use to assess the various findings to be outlined below. To begin with, we will assume that human affairs follow, more or less, a well-ordered sequence of actions. For example, most people do not start work before going to school, people cannot get divorced before they are married, and one does not order a meal in a restaurant after eating it. In general, then, it seems reasonable to assume that the various periods of our lives proceed in some potentially identifiable order and that within a culture many people may have similarly ordered lifetime periods (e.g. infancy, school, college, work, marriage, parenthood, middle age, retirement, old age).

Within a lifetime period there may be further chronological orders such as going to infant school before attending secondary school. These orders will be referred to as 'temporal reference systems'. Temporal reference systems were originally proposed by Robinson who argued that 'it is self-evident that participation in a domain of action engenders an appropriate cognitive representation of the temporal pattern associated with it. Viewed as socially prescribed routines, these patterns function as timetables (or schedules or calenders)' (1986b: 159). Robinson's work is discussed in more detail later in this chapter. Here we are mainly concerned with the temporal reference system relating to a person's whole life.

Thus our first assumption is that people have a life-timetable made up of distinctive periods which are arranged in some loose temporal order. These might be periods such as, 'before I went to school', 'infant school', 'secondary school', 'sixth form', 'college', 'first job', 'early married life', 'after the children were born', and so on. Or they might be periods such as single years, months, weeks or days from a person's life. In addition to this orderly temporal division we assume that a person listing all the memories of their life would sample each time period equally, and that in each period roughly the same number of memories were encoded. This is the simplest assumption to make and it predicts that a more or less flat distribution of ages of memories should result from our memory-listing experiment (i.e. the same number of memories are recalled for each period sampled). Distribution in ages of memories which are not flat will show us that the equal-sampling hypothesis (which encompasses all the three above assumptions) is incorrect or incomplete and that the life-span temporal-reference system is determined by factors other than, or in addition to, equal sampling. Note also, that this equal-sampling hypothesis assumes that either there is no forgetting, or that memories are lost at an equal rate from each lifetime period – an assumption which is undoubtedly incorrect, as we shall shortly see.

Sampling memory: Galton's original data

Galton in his orginal study of the production of ideas produced per unit time to single words (see Chapter 2 for an extended account of this experiment) found that many of the 'ideas' which came to mind were in the form of images of past events or autobiographical memories. In fact, Galton was able to date these memories and sort them into three general groups: memories dating from before the age of 22, memories from the period 22 years and subsequent manhood, and memories of 'quite recent events'– Galton was 57 years old when he undertook the experiment. Galton reports that 39 per cent of the memories were from before the age of 22, 46 per cent were from manhood, and 15 per cent were of recent events. Clearly, this distribution of memory ages is not flat and would seem to contradict the equal-sampling hypothesis. There are, however, some problems with Galton's experiment (although it should be noted in Galton's favour that his experiment was never intended to test the sampling hypothesis!).

To begin with, Galton did not attempt to sample his whole life. In fact Galton was not originally concerned with the production of memories but more with the variety of his 'ideas'. This, however, is not a serious objection because we can assume that in response to different stimuli (single words in Galton's case) different time periods will be sampled equally often and to an equal extent – if the equal-sampling hypothesis is correct. Given only a limited sampling of memory we might expect a distribution which is somewhat less than flat (because not all time periods are sampled) but not one which has a large peak in the middle and rapidly declines at the end!

Another problem is that Galton's division of his life into three very large time periods of unequal duration may have artificially distorted the distribution. If it were possible to rescore Galton's memories so that we could plot the number of memories recalled in, say, every five-year period then we might find a less peaked distribution of memory ages, i.e. about 9 per cent of memories occur in each five-year period. One final problem relates to the type of words used by Galton to cue his memory, many of which were uncommon words hardly likely to relate to everyday experiences ranging across the life-span, e.g. abyss, abasement, abhorrence, etc. Thus the cue words may themselves have distorted the sampling procedure.

Short lives: sampling the memory-age distributions of young people

The distribution of Galton's memories across his life clearly does not support the equal-sampling hypothesis, although problems with the study leave the findings open to alternative interpretations. In order to remedy some of the shortcomings of Galton's study Crovitz and Schiffman (1974) conducted a considerably modified version of the experiment. In the Crovitz and Schiffman study 92 undergraduates read a list of 20 words and brought to mind a personal memory associated with each word. The words had been selected so that they represented highly familiar concrete nouns which were also judged to be highly imageable and meaningful. As they recalled each memory the students wrote down a few words describing the memory and, after completing the whole list, went back and dated each memory using the natural language-time units: seconds, minutes, hours, days, weeks, months, and years.

In order to examine the distribution of memory ages across the life-span Crovitz and Schiffman allocated memories to temporal classes based upon the time units employed by subjects. The number of memories falling in each of the temporal classes were counted and the resulting distribution of memories by time class showed that most memories were recalled from recent time periods, least from the earliest time periods, and that frequency of recall of memories from other time classes decreased linearly with increasing age of the time class. (Note that the data were further transformed prior to being plotted and the reader should see Crovitz and Schiffman 1974 for details.) Contrary to Galton's initial report, then, Crovitz and Schiffman's findings indicate that frequency of autobiographical memories decreases with increasing remoteness of the time period sampled and this is the case across a large group of people; we will see later, however, that there are problems in comparing these two studies. It is also clear that this distribution runs counter to the equal sampling hypothesis outlined earlier and this also we shall consider in further detail shortly.

If it is the case that fewer memories are recalled from remoter time periods, then it should also be the case that, when memories are sampled from a short time period, say the first eight years of life, a similar linearly decreasing memory age distribution should be observed. This distribution should be present when subjects recall one memory to each word in a list of words and when they recall many memories to a single word. Crovitz and Quina-Holland (1976) conducted two experiments using the cue-word method of Crovitz and Schiffman which explored these possibilities.

In the first of Crovitz and Quina-Holland's experiments, college students recalled a single memory from their childhood to each of the following words: *safety, product, ship, clock, owner, time, blessing, author, table, bird, pride*, and *inhabitant*. In a second experiment students recalled 10 to 15 memories to single words taken from the first experiment. In both studies the students wrote a short description of their memories and subsequently dated each memory. In addition to this Crovitz and Quina-Holland also included in their analysis the dates of memories collected by Waldfogel (1948: see Chapter 2 for full description of this study and Chapter 8 for an extended account of 'childhood amnesia'). Waldfogel had collected childhood memories from 124 college students using the exhausting procedure of requiring the students to recall all their memories from below the age of eight years and to date each memory. Figure 3.1 shows the proportion of memories recalled in each year in each of the three experiments. The distributions are virtually identical in all three studies and show that the amount of memories recalled decreases linearly with increasing age of the time period sampled. Note that no memories were reported for the period 0 to 12 months.

These findings demonstrate that fewer memories are recalled from remoter life periods and most memories from recent life periods, and that this is the case across the whole life-span, across shorter time periods, in response to single words or lists of words, and when an exhaustive attempt is made to recall memories. One interpretation of these findings is that memories are forgotten over time and that the longer the retention interval the greater the loss of memories. Thus the distribution of memory ages across the life-span may reflect some type of retention function of autobiographical memories. If this is the case, then, of course, our original simplistic assumption of equal sampling, with either no forgetting or constant forgetting, is clearly incorrect.

A retention function for autobiographical memory was originally proposed by Rubin (1982). Rubin suggested that autobiographical memories are retained across the life-span in the same way as stimuli learned in laboratory experiments are retained across shorter time periods (i.e. minutes and hours). In the laboratory-based memory experi-

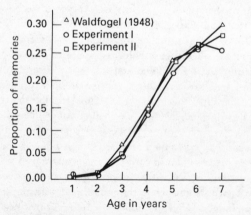

Figure 3.1 Proportion of childhood memories recalled for each of the years 1 to 8 (based on, Crovitz and Quina-Holland 1976, figure 1, p. 62)

ment a subject may be presented with a list of words to study and some time later asked to recall the word list. If all other factors are held constant (i.e. original depth of learning, nature of intervening events between learning and recall), then retention is found to be chiefly a function of time. In other words as the retention interval increases, recall rates decrease.

In order to explore a retention function for autobiographical memory Rubin (1982) conducted a series of autobiographical memory retrieval experiments. In the first of Rubin's experiments a large group of undergraduate students, all under 22 years of age, recalled a single memory to each word on a 125-word list, and dated their memories. In the second experiment a further large group of 18-year-old students free recalled and dated 50 autobiographical memories. In his analysis of the memory-age data Rubin was primarily concerned with describing the resulting retention functions in terms of different mathematical models. This aspect of Rubin's studies need not concern us here and the important finding was that, over both studies, most memories were recalled from recent time periods, least from remote time periods, and there was a steady decrease in amount of memories recalled as age of time period increased. Thus the retention function observed by Crovitz appears to be a robust phenomenon.

There are, however, a number of criticisms of these studies. To begin with the retention function is obtained by averaging memory ages across cues and subjects and so it is possible that no single subject shows such a function, and that different cue words may give rise to different retention functions which are obscured by the averaging process. Rubin attempted to meet this later criticism by reanalysing data reported by Robinson (1976: see Chapter 6). Robinson had required subjects to recall memories to cue words which specified objects, actions, or feelings, and to date their memories. If it is the case that certain cue words systematically give rise to different retention functions, then it is possible that this will be evident in response to different categories of words. Rubin found the same retention function for each of the three categories and this function was very similar to that found in Rubin's first two experiments. The only notable difference was that the slope of the retention function was steeper for the ages of memories recalled to words naming feelings and this reflects the preponderance of recent memories in this category (emotions and autobiographical memory are considered in further detail in Chapters 4 and 5).

Rubin's third experiment examined the possibility that the retention function for individual words (rather than classes of words) may vary. In this experiment students recalled a single memory to each of five words and dated their memories. The five words were selected from Rubin's first experiment on the basis of the average age of the memories they had evoked. The words and the mean ages from the earlier experiment were: *paper* (10 days), *plant* (25 days), *wine* (44 days), *hospital* (61 days), and *fire* (334 days). The retention function for each cue word was calculated separately, although within a cue word memory ages were averaged over subjects. In general, the same retention function was observed for each cue word, demonstrating that the retention function was not an artefact of averaging over cue words.

Rubin next dealt with the problem of averaging memory ages over different subjects. In his fourth experiment seven students recalled and dated memories to a set 326 cue words, and retention functions were calculated separately for each student. Each student showed retention functions highly similar to the group retention function found in all the previous studies (except of course for Galton's study). This clearly suggests that the retention function is not an artefact of averaging over people. Interestingly Rubin also found that, although all his students showed a retention function similar to the group retention function, they differed significantly from one and other in the slope of their functions. In other words, some of the students recalled a lot of recent memories, whereas others recalled comparatively fewer recent memories. Unfortunately Rubin did not investigate these individual differences in further detail and it is not clear what they might mean. One likely possibility, however, is that different people use different retrieval strategies and these strategies determine the total number of memories recalled from different time periods.

In his final experiment Rubin attempted to assess the accuracy of memory dating. If it is the case that people are wildly inaccurate in dating their memories, then this would suggest that the retention function may be only marginally related to memory. For instance, perhaps people *believe* that they will remember less from the remote past and more from the recent past and, in the absence of any knowledge of when events occurred, date their memories to support this belief. Intuitively this seems implausible, and we know from our own experiences of our own memories that we do have knowledge of when events occurred; nevertheless this knowledge may be relatively impoverished (i.e. not include exact dates – see below) and so, perhaps, beliefs about memory do guide memory dating in some small but significant way.

In Rubin's fifth study a small group of diary keepers were recruited who free recalled and then dated 100 memories. The retention function for these memories was the same as that observed in the previous studies, although the slope of the function was considerably shallower. In other words, subjects who kept diaries recalled more older memories than subjects in the earlier studies. The reason for this difference is unclear, although it could possibly be due to a tendency of diary keepers to dwell more extensively on the past than non-diary keepers, or maybe in the context of the study these subjects actively tried to recall events recorded in their diaries.

Memory-date accuracy was established for over 25 per cent of the memories recalled by each subject by consulting the diaries. Memory-date accuracy for the datable memories was found to be high and 74 per cent of memories were dated accurately to within a month, and 93 per cent to within a year. There were, however, some errors, the largest being the misattribution of a visit to Niagara Falls to 1970 when, according to the diary entry, this occurred in 1980 – an error of 3,696 days!

The studies of Crovitz and his colleagues and of Rubin quite clearly demonstrate that across the life-span most memories are recalled from recent time periods and least from remote time periods. This 'retention' function is evident in individual subjects, across groups of subjects, in response to single words, categories of words, heterogeneous lists of words, in recall from specific lifetime periods, and in free recall. The generality of the function suggests that the life-span temporal reference frame has little to do with ordered sequences of activities – as Robinson (1986b) proposed – but rather depends upon some general property of the memory system. Perhaps older memories are subject to some form of decay and so are not retained. On this account, then, our original assumption of equal sampling would have to be modified to include forgetting. Maybe all time periods are sampled equally – that is, the same amount of time and effort is expended in searching each period – but for remoter periods less memories are retained and so fewer memories can be retrieved. The effects of forgetting on more recent time periods are less marked and so more memories are available for retrieval and, for the same amount of time and effort, more memories can be recalled.

Despite the apparently robust nature of this retention function there are good reasons for doubting its generality. The distribution of the ages of memories recalled by Galton did not correspond in any way to the retention function found in subsequent studies. Apart from the many obvious differences in methodology between the Galton and the Crovitz *et al.* and the Rubin studies, the critical difference may concern the age of the rememberer: Galton was 57 years old when he sampled his memory, whereas the subjects in the Crovitz and the Rubin studies were all less than 22 years old, and usually were all 18-year-olds. The retention function may simply be a property of short life-spans and developing memories. After all, 18-year-olds have yet to experience many of the major events of their lives and these events may themselves lead to the preferential encoding and/or retrieval of autobiographical memories. Similarly, some events, perhaps because of their personal significance for the individual, may be encoded in such a way as to render them relatively immune to the processes which mediate forgetting (see page 53 for a discussion of 'landmark' events). It seems possible, then, that the distribution of memory ages may vary with the length of the life-span sampled and it may be that longer life-spans do not show a simple retention function such as that observed for 18-year-olds.

In fact there is a hint of this in both Crovitz's and Rubin's studies. In some of these experiments memories from the earliest ages, e.g. 1 and 2 years of age, were either not present or were so few that they were excluded from the analysis because they would have distorted calculation of the retention function. Evidence from other studies (see Chapter 8) indicates that there is a period in early life, from birth to about 5 years of age, from which very few memories are ever recalled. The retention function, then, rather than gradually decreasing with increasing age, is probably subject to a sharp and marked decrease for this period. As we shall see in the next section, such variations in the distribution of memories across the life-span are more clearly marked in older subjects.

Long lives: sampling the memory-age distributions of older people

Clearly it is crucial to discover the characteristics of memory retention for older people if we are to develop a general model of autobiographical memory. In order to explore retention over much longer lives, Franklin and Holding (1977) required subjects to give 'an immediate association involving personal reference' (p. 528) to each of 50 words and to date each reference. One hundred subjects were employed in five age groups, 25–34, 35–44, 45–54, 55–64, and 65–74. The distribution of memory ages for each of these groups is shown in Figure 3.2.

If the memory ages are transformed logarithmically and summed over subjects the resulting distribution is similar to that found by Crovitz and Schiffman (1974), and it was found that the number of memories recalled decreased with increasing age in a

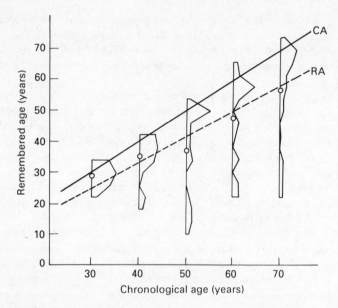

Figure 3.2 Mean remembered age (RA) plotted against chronological age (CA). The vertical frequency polygons are the distributions of individual median remembered ages (reproduced by permission of the authors and publishers, from Franklin and Holding 1977, figure 1, p. 530. © The Experimental Psychology Society)

regular fashion. However, it can be seen from Figure 3.2 that the distribution of memory ages is hardly linear or regular within the age groups and it is clear that the distributions differ across age groups. Franklin and Holding found that the distribution of memory ages for the 30-year-olds differed significantly from all other groups who did not differ reliably from each other. All the groups, with the exception of the 30-year-olds, show more or less bimodal distributions. That is, many memories are recalled from recent time periods and this decreases with increasing age but only for a limited period. After the sharp decline in the recall of recent events the distribution rises again, and all the older groups show an increase in memories retrieved from the time period 20 to 40 years of age (which is especially noticeable in the 50-year-old group – see Figure 3.2). These data then are not as clearly in favour of the retention function described by Rubin as were the data collected from younger subjects.

One problem with the Franklin and Holding study is that subjects were not required to recall specific memories to the cues but only to bring to mind a 'personal reference'. In fact the authors report that just under a third of the memories were generic in nature (i.e. were memories of frequently repeated experiences, or factual in nature – see Chapter 1). Thus it may be that the memory-age distributions were distorted by the inclusion of a large number of memories which we would not want to class as being memories of specific experiences.

McCormack (1979) conducted a series of experiments with elderly subjects where memories of specific experiences were retrieved to cue words and dated. In order to examine the distribution of memory ages McCormack divided each person's life into quarters and summed the number of memories in each quarter. Figure 3.3 shows the distribution of memory ages obtained in three separate experiments employing subjects older than 72 years. (Note that McCormack later required subjects to redate their memories and found high consistency between original dates and redates.)

The remarkable finding here is that most memories are recalled from the first quarter of life with the third quarter representing the point of lowest recall. Recall rates across the second and fourth quarters do not differ reliably, although the fourth quarter generally led to recall rates which were reliably higher than recall rates in the third quarter. One problem with McCormack's analysis was that subjects who recalled most of their memories from only one quarter of their lives were eliminated from the data set on the assumption that they had not sampled across their life (as instructed) but rather had adopted some form of retrieval strategy they judged appropriate for the experiment. It seems possible that these subjects recalled most memories from the fourth quarter of their lives and so the number of memories shown in Figure 3.3 for the fourth quarter may be an underestimation. If this is the case then, it may be that

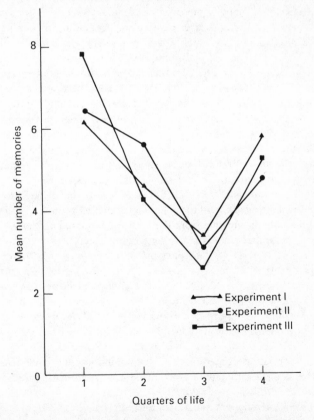

Figure 3.3 Mean number of memories recalled for each quarter of life (based on McCormack 1979, figure 3, p. 120)

McCormack's distributions are more similar to those reported by Franklin and Holding (1977) than would be apparent by comparing Figures 3.2 and 3.3. In other words, McCormack's memory-age distributions may be more clearly bimodal than Franklin and Holding's and may show (if the missing data were included!) that most memories are recalled from the fourth and first quarters of life.

Interestingly, McCormack further divided up memories from the first quarter of life by quartering this period and then plotted the distribution of the first-quarter memory ages. The first quarter of life for McCormack's subjects roughly corresponds to the full life period of the younger subjects studied by Crovitz and his colleagues and by Rubin. McCormack found that the distribution of memories in the first quarter of life corresponded to the distribution observed by Crovitz and Schiffman (1974). In other words the Rubin retention function describes the first 20 to 25 years of life but not the whole life-span of elderly subjects.

Further evidence for age-related variations in memory age distributions was reported by Fitzgerald and Lawrence (1984) who employed the cue-word method and studied groups of subjects aged 11 to 14 years, 17 to 22 years, 35 to 55 years, and 60 to 74 years. (Note there were a number of other variables in this experiment such as speed of retrieval – see Chapters 6 and 7 for coverage of these types of measures and Chapter 8 for further analysis of memory ages.) The principal finding of importance for the present discussion was that the distribution of memory ages corresponded closely to the retention function reported by Rubin (1982). There was, however, a discrepancy for the older groups in the study, who recalled equal numbers of memories over the periods from birth to 40 years old. For these groups there was a rapid and steady decline in the number of memories recalled with increasing age but this decline levelled out for the first half of a person's life and more memories were recalled from earlier time periods than would be predicted by the Rubin retention function. Again the distribution of memory ages across the life-span for older subjects does not appear to fit easily the retention function observed with younger subjects.

In an attempt both to explain and resolve these unexpected findings with older subjects Rubin, Wetzler, and Nebes (1986) decided to compare the findings from all the studies reported thus far, and to include a further set of memory-age data. Rubin *et al.* were able to obtain the data from the Franklin and Holding study, the Fitzgerald and Lawrence study, and a study featuring amnesic subjects (see chapter 9). In addition, Rubin *et al.* collected a further set of memory ages using the cue-word technique from subjects aged 18 to 22 years and 68 to 76 years. The distribution for memory ages in these studies is shown first for 50-year-old subjects in Figure 3.4 and second for 70-year-old subjects in Figure 3.5.

Note that, for illustrative purposes, memories which dated from less than one year prior to the experiments are not included in these graphs. Also note that the affect and noun words employed by Fitzgerald and Lawrence are plotted separately. It should be clear that the distribution of memory ages is not a monotonically decreasing function of age and this is most strikingly evident in the plot representing the sum of all the distributions.

In order to examine recent memories for different age groups Rubin *et al.* plotted the distribution of memory ages for the most recent 20 years of life collected from their 20-year-olds and 70-year-olds. In other words, all the memory ages from the 20-year-olds were plotted and all the memory ages for the period 70 to 50 years were plotted

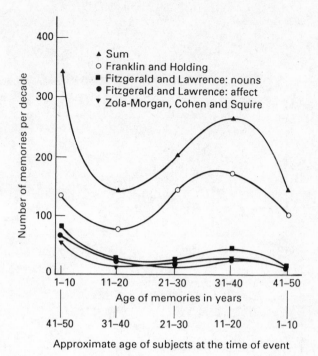

Figure 3.4 Number of memories recalled per decade by 50-year-old subjects (reproduced by permission of the authors and publishers, from Rubin, Wetzler, and Nebes 1986, figure 12.1, p. 211. ©Cambridge University Press)

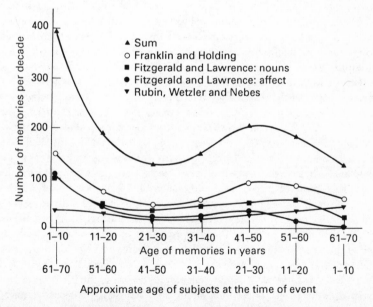

Figure 3.5 Number of memories recalled per decade by 70-year-old subjects (reproduced by permission of the authors and publishers, from Rubin, Wetzler, and Nebes 1986, figure 12.2, p. 212. ©Cambridge University Press)

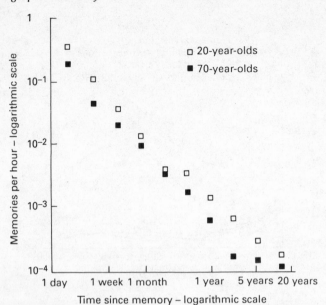

Figure 3.6 Distribution of memories for the most recent 20 years, log-log plot (reproduced by permission of the authors and publishers, from Rubin, Wetzler, and Nebes 1986, figure 12.5, p. 216. ©Cambridge University Press)

for the 70-year-olds and the resulting distributions are shown in Figure 3.6. Note that the memory ages in Figure 3.6 are plotted on logarithmic scales. Figure 3.6 then clearly shows the retention function previously observed only with 20-year-olds. Figures 3.4, 3.5, and 3.6 suggest that in subjects older than about 35 years there are at least three components to the distribution of memory ages across the life-span. Consider the distribution for 70-year-olds shown in Figure 3.5: for the most recent 20 years or so (50 to 70 years of age) there appears to be a retention function where very recent memories are frequently recalled and frequency of recall steadily declines with increasing age. Frequency of recall starts to recover, however, between 20 and 30 years ago (40 to 50 years of age) and shows a marked increase in the period 30 to 50 years ago (when the subjects were 10 to 30 years of age). Finally there is marked decline in the amount of memories recalled from the early years of life and few memories are recalled from 60 plus years ago (when the subjects were less than 10 years old).

Rubin *et al.* propose that these peaks and troughs in the distribution of memory ages across the life-span represent three separate components of retention. The first component is a retention function which applies to the most recent 20 to 30 years of a person's life. The retention function is represented by a monotonically decreasing function of number of memories recalled and increasing age of memories, and most memories are recalled from the very recent past and least from 20 to 30 years ago. Thus this retention function accurately describes the life-span distribution of memory ages for subjects less than about 35 years of age but only describes the most recent 20-to-30-year period for subjects older than 35.

The second component of retention is marked by the rise in recall of memories from the middle period of life (when subjects were about 10 to 30 years of age) and this is often referred to as a 'reminiscence' peak. Rubin *et al.* argue that the reminiscence peak arises because of differential sampling of memories from this time period and point out that other explanations for the peak seem somewhat unlikely. For instance, it might be argued that more memories are encoded between the ages of 10 to 30 – a differential encoding explanation. But subjects aged between 20 and 30 show monotonically decreasing retention functions which in terms of both distribution and absolute amount of memories recalled are virtually identical to the distribution of memories recalled by older subjects for their most recent 20 years of life. Thus there is no evidence that memories are differentially encoded in early adulthood.

Another version of differential encoding might argue that the reminiscence peak represents a period of highly memorable events occurring in the life of the older subjects only – events occurring around the time of the Second World War, for example. If this were the case, however, the reminiscence peak should depend on the age of the precipitating events (i.e. late 1930s to mid-1940s) and not, as it does, on the age of the subject at the time of encoding. Finally, it might be argued that certain memories are somehow resistant to decay and hence the reminiscence peak. Again this seems unlikely because the increase in frequency of recall depends on the age of the subjects at encoding and not on the age of the memory. Thus the reminiscence peak may reflect preferential sampling of memories of events originally experienced in early adulthood.

The third component of the memory-age distribution across the life-span is shown in the paucity of memories recalled from early childhood and infancy. The dramatic fall in frequency of memories recalled from this period, evident for all subjects of all ages, cannot be accounted for by either the Rubin retention function or by a differential-sampling function. This period of childhood amnesia is discussed in detail in Chapter 8 and one possible account of this phenomenon is that equal numbers of memories were encoded during early childhood but for various reasons are no longer accessible. Perhaps memories from early childhood were encoded in terms of knowledge which adults no longer use and therefore no effective cues can be located to facilitate retrieval.

The life-span temporal reference system appears to be comprised of a number of components. Memories spanning a 20-to-30-year period are best characterized by a retention function in which memories of recent events are well retained and retention diminishes over time. Memories over 30 years in age may be subject to reminiscence and so become more available for recall, but memories relating to the very early years of life, even though these may be 30 years or older, are less available and therefore are less often recalled. On the basis of these findings we might modify our original assumption of equal sampling as follows: for the most recent 20 years of so of older people's lives, and for the whole life-span of people under about 30 years, time periods are sampled equally but for remoter time periods fewer memories are retained and so the distribution of memory ages can be described by a retention function. In other words a forgetting component must be added to the simplistic equal-sampling view. For older people only, the period of life corresponding to late adolescence and early adulthood is preferentially sampled and this may be because older people have rehearsed (i.e. thought and talked about) events from this period. Effectively this means that the period 10 to 30 years of age is preferentially sampled – memories in this period have been well rehearsed and are easily available to retrieval processes. Finally, for people of all ages few memories can be retrieved from the early years of life and this may represent a failure of sampling – effective cues with which to access memories are simply not available to retrieval processes for this period. Thus equal sampling may be modified, at different points in the life-span, by forgetting, by rehearsal, and by the systematic failure of retrieval processes. So if you undertook the memory-listing experiment mentioned at the start of this chapter, the distribution of your memories would critically depend upon your age at the time you undertook the experiment.

The distribution of memory ages across the life-span reconsidered

It might be thought, on the basis of the preceding sections, that the broad temporal qualities of the distribution of memories across the life-span have been firmly established. But, as we shall now see, such confidence would be misplaced: autobiographical memory retrieval is a much more flexible and task-sensitive process than the previous studies have suggested.

One finding which remains highly anomalous with the memory age life-span distribution identified by Rubin *et al.* (1986) is the distribution reported by McCormack (1979). It will be recalled that McCormack found that most memories were recalled from the first (oldest) quarter of a person's life and not from the last (most recent) quarter. McCormack's dating method differed in an important respect from the dating method used in other studies. Subjects in the McCormack study dated memories as they retrieved them, whereas subjects in the other studies dated their memories only after they had recalled all the memories required by the experiment. Holding, Noonan, Pfau, and Holding (1986) point out that 'serial' dating (the method used by McCormack) may bias subjects to recall earlier memories. This may occur because, in the course of dating a memory (say the first memory recalled), subjects may search autobiographical memory for time markers which help infer the date (e.g. Did this event occur before or after I started school? Did this event occur after I was married? See page 53, for further evidence of the role of landmarks in dating memories). In the course of locating time-marking events other memories may be retrieved and subsequently employed in response to the next cue word in the list. As these other memories will be chronologically close to the first memory, then memories will tend to be retrieved from within time periods when serial dating is employed. In this way then, the number of childhood memories recalled may be increased and the number of recent memories may be decreased. (Of course, this argument only holds if subjects, for whatever reason, retrieve older memories at the outset of the experiment! If subjects retrieve recent memories at the outset of the experiment, then we might expect more recent than old memories to be retrieved.)

Holding *et al.* (1986) directly investigated differences in retrieval strategies by requiring groups of young and elderly subjects to recall memories to cue words and to date each memory either as it was recalled (serial dating), or go back and date each memory after all memories had been recalled (standard dating). The serial dating procedure corresponds to the dating procedure employed by McCormack and standard dating to the procedure used in the other studies. Holding *et al.* plotted the proportion of memories recalled in each of the four quarters of the life-span and this was done in two ways. First of all, proportions of memories in each life quarter resulting from serial and standard dating methods were plotted separately but within each dating method memories were averaged over young and old subjects. Second, the distributions of memory ages for young and old subjects were plotted separately. These last two distributions were 'corrected' following the procedure employed by McCormack, in which memory dates from subjects who recalled more than two-thirds of their memories from any single quarter of life are omitted from the distribution. Figure 3.7 shows the resulting four distributions.

It is clear from Figure 3.7 that, for all groups, most memories were recalled from the most recent quarter of life. For the serial-dating group, however, this effect is not as marked as it is in the standard-dating group. The serial group recall more memories from the first three-quarters of life than the standard group and slightly fewer memories from the most recent quarter of life than the standard group. Thus method of dating appears to modulate the Rubin retention function. This modulation is much

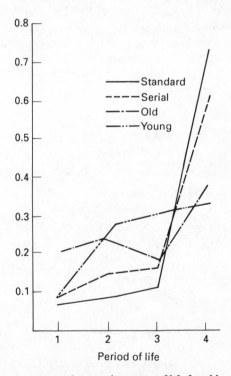

Figure 3.7 Proportion of memories from each quarter of life for old and young subjects using different dating procedures (reproduced by permission of the authors and publishers, from Holding *et al.* 1986, figure 2, p. 484. © The Gerontological Society of America)

more evident when the proportions are corrected for subjects who recall many memories from one quarter of life only, as the curves in Figure 3.7 for the young and old subjects show.

What do these findings mean? Holding *et al.* conclude that, as their findings for the standard-dating method are very similar to the findings of Rubin *et al.* (1986), they lend further support to the claim that memories become less readily accessible with increasing retention interval. However, it seems possible that the distributions of memory ages resulting from both the standard- and serial-dating procedures may have a common cause. Recall that the 'corrected' distributions omitted data from subjects who recalled more than two-thirds of their memories from a single quarter of their lives. Holding *et al.* found that these omitted subjects reliably recalled most of their memories from the most recent quarter of their lives. This suggests that there may be large individual differences in sampling autobiographical memory and this is in addition to any differences resulting from dating methods. A reasonable conclusion would seem to be that different distributions of memory ages occur when subjects use different strategies for searching memory. Many subjects may, however, have a bias to use a backwards-search strategy, that is, they start from their most recent memories and work backwards to remoter memories (see Whitten and Leonard 1981, discussed in Chapter 7), and this may account for the preponderance of recent memories observed in the majority of memory-dating studies. This means, of course, that older memories may only appear less accessible in the context of a particular retrieval strategy, and in the context of other types of retrieval strategies it is recent memories which appear less accessible.

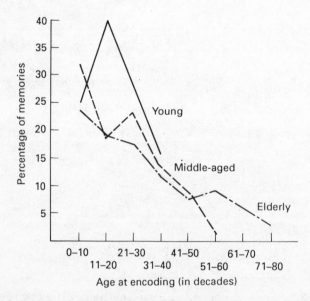

Figure 3.8 Distribution of memories across the life span for three age groups (reproduced by permission of the authors, from Cohen and Faulkner 1987, figure 1, p. 10a)

In a study reported by Cohen and Faulkner (1987) a very different distribution of memory ages was observed. Cohen and Faulkner required three groups of subjects (a young, a middle-aged, and an elderly group) to recall six highly vivid memories and, in addition, to recall a further vivid memory for each decade of their lives not represented in the initial sample of memories. Subjects then dated the memories and rated each memory for vividness, emotion, personal importance, and frequency of rehearsal. Figure 3.8 shows the distribution of memories for each of the age groups.

Remarkably most memories were recalled from the earlier decades of life, and the proportion of memories recalled steadily declined with decreasing retention interval so that fewest memories were recalled from most recent time periods. This distribution of memory ages is virtually the exact opposite of the distributions observed in the majority of the earlier studies.

Cohen and Faulkner argued that their distribution may have been a product of a sampling bias induced by the experimental demands. In the Cohen and Faulkner study, subjects were instructed to 'think over their past lives' and recall six highly vivid memories. This instruction may have predisposed subjects to review their lives starting from the earliest years to the present – in other words, subjects employed a forward-search method. In order to examine this, the authors classified subjects' retrieval attempts in the following way: where three consecutive memories were in increasing order of age of encoding, then this was counted as an instance of *forward retrieval*; where three consecutive memories were in decreasing age of encoding, then this was counted as an instance of *backward retrieval*; where three consecutive memories were from the same category (e.g. three holidays), then this was counted as an instance of *clustering*; and if the clustered memories also referred to three major life events (e.g. three births of children in chronological order), then the instance was classified as a *landmark retrieval*. Table 3.1 shows the percentages of different retrieval strategies for the three age groups.

Analysis of the distribution of retrieval strategies showed that all subjects reliably employed a forward-search –'begin at the beginning' – strategy more frequently than any other strategy. Cohen and Faulkner conclude that 'the relative density and accessibility of personal memories at different parts of the life-span appears to shift as autobiographical memory is sampled in different ways' (1987: 13).

The research on memory dating then demonstrates one outstanding feature of autobiographical memory, namely that autobiographical memory access is highly flexible and different methods of access produce sets of memories with different

Table 3.1 Types of retrieval strategies, in percentages, used by three different age groups

	Type of strategy			
	Forward	Backward	Clustering	Landmarks
Young	32.1	13.6	28.4	25.9
Middle-aged	38.8	11.8	30.6	18.8
Elderly	47.1	9.2	20.7	22.9

(Reproduced by permission of the authors, from Cohen and Faulkner 1987, table 1, p. 12)

properties (e.g. different age distributions). It will be seen in later chapters that this flexibility of access is reflected in many different types of studies and indeed appears to be something of a hallmark of autobiographical memory.

But where does this leave our already modified, equal-sampling assumption? To begin with, we must acknowledge that autobiographical memory is always accessed in the context of some task (such as cue-word prompts, free recall, vivid memory retrieval, etc.) and that different tasks induce different sampling procedures. Thus the memory-age distributions we have considered so far demonstrate the flexibility of autobiographical memory access and highlight the role of retrieval strategies in determining the broad temporal characteristics of retrieved memories. What seems clear is that different temporal periods across the life-span are not sampled equally but, rather, are sampled strategically.

Memory-age distributions from short and verifiable time periods

Apart from the cue-word methodology for studying autobiographical memory an additional legacy of Galton's original study has been the selection by experimenters of their own memories as objects of study – a sort of participant-observation methodology. This type of experiment typically requires an experimenter to record events from her/his life in some systematic way over a specific period of years and then to assess memory for the recorded events. One of the great advantages of this type of study is that memory for a very large number of verifiable events can be examined. In particular, the rate of forgetting can be uniquely assessed. (In the studies considered previously there was no way in which forgetting could be directly assessed.) If the retention function described by Rubin (1982) primarily reflects the number of memories retained, rather than a sampling bias of some (unspecified) retrieval strategy, then, of course, it should be the case that the amount of memories forgotten should steadily increase with the passage of time. Note, also, that a second advantage of these studies is that the cues which are employed to prompt retrieval are much more specific and directed than the cues employed in the cue-word method. This cue specificity may have the advantage of rendering all memories, regardless of their age, more accessible than the general cues typically employed in the cue-word paradigm.

One of the most well-known participant-observation studies of autobiographical memory was reported by Linton (1975, 1978, 1982). Linton recorded two to three events from her life each day for a period of six years. The events recorded were selected as far as possible to represent comparatively unique or distinctive events in her life. Each event was recorded on the day it occurred in the form of a brief description, dated, and rated on a number of scales (these latter aspects of Linton's study are discussed in Chapters 4 and 6). At the end of each month Linton selected, in a nonsystematic way, items from the accumulating pool of records and (among other judgements) attempted to date each event. Linton (1982: 78) comments 'After six years the experiment had reached imposing dismensions. I had written 5,500 items . . . and tested (or retested) 11,000 items (about 150 items each month).' Linton found that in the first 18 months less than 1 per cent of memories were forgotten. After 18 months the forgetting rate increased to about 5 to 6 per cent and remained at that rate for all subsequent years, so that after six years about 32 per cent of the events had been forgotten. Thus, after an initial period of very high retention, forgetting remained constant with increasing retention interval – a clear contradiction of the 'forgetting' version of the retention function.

Recall that Linton tried to select unique and distinctive events to record in her diary study. In fact she was not totally successful in this endeavour (after all, who experiences three unique events every day of his or her life?) and found that the (few) events she recorded which were repeated in her life, or formed part of very similar sequences of events, were barely remembered at all. Related to this, White (1982) performed a diary study in which he recorded one event from each day of his life for a period of a year. White, however, selected the to-be-recorded events in an unsystematic way and consequently included many non-unique events in his sample. When he tested himself for recall of these events, by rereading a short description of the event, he found that he remembered only 23 per cent of the events. When he provided himself with fuller descriptions of the event his recall rate rose to 41 per cent – still impressively less than Linton's recall rate (and also far less than Wagenaar's 1986 rate – see page 48). Dating of memories in White's study was highly inaccurate, although more distinctive memories were dated with more accuracy. In fact in White's study the rated vividness of the event (at or near the time of occurrence) and rated frequency of rehearsal were the best predictors of remembering. White argues that many events are forgotten and this occurs because of interference by the encoding in memory of many similar events. Thus Linton's findings of a very gradual forgetting rate should be treated with caution – only distinctive events are forgotten slowly. Memories of less distinctive events may rapidly become inaccessible in memory.

In a study similar to Linton's, Wagenaar (1986: see Chapter 7 for more details of this study) recorded 2,402 events from his life over a six-year period. For each event Wagenaar listed four cues (*who, what, where,* and *when*) and recorded a critical distinguishing detail of each event. At test, the events were re-presented in random order in the following way. First, one cue was randomly presented and Wagenaar attempted to recall the other three cues; then the first cue plus a second cue were presented and the remaining two cues recalled; the first two cues plus a third cue were presented and the final cue was recalled; and finally all four cues were presented and the critical details recalled – (recall took place over a period of one year and Wagenaar describes it as 'somewhat torturous' (1986: 231). Figure 3.9 shows retention as a function of the number of cues used to probe memory and shows the number of memories judged not to be totally forgotten.

It is clear from Figure 3.9 that very few memories were totally forgotten and that forgetting was not a monotonically decreasing function of time. In fact, the retention curves from Wagenaar's study are very similar to those reported by Linton (1978) and White (1982, for distinctive events). The clear discrepancy in these retention curves and those reported by Rubin (1982) and Crovitz and Schiffman (1974) is almost certainly due to the effect of different retrieval strategies induced by the experimental task. Wagenaar argues that the specific cues employed in his study facilitate access to older memories, whereas the non-specific cues used in the cue-word paradigm bias subjects towards accessing recent memories – perhaps by forcing a backward-search strategy. It is clear that there may be a whole range of memories, any one of which a

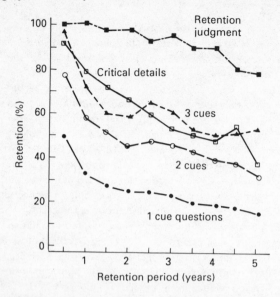

Figure 3.9 Percentages of memories recalled to different numbers of cues or judged not totally forgotten (reproduced by permission of the authors and publishers, from Wagenaar 1986, figure 3, p. 235. ©Cognitive Psychology)

subject could legitimately retrieve to a non-specific cue. If subjects initially adopt a backwards-retrieval strategy, then obviously retrieval of most recent memories will dominate (on the assumption that there will be many recent memories which will 'fit' the cue words) and consequently older memories will be underrepresented. As Wagenaar (1986: 233) concludes 'retention curves in Crovitz and Schiffman-type studies underestimate the accessibility of older autobiographical memories considerably, because they represent elicitation by unspecific cues'. Strategic sampling may be most evident then, when the cues used to probe memory are general and do not correspond in any specific way to the encoded memories. On the other hand, when more specific cues are employed (i.e. cues which relate directly to a subject's life), the effects of strategic sampling may be reduced and the rate of forgetting is found to be far lower than that suggested by studies employing general cues.

Let us briefly review the principal findings so far. We started with a very simple hypothesis, namely that there is either no forgetting or constant forgetting and that, when a person attempts to recall memories, they sample all time periods equally. As all time periods are assumed to contain the same amount of memories, then it follows that about the same number of memories should be recalled from every period. We quickly found that this hypothesis was untenable. The work of Crovitz and later Rubin and their colleagues demonstrated that there were at least three components to memory retrieval. First of all, some memories appeared to be inaccessible and these were memories for events experienced in the first few years of life. Second, some memories – those relating to events from early adulthood – appeared to be highly accessible and this may be because they have been frequently retrieved in the past. Third, memories which are not otherwise inaccessible or well rehearsed appear to be subject to a forgetting function such that older memories are forgotten at a faster rate than more recent memories. Subsequent research demonstrated that this third component may be dependent upon the use of certain retrieval strategies. When backwards search is employed, then this favours the retrieval of memories of recent events whereas forwards search favours the retrieval of older memories. In the present section we have seen that the specificity of a cue may completely eliminate the third component and, by implication, the second and first components. For, when sufficiently specific cues are available, retrieval from any time period should only be subject to a constant forgetting rate (about 5 per cent of memories per year). Taken together, these findings demonstrate that ages of retrieved memories are mediated by two main factors, retrieval strategy and cue specificity.

Sampling structured time periods: the school year

Retrieval of memories across the life-span and across shorter time periods appears to be highly sensitive to the type of retrieval strategy adopted and to the sorts of cues available to the retrieval process. But is the same sort of flexibility in retrieval evident when a person searches for memories from a more clearly structured time period? Robinson (1986b) investigated this question by exploring memory retrieval for events occurring in the academic year. Robinson argued that events occur in the context of various sorts of activities (e.g. attending college) and that within activity contexts events are organized in some chronological order (e.g. attending lectures and completing course work precede examinations). In two preliminary studies Robinson (1986b) established that the academic calendar year divided into three main periods winter/spring, summer, fall (autumn). He also found that the months of the year, when arranged in terms of the academic calendar, facilitated college undergraduate recall of groups of common words, demonstrating that the temporal structure of the school year can indeed influence memory.

Having established that the academic calendar appeared to facilitate memory in a word-recall task, Robinson then decided to use the calendar to cue autobiographical memory retrieval. The hypothesis of his first study was that memories should cluster around the three temporal units, winter/spring, summer, and fall, and that some months (i.e. those marking the beginnings and endings of the three temporal units) should act as better recall cues than other months. Two groups of college undergraduates took part in the study and both groups were required to recall 20 autobiographical memories of events occurring in the preceding year or two. One group recalled their memories in November (the ending of the preceding semester occurring in May) and the second group recalled their memories in April (the ending of the previous semester occurring in December). After recalling each memory subjects also dated the memories and rated the importance and the frequency with which those memories had been recalled prior to the experiment. The main finding, for both groups, was that fewest memories were recalled from the middle parts of the three temporal periods and that discontinuities in the proportion of memories recalled across the year reflected the three time periods, winter/spring, summer, fall. Most memories were, however, recalled from the endings of the three time periods. Neither ratings of importance nor ratings of frequency of rehearsal proved to be reliably related to the amount of memories recalled across the year.

One problem with this study is that subjects may have adopted a backwards-retrieval strategy and this strategy may have led to increased recall for the end of the time periods. In order to obviate this objection Robinson conducted a further memory-retrieval study. In this study the names of the months of the year were used as retrieval cues and subjects were required to recall as many memories as they could in a fixed period of time to each month. The months were presented in either chronological or random order and in either forwards or backwards order. Different groups of subjects recalled memories to one of these four cue groups. If the endpoint advantage noted in the earlier study is a product of a specific retrieval strategy, then the recall pattern should not be present when different retrieval strategies are employed (if we assume, of course, that these are induced by the different orders of presentation of months). Robinson found that there were no differences between the different cue orders and the endpoint advantage for number of memories recalled was present in all groups and this is shown in Figure 3.10.

It is clear from Figure 3.10 that Robinson's original hypothesis, that both beginnings and endings of time periods would be marked by more memories, must be revised: the findings indicate that only the endpoints of the time periods are reliably marked by an increase in the number of memories recalled.

In a final study Robinson (1986b) assessed memory-dating accuracy using school year or birthday as temporal reference points. In this study subjects recalled memories to

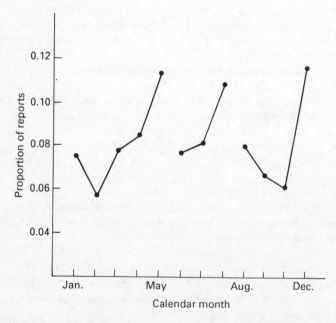

Figure 3.10 Proportion of memories recalled per month in temporally cued recall (reproduced by permission of the author and publisher, from Robinson 1986, figure 10.8, p. 179. ©Cambridge University Press)

31 cue words and dated each memory. The cue words were selected so as to refer to subjects and activities associated with school, work, recreation, and interpersonal relations and, in addition, subjects were instructed to focus on their adolescent years (12 to 18 years) when recalling events. Two weeks after the initial recall phase, subjects returned to the laboratory and redated their memories. In this phase of the experiment one group of subjects first judged whether a remembered event had occurred before or after their birthday in the year of the event and then dated the memory. A second group of subjects judged whether the remembered events had occurred in a school term (and if so which one) or during vacation and then dated each memory.

One measure of interest is how consistent subjects were in redating their memories. Robinson found that the birthday group were highly consistent and the two sets of dates for this group correlated at .84. The school-year groups were less consistent and their two sets of dates correlated at .66. Further analyses indicated that, when an error in dating was made, it was most likely to be an error in the month of the date for the birthday group and equally likely to be an error in the month *and* the year for the school-year group. What this means is that the school-year group tended to change the year of the memory more frequently than the birthday group and, when such changes occurred, these were most likely to locate the memory in a more recent time period. This phenomenon is known as 'forward telescoping' and we shall see shortly that other research has shown that the effect of forward telescoping can be reduced by providing subjects with temporal landmarks such as birth dates.

The selective effect of forward telescoping in the school-year group is also evident when the discrepant dates are considered. In order to perform this analysis Robinson assigned the discrepant dates to three classes, same unit, similar unit, and other unit. For example, if a memory had been initially dated in October and was subsequently dated in July, then this would be assigned to 'other unit' because July does not fall in a school term. If, however, the memory was inconsistently redated in May, then this discrepancy would be assigned to 'similar unit' because May falls in a school term. Finally, if the memory was inconsistently dated as occurring in November, then, in this example, it would be assigned to 'same unit' as it is still dated as occurring in the same school term. Figure 3.11 shows the distributions for the birthday and school-year groups of the classified discrepant dates.

It can be seen from Figure 3.11 that the birthday group's discrepant dates occur most frequently in the same unit and less frequently but equally often in the classes of 'similar unit' and 'other unit'. This strongly suggests that the birthday group were not employing the school year to guide their dating. In contrast the school year group shows a tendency for discrepant dates to fall in the class 'similar unit' rather than 'other unit'. In other words the school-year group, when making an inconsistent redating, tended to redate their memories as occurring in a subsequent school term rather than as occurring in a temporally more contiguous period, i.e. the non-school period, summer.

Robinson's (1986b) findings show that the retrieval of memories from a short and structured time period (the school year) reflect the temporal structure of the period in an interesting way: endpoints of temporal units within the period are marked in memory by the availability of comparatively large numbers of memories. Beginnings of temporal units in the period are better marked than the middle points of the temporal

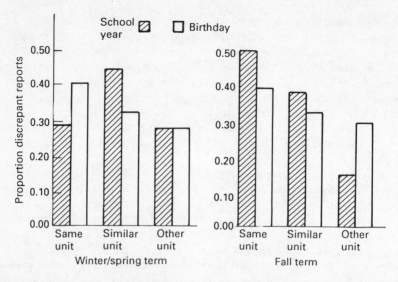

Figure 3.11 Proportion of incorrectly dated memories by school term, structural unit, and dating condition (reproduced by permission of the author and publisher, from Robinson 1986, figure 10.9, p. 185. ©Cambridge University Press)

units in terms of the number of memories recalled, but this is a small and not particularly reliable difference. Finally, the structure of the period can guide memory dating and in the case of the school year may induce forward telescoping in dating consistency. In contrast, dating by a landmark, such as a birthdate, reduces forward telescoping, generally increases dating consistency, and removes dating by the structure of a specific time period (i.e. the terms and holidays of the school year).

Thus it seems likely that strategic sampling of autobiographical memory may also be guided by the temporal structure of the particular time period sampled. Yet we cannot decide on the basis of the experiments considered so far whether or not the effect of temporal structure occurs by directing the retrieval process, by the differential encoding of memories within the period, or by differential forgetting of memories. We might speculate though that the effects found by Robinson may reflect differential forgetting in the following way: perhaps the middle sections of time periods are dominated by rather familiar and routine activities which are frequently repeated. If so then, following White's (1982) findings discussed above, we might argue that these events are highly likely to be forgotten because of the interfering effect of encoding many similar events. Of course, this does not explain why the endpoints of temporal units are better marked, in terms of memories retrieved, than their beginnings and these findings will require further research before we can even begin to speculate as to possible causes (but see Chapter 7 for additional details concerning such 'recency' effects).

Dating by landmarks

One implication of Robinson's finding that memory dating with a landmark event (i.e. birth date) reduces forward telescoping in dating is that provision of landmarks may reduce the number of recent memories recalled in autobiographical memory-retrieval experiments. Clearly this has strong implications for the retention curves reported by Crovitz and Schiffman (1974) and Rubin (1982) for it could be the case that subjects in those studies inaccurately dated at least some of their memories. In the absence of landmark events to guide memory dating, any inaccuracies may have telescoped the date of the memories to a more recent period and this may be one of the factors contributing the large recency effect observed in the studies. Some evidence for this is provided by Garofalo and Hindelang (1977: cited in Loftus and Marburger 1983) who found that up to 20 per cent of crime victims, when asked for dates of victimization episodes occurring in the preceding six months, erroneously dated victimization episodes as having occurred within the six-month period, when in fact these episodes had occurred prior to the six-month period being sampled.

In an interesting study, Baddeley, Lewis and Nimmo-Smith (1978) demonstrated that landmarking may enhance the accuracy of memory dating. Their subjects, who were members of the Applied Psychology Unit subject panel in Cambridge, were asked to recall and date their preceding visit to the Unit. These subjects also listed various strategies they had employed in dating their memory. Detailed records of subject's last visit to the Unit were available to the experimenters, so dating accuracy could be easily verified, and the retention intervals for the subjects varied between 2 and 540 days. The main finding was that error dating increased with retention interval so that there was an average error date of about 19 days for every 100 days of retention. However, subjects who reported relating their last visit to some specific personal event (e.g. a wedding anniversary) were more accurate in dating their memories than subjects who used other strategies. Thus autobiographical memories of events, the date of which are known, may act as landmarks in dating other events.

In an ingenious study reported by Thompson (1982), college undergraduates kept diaries for 14 weeks and recorded events for four days in each week. These diary keepers recorded events which they themselves experienced and events which their roommates had experienced – the roommates were, of course, unaware they were being recorded in this way. In a subsequent memory test for the recorded events remarkably few differences were found in recall between the roommates and diary keepers. A particularly important finding in the study was that memory for *when* an event occurred and memory for *what* occurred were related, but only for the first few weeks of retention. After this period memory for when an event occurred and memory for details of the event became relatively independent. One consequence of this is that when an event is remembered and no date is recalled, then a date must be inferred in some way. Inferences about dates are hardly likely to be exactly correct, and this may explain why Thompson also found that dating error (subjects only dated events they remembered) steadily increased at a rate of about one day for each week of retention, a slightly lower rate than that observed by Baddeley *et al.* (1978). Moreover, in a post-test interview Thompson found that subjects who were comparatively accurate in dating their memories reported using landmark strategies. One notable example of this provided by Thompson (1982: 330) is that of a female student who had, during the study, separated from her boyfriend and who thought of events as 'before Jeff and after Jeff'.

The effect of improving dating accuracy by landmarking recalled events was studied directly by Loftus and Marburger (1983). These authors were partly concerned with some of the practical implications of forward telescoping and in particular with people's responses to questionnaire studies of crime victimization, health, drug use and so on. In their first study Loftus and Marburger interviewed people waiting in an airport and asked them a list of questions relating to recent crime victimization (e.g. has anyone tried to steal anything from you?). For one group of subjects each question was preceded by the phrase 'During the last six months'. For a second group of subjects each question was preceded by mention of a landmark event which, in this case, was the first eruption of Mt St Helen, hence questions for this group read: 'Since the first major eruption of Mt St Helen'. In the six-month group 9.2 per cent of people sampled reported a victimization in the sampled period but in the landmark group only 1.5 per cent (a single subject) reported a victimization episode.

A second study repeated the same basic experiment but with the following modifications: half the subjects were tested exactly six months after the eruption and others eight months after the eruption and 'eight months' was substituted for 'six months' in their questions. Additional questions were also asked and, in particular, subjects were asked if they had had a birthday in the sampled period and if the failure to rescue the American hostages in Iran had occurred in the sampled period. Finally, all subjects first completed the six/eight-month version of the questions and at a later date the Mt St Helen version. The principal finding was that subjects occasionally revised judgements that something had occurred in the six/eight-month period when confronted with the Mt St Helen version of the question, suggesting increased dating accuracy induced by the landmark question. More importantly, a greater number of subjects correctly judged the date of the hostage crisis when provided with the landmark question than with the six/eight-month version of the question. Remarkably, two subjects incorrectly judged their birthdays to have fallen in the six/eight-month condition and revised this when provided with the landmark question – all other subjects correctly judged the occurrence of their birthdays in response to both types of question. In other studies Loftus and Marburger (1983) found that the landmark effect improved dating when the subject provided his/her own personal landmark, when New Year's Day was used as a landmark, and even when a specific date (6 December) was employed as a landmark, although this later effect was less than that induced by the other landmarks. Using a landmark event when dating a memory reduces forward telescoping and may improve dating accuracy. The landmark effect may partly occur because a specific date is specified and this leads the subject to be generally more accurate in dating their memories. However, the landmark effect was greater when the landmarks referred to distinctive events (eruption of Mt St Helen, New Year's Day) than when the landmark referred to a specified date (6 December) indicating that the effect of landmarks in improving dating entails more than just the specification of a date as a reference point.

Friedman and Wilkins (1985) directly investigated people's ability to date public events which had received extensive media coverage. Subjects were asked to date the events on the following time scales, hour, day of week, day of month, and year. They hypothesized that, if subjects dated events by retrieving fragmentary knowledge relating to the event and then inferred a specific year and month, dating accuracy for fine time scales (i.e. hour and day of week) should be more accurate than dating accuracy for more coarse time scales (month and year). This is because the former are retrieved directly from memory, whereas the latter are inferred on the basis of retrieved knowledge. Their findings confirmed this hypothesis and subjects made less errors in dating day of the week and hour of an event than in dating year and month. Moreover, Friedman and Wilkins also found that their subjects frequently recalled autobiographical memories when dating public events, the implication being that these formed the basis of the inference process for estimates of the year and month dates. Finally recent research has further emphasized the role of estimates in dating events. Huttenlocher, Hedges, and Prohaska (1988) proposed that the nature of the time scale used in searching memory and in making a date inference is critical in accurate dating: fine time scales leading to more accurate dating than coarse time scales. Employing a somewhat different model Rubin and Baddeley (1989) argued that the dates of older events are less accurately preserved in memory than the dates of more recent events and consequently that older events are more likely to be misdated.

The implication of these findings is that memory dating may, in general, be an inferential process and that retrieved memories are strategically dated. One common strategy appears to involve calculating a *relative date* for a memory, i.e. calculating when an event might have occurred on the basis of its closeness or distance from an event the date of which is known.

The process of dating

The landmark strategy for dating memories may improve accuracy because more is known about landmark events than arbitrarily selected events (e.g. either the exact date is known or can be easily inferred) and this additional knowledge may facilitate the dating process, but, as we shall see, increased knowledge about an event may introduce further biases into the dating process. Brown, Rips, and Shevell (1985) investigated people's dating accuracy for well-known and less well-known public events. Some of these events were political in nature, e.g. 'Government forces AT&T to break up holdings' (well known), 'Antitrust case against IBM dropped' (less well known), some referred to cultural events, e.g. 'John Lennon dies' (well known), 'Keith Moon of the "Who" dies' (less well known), and some referred to 'natural' occurrences, e.g. 'Chicago experiences coldest day on record' (well known), '25 die in California mud slides' (less well known). Brown *et al.* predicted that the dates of well-known events would tend to be shifted towards the present – in other words well-known events would seem more recent. The principal findings across a series of such dating studies were that, although people were able to accurately judge the correct order of events, they nevertheless dated well-known events as happening more recently than they had and dated less well-known events as being more remote than they were.

These findings quite definitely implicate the role of inferencing in dating memories and show how dates might be inferred on the basis of the amount recalled (or recallable). In a second study, Brown, Shevell, and Rips (1986) argued that two further factors may guide the relative dating (ordering) process. First of all, public events are structurally comparable to stories in that they generally have some theme and actions occur in a more or less fixed order. For example, Richard Nixon could not have resigned as president before he became president! The Watergate scandal must have preceded his resignation and the theme of a duplicitous and secretive administration may suggest that the US bombing of Cambodia most probably occurred sometime during Nixon's tenure as president. Second, public events occur in the context of a perceiver's own personal history and may be associated in memory with records of personal experiences (see Chapter 7 for further discussion of the intersection of public and private events in memory). Thus the structure of public events and their personal context may help determine the relative dates of a set of events.

In two experiments Brown *et al.* investigated the relation of public events and their personal context. In their first experiment subjects dated a set of political and non-political events drawn from the period 1978 to 1982 and these were selected so that all the events were well known to the subjects. The critical manipulation was that subjects should 'think aloud' while dating the events. Brown *et al.* predicted that subjects would mention information other than the date indicating that dating involved an inference process. Subjects should also mention autobiographical details and so show the interrelation of public and private events in memory. It was also expected that subjects, when dating events, would mention other public events thematically related to the target event, indicating the thematic nature of public events. Finally, it was predicted that protocols to dating political events should contain frequent mentions of presidents and presidential administrations but these details would not occur in the protocols for non-political events.

Over 70 per cent of the responses featured non-temporal information and this was the case for 77 per cent of the protocols to political events and 64 per cent of the protocols to non-political events. The non-temporal details in subjects' protocols were sorted into five categories and examples of these are shown in Table 3.2.

The percentages of protocol details falling in each of the five classes for the two types of event – political and non-political – are shown in Table 3.3.

It can be seen from Table 3.3 that over 40 per cent of responses contained at least one autobiographical detail and, although not reliably different, more autobiographical details were mentioned when dating non-political as compared to political events. Thematically related public events were also evident in the dating of political events but not in the dating of non-political events. Finally, as predicted, many more references to presidents and presidential terms of office emerged in the dating protocols for political than non-political events. These findings support Brown *et al.*'s proposal that public events may be dated with reference to private events and this is especially marked for non-political public events. Although political public events are also dated by means of autobiographical details, non-autobiographical thematically related details apparently supplement the dating process for these events.

In order to investigate this pattern of findings further Brown *et al.* conducted a second experiment. They hypothesized that it should be easier to locate a political event temporally during a period bounded by other political occurrences and dif-

Table 3.2 Examples of types of dating protocols

Specific temporal information
Congress extends the ERA deadline: 'That was three years before last June, so it would have been about June of '79.'

Presidential reference
Andrew Young leaves UN post: 'It happened near the end of . . . Carter's term, so . . . May of '79.'

Datable public events in same narrative
Sadat and Begin win the Nobel Prize: 'It was a little while after Camp David, which was in '77, I'd say . . . February of '78.'

Datable public events not in same narrative
Paul McCartney arrested by Japanese police: 'Was approximately during the hostage crisis in Iran, because *Saturday Night Live* had this great take-off on it, doing the whole thing of the hostage crisis, day one of Paul McCartney in Japan. . . . So the hostages, what I was saying, the hostages were freed in January of 1981, they'd been in 180 days, approximately, I think, which would have been halfway back to 1980; Paul McCartney was arrested in 1980, then, we'll say, say September 1980.'

Autobiographical reference
François Mitterrand becomes French premier: 'I got in an argument with somebody about Mitterrand, I was in favor of him, and this person wasn't, and I think it was in the spring of, say, April or something, of 1981 that he was elected.'

(Reproduced by permission of the authors and publishers, from Brown, Shevell, and Rips 1986, table 9.2, p. 148. ©Cambridge University Press)

Table 3.3 Proportions of classified protocols

	Event type	
Response category	Political	Non-political
Unjustified responses	.22	.34
Justified responses		
Specific temporal facts	.07	.08
Presidential term of office	.35	.04
Datable event from same narrative	.32	.09
Datable event not in same narrative	.12	.13
Autobiographical event	.31	.50

(Reproduced by permission of the authors and publishers, from Brown, Shevell, and Rips 1986, table 9.3, p. 148. ©Cambridge University Press)

ficult if the period is bounded by personal occurrences. In contrast it should be easier to date a non-political event in a period bounded by personal occurrences than in one bounded by political occurrences. Taking advantage of the fact that their undergraduate students had attended high school during the Carter presidential administration (1978 to 1980) and college during the first three years of the Reagan administration (1980 to 1983), Brown *et al.* constructed the following experiment:

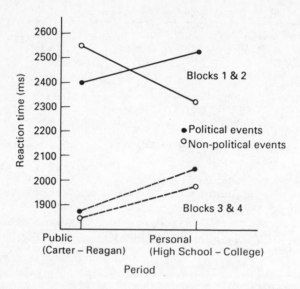

Figure 3.12 Mean reaction time to judge whether events occurred during personally described or publicly described times periods (reproduced by permission of the authors and publisher from Brown, Shevell, and Rips 1986, figure 9.1, p. 154. ©Cambridge University Press)

Two sets of political and non-political events were selected, half of each occurring in the two time periods (1978 to 1980 and 1980 to 1983). Subjects were required to judge whether an event occurred either during high-school years or during college years and, in another condition, whether the same event had occurred during the Carter administration or during the Reagan administration. Subjects registered they had a date in mind by pressing a button and reaction time from presentation of the event to button press was recorded. In a blocked presentation half the subjects judged high school vs. college first (blocks 1 and 2) and Carter vs. Reagan second (blocks 3 and 4), the order being reversed for the remaining subjects.

Figure 3.12 shows the reaction times for blocks 1 and 2 and blocks 3 and 4 separately.

Before considering the findings we should first note an unfortunate methodological flaw with the experiment which may have obscured the experimental effect in blocks 3 and 4 of the experiment (bottom part of Figure 3.12). Because all subjects responded under all conditions, both personal and political time periods were available to subjects when completing blocks 3 and 4. It seems almost certain that subjects would have noticed that, although differently named, the two sets of periods refer to the same times (i.e. 1978 to 1980 and 1980 to 1983). Thus, on the latter two blocks of trials subjects may have elected to use only one set of named periods. For example, when presented in a later block with the personal time periods high school vs. college, a subject may have simply covertly renamed these Carter vs. Reagan. So the findings from the last two blocks of the trials will not be considered here.

The main findings of interest come from the first two blocks of trials (upper portion of Figure 3.12) when subjects were unaware of all the time periods to be used in the experiment. It can be seen that the reaction times confirm Brown *et al.*'s predictions and political events are dated more quickly in the context of political periods than personal periods, whereas non-political events are dated more quickly in the context of personal periods than political periods. Conversely, political events are dated more slowly in the context of personal periods, whereas non-political events are dated more slowly in the context of political periods.

It seems, then, that the representation in memory of public political events may be more closely associated with thematically related political events than with autobiographical knowledge, although, as Brown *et al.*'s protocol study shows, political events are, none the less, associated with at least some autobiographical knowledge. Non-political events appear to be more closely associated with autobiographical details, possibly because they are less cohesive thematically or maybe because they make more personal impact than the somewhat personally remoter political events. Just exactly how these effects arise will require additional experiments which have yet to be reported.

In conclusion, the studies of Brown, Rips and Shevell (1985) and Brown, Shevell, and Rips (1986) show that memory dating may be biased by the amount known about an event. Brown *et al.* (1985) refer to this as the *accessibility principle* and argue that, when the date of an event is not known, then the more information that can be retrieved from memory about that event the more likely the event is to be (erroneously) dated as being from a recent time period. Conversely, when little is known about an event, the probability of the event being (erroneously) dated to some remote time period increases (but see Thompson, Skowronski, and Lee, 1988, for a different interpretation of these findings). Brown *et al.* (1986) demonstrated that the dating process is largely inferential and inferences are primarily based on autobiographical details which may be supplemented and partly superseded by information thematically related to the target event, when such information is available.

Summary: memory retrieval and memory dating – complex processes in autobiographical memory

We started this chapter with two main questions: 'What would the distribution of memory dates look like if you tried to list as many memories as you could from your life?' and 'How could we explain the distribution of the ages of the memories?' It turns out that the answers to these questions are complex and many factors influence just which memories are retrieved and the eventual dates which are assigned to them. Certainly our original simple assumption that all time periods in memory are sampled equally appears no longer tenable. Nevertheless the research reviewed in this chapter suggests some specific features of memory retrieval and memory dating:

1 Recent events are well remembered

Most of the studies reviewed above quite clearly demonstrate that more memories of recent than remote events are retrieved across a range of different retrieval tasks.

2   The process of memory retrieval is highly flexible

Autobiographical memory retrieval is highly task dependent and cue sensitive. Different tasks will lead to the sampling of different sets of memories. General cues allow retrieval strategies to dominate the retrieval process, whereas specific cues appear to focus the retrieval process and minimize the effect of retrieval strategies.

3   Exact dates are not stored in memory

The dates of remembered events are inferred after retrieval and coarse-grained exact temporal information is not, in general, represented along with memories of events. Although for some landmark memories exact dates will be known.

4   Distinctive events are remembered, routine events are forgotten

Most recalled memories are of events which were, in some way, distinctive. Memories for routine events appear to be rapidly forgotten and this may be because of the interference effect of encoding many memories of similar events.

5   The nature of memories and the nature of time periods influence both retrieval and dating

Events about which much is known, but not the date, may be telescoped forwards in time. The temporal structure of a time period from which a memory is drawn can determine accessibility of a memory and inference of a date.

In sampling autobiographical memory across the life-span it seems likely that most, if not all, of these factors would influence the resulting distribution of memory ages.

4 • VIVID MEMORIES

Perhaps one of the most obvious observations we can make about autobiographical memory is that some events are remembered in more detail and clarity than other events. For example, I can remember in great detail important job interviews, the birth of my sons, and the death of my grandmother. In contrast, I cannot remember what I had for breakfast three weeks ago, what clothes I wore last Christmas day, or who came out to eat with the visiting speaker after the last talk I attended. Of course, I could make pretty good guesses about the details of these events but I could not remember them in the sense that I can remember the details of the personally significant events listed previously. Interestingly, I undoubtedly would be able to remember what clothes I had worn on Christmas day if you had asked me on 26 December, although by January my memory would have become hazy and maybe by that time I simply wouldn't remember.

Why do some memories retain this vivid quality as though the events they relate to 'only happened yesterday'? Do such memories constitute a special class of autobiographical memories? Are vivid memories correct? That is to say, do these memories accurately represent the details of past occurrences or can they contain minor, or even major, errors – could a vivid memory be a total fabrication? What possible purpose could such memories serve? The study of vivid memories by cognitive psychologists has brought some of these questions into sharper focus and it is these studies which are the subject of this chapter.

Flashbulb memories

The term 'flashbulb memories' was originally used by Brown and Kulik (1977) in a landmark paper which set the scene for the study of vivid memories. We will consider the Brown and Kulik paper shortly but here we might note that the memories which are examined in flashbulb-memory research are typically (but not always) memories of events of national or international significance – the assassination of John F. Kennedy, the space-shuttle disaster, and so on. The focus of flashbulb-memory studies is on what people can remember of the circumstances in which they learned of an outstanding and usually surprising national/international event.

Almost a century before the Brown and Kulik study Colegrove (1899, see Chapter 2) reported a survey of people's memories for their circumstances when they learned of the assassination of Lincoln. Colegrove questioned 179 people and found that 127 were able to provide full descriptions of where they were, who they were with, and what they were doing, when they heard the news of Lincoln's death. What's remarkable about this is that the assassination of Lincoln occurred 33 years before Colegrove conducted his interviews! In order to appreciate the detail and clarity of these 33-year-old memories, consider the following account provided by one of Colegrove's subjects:

> My father and I were on the road to A– in the state of Maine to purchase the 'fixings' needed for my graduation. When we were driving down a steep hill into the city we felt that something was wrong. Everybody looked so sad, and there was such terrible excitement that my father stopped his horse, and leaning from the carriage called: 'What is it my friends? What has happened?' 'Haven't you heard?' was the reply –'Lincoln has been assassinated.' The lines fell from my father's limp hands, and with tears streaming from his eyes he sat as one bereft of motion. We were far from home, and much must be done, so he rallied after a time, and we finished our work as well as our heavy hearts would allow.

Of course, not all the memory descriptions were of this vividness or length, but all contained information about time of day, exact location, and informant. It is worth considering at this point the histrionic, almost journalistic, nature of the above account. It has the feel of a story which has been told many times and which has been embellished with literary devices such as 'the lines fell from my father's limp hands', 'he sat as one bereft of motion', etc. The structure of the account carefully builds up to the shocking news and then tails off into the resulting sadness. Later on we will consider what these types of narrative conventions may suggest about the origins and functions of vivid memories.

Brown and Kulik (1977) undertook the first systematic study of flashbulb memories and their starting point was people's memories for the assassination of the American president, John F. Kennedy, which occurred in 1963. Brown and Kulik provide the following accounts of their own flashbulb memories of hearing the news of the assassination:

> I was on the telephone with Miss Johnson, the Dean's secretary, about some departmental business. Suddenly, she broke in with: 'Excuse me a moment; everyone is excited about something. What? Mr Kennedy has been shot!' We hung up, I opened my door to hear further news, as it came in, and then resumed my work on some forgotten business that 'had to be finished' that day.
>
> (Brown)

> I was seated in a sixth-grade music class, and over the intercom I was told that the president had been shot. At first, everyone just looked at each other. Then the class started yelling, and the music teacher tried to calm everyone down.

About ten minutes later I heard over the intercom that Kennedy had died and that everyone should return to their homeroom. I remember that when I got to my homeroom my teacher was crying and everyone was standing in a state of shock. They told us to go home.

(Kulik)

Brown and Kulik called these types of memories 'flashbulb memories' because they wanted to convey the surprising quality of the initiating event and the indiscriminate preservation in memory of apparently trivial details. Clearly it is important that major events are retained in memory, but why should the circumstances in which one heard some news also be retained? What possible function could be served by Kulik remembering that he had been in a music class when he heard the news of the assassination, or by Brown remembering that he had been on the telephone to the Dean's secretary? Although it is unusual that such details are retained in memory, it is also clear that many other details are forgotten. As Brown and Kulik point out, flashbulb memories are not indiscriminate records of a prior event but rather are incomplete records containing only specific types of information.

In order to account for flashbulb memories Brown and Kulik postulated that some special type of encoding takes place for certain types of events. In particular, they drew upon a concept put forward by Livingston (1967) termed 'Now print!'. The 'Now print!' hypothesis proposes that, when an event is recognized as being highly novel or unexpected and is seen as being of biological meaning, then lower brain areas involved in emotions (the limbic system) massively activate cortical areas causing all recent brain events to be permanently recorded in memory. The term 'biological meaning' is meant to convey the idea that some events directly impinge upon the durability of the self. In evolutionary terms, we could imagine a special memory mechanism developing which served to record, in some detail, features of events which were markedly life threatening or, maybe, life enhancing. These details would then be available to the encoding organism for reflection and might serve as a basis for action in similar biologically meaningful events and so confer a survival advantage upon organisms that could create such memories: vividly remembering how you escaped from the lion, when attacked a second time, might help you quickly to formulate and implement an effective escape routine appropriate for current circumstances. Of course, in modern society we no longer have to worry over much about marauding lions but presumably the flashbulb-memory mechanism still operates and operates in response to brain states which involve excitatory input from the limbic system to the cortex. Thus Brown and Kulik start with the assumption that there is something special about flashbulb memories and that this may be related to a privileged form of encoding – the 'Now print!' mechanism.

One further caveat is that the 'Now print!' mechanism, as conceived by Brown and Kulik, does not lead to the indiscriminate recording in memory of brain states. Rather this mechanism leads to records of brain activity above a certain 'level of organization'. What Brown and Kulik mean by this is that the memory contains comparatively literal or veridical records of the contents of consciousness associated with the precipitating event, e.g. talking to the Dean's secretary, observing a teacher crying, etc. We shall see later in this chapter that this aspect of the Brown and Kulik version of 'Now print!' is particularly problematic.

In their study Brown and Kulik selected ten events, nine of which featured the death or injury of political figures. The assassination events were: The shooting to death of Medgar Evers (1963), John F. Kennedy (1963), Malcolm 'X' (1965), Martin Luther King (1968), and Robert F. Kennedy (1968). The non-assassination events were: Ted Kennedy's involvement in a drowning incident (1969), the failed assassination attempts on George Wallace (1972) and Gerald Ford (1975), and the death by natural causes of General Franco (1975). The tenth event required subjects to recall a personal unexpected shock such as the death or sudden illness of a relative or friend. These events were chosen for two reasons. First, they all satisfy the proposal of the 'Now print!' hypothesis that flashbulb memories are created in response to novel events. Second, the events will be of differential importance to different ethnic groups. For instance, the murders of Medgar Evers, Martin Luther King, and Malcolm 'X', and possibly the attempt on George Wallace's life, might all be of some consequence to black Americans but not necessarily of any consequence to white Americans. In contrast, the assassination of John F. Kennedy and Robert Kennedy and the incidents involving Wallace and Ford might be of consequence to white, but not black, Americans.

In the study 40 white and 40 black Americans were asked to recall the circumstances in which they learned about each of the ten events – specifically they were asked 'Do you recall the circumstances in which you first heard that . . .', followed by one of the ten target events. In response to this query the subjects first of all indicated if they could or could not remember the circumstances in which they learned about the target event and then wrote accounts of their circumstances in any order and at any length. After recording a memory, a subject then rated the consequentiality of the event on a 5-point scale. The critical instruction here was 'Probably the best question to ask yourself in rating consequentiality is "What consequences for my life, both direct and indirect, has this event had?" ' Subjects also estimated how frequently they had related the account of their memory on previous occasions.

In scoring the accounts as flashbulb memories Brown and Kulik used the following scheme. First of all, they noted that six 'canonical' categories of information appeared in nearly all the accounts. These were *place, ongoing event, informant, affect in others, own affect*, and *aftermath* – examples of all these canonical categories can be easily seen in the account cited above from Colegrove (1899). Note that the categories themselves are abstractions and that the subjects differed radically in their specific responses. For the tenth event – the personal event – an additional two categories were observed, *event* and *person*. These categories were not, of course, present in response to the public events because they were specified by those events.

In order for a memory to be classified as a flashbulb memory, Brown and Kulik required a 'Yes' answer to the question 'Do you recall the circumstances in which you first heard that . . .?' and mention of at least one of the six canonical categories. Table 4.1 shows the distribution of subject's flashbulb memories, by ethnic group, to each of the target events.

The two most important findings from Table 4.1 are for the incidence of flashbulb memories linked to Malcolm 'X' and Martin Luther King. Both these men had been major figures in the black civil-rights movement of the 1960s and their assassinations were rated as being highly consequential by the black subjects – but not by the white

Table 4.1 Numbers of white and black subjects with flashbulb (FB) memories for different events

Event	FB Whites (N = 40)	FB Blacks (N = 40)
*1 Medgar Evers	0	5
2 John F. Kennedy	39	40
***3 Malcolm X	1	14
***4 Martin Luther King	13	30
5 Robert F. Kennedy	25	20
6 Ted Kennedy	13	10
**7 George Wallace	11	20
8 Gerald Ford	23	16
9 Gen. Francisco Franco	17	13
10 A personal, unexpected shock	37	32(36)

*Frequency of flashbulb memories for these events differed reliably across the two groups.
(Reproduced by permission of the authors and publisher, from Brown and Kulik 1977, table 2, p. 89.
©Elsevier Science Publications B.V.)

subjects. As Table 4.1 shows, black Americans, in this sample at least, had far more flashbulb memories of hearing about these two assassinations than did white Americans. This then would seem to support Brown and Kulik's claim that consequentiality is critical in the formation of flashbulb memories and, by implication, the 'Now print!' hypothesis is also supported.

But what about the distribution of flashbulb memories for the assassinations of the Kennedys? Remarkably, virtually all the subjects had flashbulb memories of hearing the news that John F. Kennedy had been assassinated and there was no reliable difference between the number of black and white subjects who had flashbulb memories of hearing of the news of Robert Kennedy's assassination. As Brown and Kulik point out, both the Kennedys were, however, prominent in civil rights and both seemed to hold out the promise of an equal and generally better society for all. This aspect of the Kennedys may have made their deaths of equal perceived consequence for both black and white Americans and hence the distribution of flashbulb memories shown in Table 4.1.

In further analyses Brown and Kulik found that ratings of consequentiality were highly correlated with length of memory description so that more consequential events received more elaborate memory descriptions. Similarly, ratings of rehearsal were highly correlated with elaborateness of memory descriptions and with ratings of consequentiality. These correlations varied somewhat for the two different ethic groups but overall the results were the same: consequentiality, rehearsal, and elaborateness of memory description were all positively interrelated.

Brown and Kulik interpret these findings as follows: flashbulb memories are the result of surprising and consequential events. The assassinations of the black civil-rights leaders were consequential events for members of the black community and gave rise to flashbulb memories for members of this group but not for members of other racial groups. The assassinations of John and Robert Kennedy were of consequence to both black and white Americans and so generally precipitated flashbulb memories. Personal shocks were rated as being of slightly higher consequentiality than public events and, together with the assassination of John F. Kennedy, gave rise to the highest number of flashbulb memories. Thus consequentiality appears to be a critical determinant of flashbulb memories. The personal circumstances associated with surprising and consequential events, enshrined in flashbulb memories, are often recounted to other people and hence the memories of these events are associated with high levels of rehearsal.

There is, however, a problem here: do flashbulb memories retain their vivid qualities because of some special encoding mechanism or do they retain these qualities because they have been frequently rehearsed? Clearly people will talk and think about events of great national significance and similarly will unwittingly rehearse events of more personal significance. If these rehearsals are more frequent than the rehearsals of more run-of-the-mill occurrences, then rehearsal may be sufficient to 'keep alive' the memory – to make it seem as though it happened 'only yesterday' – and so we would not need to postulate any special encoding mechanism. In Brown and Kulik's study there are no data which can allow us to choose between these alternatives but the authors see a rather different and secondary role for rehearsal and comment that 'It is our assumption then that the flashbulb memory is always there, unchanging as the slumbering Rhinegold, and serving by means of rehearsal to generate some variety of accounts.' We will see later that this assumption is highly questionable, but, before we turn to criticisms of Brown and Kulik – of which there are many of varying degrees of veracity, one more seminal study of flashbulb memories will be considered.

At the same time that Brown and Kulik were conducting their classic study of flashbulb memories, Yarmey and Bull (1978) were conducting a far larger study of groups of Canadian and American individuals' memories for the circumstances in which they learned of the assassination of John F. Kennedy. Yarmey and Bull asked 182 Americans and 215 Canadians to recall, (1) what time of day it was when they heard the news about the Kennedy assassination, (2) where they were, (3) who they were with, (4) what they were doing one hour after they heard the news, and (5) what they were doing one hour before they heard the news. The subjects were split into groups according to variations in questions (4) and (5) which required some subjects to recall what they were doing four hours or twenty-four hours before and after hearing of the assassination. Yarmey and Bull expected that, overall, Americans would have more detailed memories than Canadians and that there might be some amnesia in both groups for time periods immediately surrounding the event of hearing the shocking news. Finally, the subjects in the Yarmey and Bull study varied in ages falling into roughly four groups: 18–22 years old, 23–27 years old, 28–65 years old, and a small group who were all over the age of 66. Note that these groups contained roughly equal numbers of Americans and Canadians.

To Yarmey and Bull's surprise Americans and Canadians did not differ in the clarity of their memories for the activities that had been engaged in at the time of hearing of John F. Kennedy's assassination, amount recalled being 90 per cent to the Americans and 84 per cent to the Canadians. Similarly there were no sex differences and the recall rate for women did not differ from the recall rate for men. In fact the only difference Yarmey and Bull found was that for the youngest age group (who would have been in their early teens when the assassination occurred) memory was depressed.

Interestingly, these poorer memories differed by nationality – 85 per cent recall for Americans and 66 per cent recall for Canadians. This is, however, probably a relatively uninteresting finding: undoubtedly the Canadians – who at the time would have been schoolchildren – would have heard the news later than their American counterparts (perhaps after school hours) and would not have experienced the same interruption to their daily schedule, e.g. teachers weeping and the premature termination of the school day. Thus the event would not have the same memorable qualities for young Canadians as it did for young Americans.

What is remarkable about these findings is that twelve years after the event nearly everybody – regardless of nationality – remembered what they had been doing, where they were, and who they were with, when they heard about the assassination of President Kennedy. Consider for a moment, what events can you remember in this detail which occurred twelve or more years ago?

Yarmey and Bull also make one further very important point in their paper. As with nearly all autobiographical memory research it is impossible to know whether the remembered event is true, is veridical, or not. As Yarmey and Bull point out, however, this question is only of interest if the researcher takes a certain perspective upon memory. That is, if memories are, as it were, 'things' and these things are records of the past, then the question of veridicality is of central importance. If, on the other hand, we view memory as some type of belief system, then what is important is what people *believe* has happened, what is important is what people *claim* to remember, and the question of veridicality is only of secondary importance. Conceptualizing memory as a belief system is something of a heresy in contemporary cognitive psychology and there are few cognitive psychologists who view this as a fruitful approach to the study of memory. Nevertheless, later in this chapter it will become apparent that people's beliefs might indeed be an important and overlooked factor in the study of vivid memories.

Criticisms of the 'flashbulb' memory concept

Neisser (1982) put forward an apparently devastating critique of Brown and Kulik's concept of flashbulb memories. Neisser's critique focuses on four main aspects of flashbulb memories, their veridicality, the way in which they are created in the human brain, the role of consequentiality, and the content of flashbulb memories – let's consider veridicality first.

To begin with, Neisser argues that it is naïve to accept the proposal at face value, that people do in fact have highly detailed veridical memories of, at least some, past events. Why should we accept this proposal when, after all, it is only based upon what people claim to remember? Especially when we know from our own experience and from laboratory studies that memory is hardly reliable. Neisser cites a memory recorded by Linton (1975) of a flashbulb memory of hearing of the murder of John F. Kennedy. The remembered event featured Linton herself but she had no memory of the event; moreover she was able to demonstrate that she could not have been involved in the remembered event because she was not in the same place as the rememberer. This experience apparently persuaded Linton to abandon her own study of this class of memories. In support of Linton, Neisser offers his own (erroneous) flashbulb memory:

> For many years I have remembered how I heard the news of the Japanese attack on Pearl Harbor, which occurred on the day before my thirteenth birthday. I recall sitting in the living room of our house – we only lived in that house for one year, but I remember it well – listening to a baseball game on the radio. The game was interrupted by an announcement of the attack, and I rushed upstairs to tell my mother. This memory has been so clear for so long that I never confronted its inherent absurdity until last year: no one broadcasts baseball games in December!

Thus Neisser shows that flashbulb memories which may exist for many years can be incorrect. Clearly this is a direct disconfirmation of the 'Now print!' hypothesis, for how could one have a non-veridical flashbulb memory if flashbulb memories only arise by means of a special encoding mechanism?

One problem with the Brown and Kulik model, as we noted earlier, is that it is not clear what role rehearsal plays in flashbulb recall. Brown and Kulik argued that rehearsal played no role and that recounting a memory involved a more or less true description of what a person actually experienced. As Brown and Kulik offered no data in support of their claim, then clearly any other claim is equally plausible and Neisser's counter-proposal is that rehearsal, is in fact, the critical factor. According to Neisser, the significance of an event is assigned *after* it has been experienced, in the following hours, days, and even years. That is to say that, after an event has been experienced, the event is re-evaluated in a person's mind or perhaps more publicly in conversations and, in exceptional circumstances, an event might be extensively re-evaluated in a society at large. Neisser argues that it is this process of re-evaluation which gives rise to apparently detailed and vivid memories and not some special encoding mechanism which takes a snapshot of recent brain events.

One possible advantage of the rehearsal view is that it provides an obvious way in which inaccuracies might be preserved in memory. As an event is frequently talked and thought about, details arising from these rehearsals will become incorporated with the original memory and, eventually, a composite memory will be constructed which represents a person's flashbulb memory of an event. This proposal seems most plausible if we accept the premise that consequentiality is assigned only after an event has occurred. Certainly in the case of the assassination of leading political figures such as Martin Luther King and the Kennedys, the consequences would unfold over time and were evaluated endlessly in the media. Thus it seems possible that flashbulb memories might arise through some process of rehearsal which itself is dependent on assigning consequentiality after an event has occurred.

But consequentiality is not always assigned only after an event has occurred. For many personal and nationally important events consequentiality may be assigned long before the event occurs. For instance, the birth of a child is an event of major consequence in a person's life but it is hardly unexpected and the consequentiality of this event may be appreciated, at least to some extent, long before the event takes place. For events of national importance Neisser cites the resignation of President Nixon, an event which was hardly unexpected, but like the birth of a child has been found to be frequently associated with flashbulb memories. Consequentiality does not then appear to be a critical factor in the creation of flashbulb memories and it may be that the overlooked factor of rehearsal is in fact the more important process in flashbulb-memory creation.

Brown and Kulik also argued that the canonical categories of information – who, what, when, where and why – which were so frequently reported by subjects with flashbulb memories, indicated that some common encoding mechanism had been employed when the events were experienced. Neisser, however, sees a different interpretation and argues that these so called 'canonical' categories might reflect narrative conventions rather than a special encoding mechanism. After all, when journalists and other professional writers report an event, they focus on the who, what, when, where, and why of the event and, as Neisser points out, also include a few interesting details. We would not want to claim, however, that every reporter was recounting a flashbulb memory every time they wrote a story! Similarly people in general appear to follow something like this set of narrative conventions when they report an event but, again, we would not want to infer from this that for every report the underlying knowledge structure is a flashbulb memory. Thus, the 'canonical' categories do not necessarily support the notion of a special encoding mechanism.

Finally, Neisser considers the function of flashbulb memories. Recall that Brown and Kulik had suggested that flashbulb memories might confer a survival advantage by providing a record of critical details relating to an experience of biological significance. But if flashbulb memories can be inaccurate, arise by rehearsal and not by a special encoding mechanism, and share many features with other types of memories which are not flashbulb, then the unique evolutionary status of such memories is questionable. Instead Neisser argues that flashbulb memories represent the intersection of public and private history – the point where our lives intersect with the course of history. According to Neisser (p. 48), flashbulb memories 'are the places where we line up our own lives with the course of history itself and say "I was there" '. Thus, in Neisser's view, the accuracy or inaccuracy of flashbulb memories is of little interest; what is important is how the memory acts as a benchmark which signals the intersection of personal and public history. Memories which act as benchmarks have the quality of great vividness, perhaps because of rehearsal, or perhaps because of their intrinsic function of locating us in time and in the history of a culture.

In summary, then, Neisser argues that flashbulb memories can be inaccurate and so are unlikely to arise by way of some special encoding mechanism. On the other hand, flashbulb memories might arise by rehearsal which occurs when we think and talk about some previously experienced event. Consequentiality is unlikely to be a distinguishing feature of flashbulb memories as this can be estimated before an event occurs and in many cases is only assigned after the experience of an event. Note that Neisser also dismisses emotion as a causative factor in the creation of flashbulb memories because, he claims, emotions are associated with a narrowing of attention and therefore would not lead to detailed memories. In addition, the content of flashbulb memories, which is evident in subjects' reports of their memories, may reflect the operation of narrative conventions rather than any fixed quality of the memories. Thus flashbulb memories may not constitute a special or unique class of autobiographical memories which have arisen through the operation of a special-purpose encoding mechanism. Rather, flashbulb memories are like other autobiographical memories, the differences being that they have been frequently rehearsed and represent the intersection of personal and public history. We will consider next research which both supports and questions this alternative account of flashbulb memories.

Veridicality and the determinants of flashbulb memories

One of the major claims made by Brown and Kulik was that flashbulb memories are immune to forgetting. In order to investigate this claim researchers typically require subjects to recall an event on more than one occasion. If the memory descriptions show some agreement over time, then we can infer that, at the very least, the subject is employing the same knowledge base each time they 'remember'. Of course, we would not expect the various memory descriptions to be exactly the same and many factors might influence what a person chooses to report on each occasion. Yet if Brown and Kulik are correct, we would expect repeated descriptions of events for which there are flashbulb memories to vary in minor details only. For instance, a person might forget some trivial detail contained in a flashbulb memory but would not forget canonical categories of knowledge such as who, what, where, when, and why.

In an important flashbulb-memory study Pillemer (1984) examined people's memories of the 1981 assassination attempt on President Reagan. In Pillemer's study a large group of subjects completed a questionnaire about their memories of the circumstances in which they heard of the assassination attempt approximately one month after the event. Of these subjects a smaller sample also filled out the questionnaire six and half months later and a further group who had not been previously tested also completed the questionnaire at this time.

The questionnaire employed by Pillemer was based upon the Brown and Kulik procedure and required subjects to write a description of their memory and then answer a series of questions about the memory. Table 4.2 shows the composition of the questionnaire. Note that categories 1b and 1c are scores which Pillemer derived from the subject's memory descriptions.

Before turning to the detailed findings, consider the following flashbulb-memory description provided by one of Pillemer's subjects.

> On the afternoon it occurred, my husband and I were returning from a holiday in the Caribbean and had reached the Miami Airport. We were standing in line to check baggage or tickets or something, with other people near and people passing to and fro. I heard a man next to me say to his companion 'You heard about President?', and the other one say something like 'Yes, have they got the guy who shot him?' I cannot recall the exact wording but I know that I had learned someone had shot President Reagan and some news about it already existed. My immediate reaction was 'Oh God here we go again', and then a feeling of resignation, depression, we have been through this before and it was terrible, and an ironic recall of the superstition that Presidents elected in years 00, 20, 40, 60, 80, etc. will not finish their terms alive. We boarded the plane

Table 4.2 Flashbulb-memory questionnaire

1 Open-ended memories
   a. existence (yes – no)
   b. number of informational content categories
   c. number of words

2 Direct questions about memories
   a. memories for six canonical categories of information
   b. visual memories
   c. non-visual sensory memories
   d. thoughts following hearing of shooting
   e. number of rehearsals

3 Reactions and attitudes*
   a. intensity of emotional reaction at first hearing
   b. degree of surprise at first hearing
   c. degree of impact at first hearing
   d. degree of impact in retrospect
   e. perceived severity of injury at first hearing
   f. present opinion of Reagan
   g. opinion of Reagan prior to shooting
   h. type of emotion experienced

*Reactions a–g were rated by subjects on ordered five-point scales.
(Reproduced by permission of the author and publisher, from Pillemer 1984, table 1, p. 68. ©Elsevier Science Publications B.V.)

before we heard any more, and then I was asked by a young couple, visibly shaken, if I knew anything. Shortly after the plane took off the captain made an announcement giving all the information he had up to that time.

Compare this description to the ones listed earlier in this chapter. The memory description for the Reagan assassination attempt appears altogether less polished; it has the feel of a memory which has not been greatly rehearsed and honed into a dramatic tale like that of the memory for the assassination of Lincoln. Similarly it lacks the brevity and directness of the other memory descriptions. In short, it seems more like a memory than a story.

The principal findings of the Pillemer study were that most people had flashbulb memories of the Reagan assassination attempt and that most people experienced some surprise and emotion when they heard the news. However, not everybody regarded the event as consequential and indeed the majority of Pillemer's subjects regarded the event as low in consequentiality, once they had learned of the positive prognosis for the president. Remarkably, virtually no one in the main sample judged that they had rehearsed their memory and the majority of retested subjects judged that they had rehearsed their memory comparatively infrequently – of course, they must have rehearsed it at least once because they completed Pillemer's questionnaire shortly after the event. Finally, subjects' repeated memory descriptions were highly consistent, showing agreement on nearly five (out of a possible six) of the canonical categories.

These then are unusual findings: an event which is not judged as consequential leads to flashbulb memories; moreover, the memory receives little or no rehearsal, yet maintains its flashbulb qualities. Clearly neither the Brown and Kulik nor the Neisser views can accommodate these findings. A further finding, however, tends to favour something like a compilation of the Brown and Kulik and Neisser views. Pillemer found that affective reactions at the time of hearing the news were reliable predictors of flashbulb memories seven months later (but were not reliable predictors one month after the event). Affective reactions were also reliable predictors of the sensory nature of the memories (i.e. images of the event), consistency of memory over time and, most importantly, the stronger the affective reaction the more elaborate and consistent the memory.

Flashbulb memories one month after the event appeared to be independent of Pillemer's various measures suggesting that they had not received any special encoding. Perhaps most memories for surprising but fairly non-consequential events can be recalled in some detail up to one month after the event. The degree of emotional reaction was, however, associated with the nature of flashbulb memories after a seven-month delay, suggesting that the affective reaction had somehow maintained the vividness of the memory. One speculative interpretation of this is that events which evoke an emotional response are encoded in such a way as to preserve the details of the event in memory. This does not, however, require a special or privileged encoding mechanism. Emotional events must entail processing which involves personally important goals, processing which directly engages central components of one's own cognitive system. Possibly such processing ensures that the particular event is encoded in pre-existing knowledge structures in memory, and this may facilitate the preservation of details of the event. Indeed, Pillemer asked people what thoughts came to mind when they heard about the Reagan assassination and found that most people recalled previous successful and failed assassination attempts of political leaders (particularly prominent were memories of hearing about the assassination of John F. Kennedy).

Related to this Conway (1988b) asked first-year Cambridge undergraduate students to rate the vividness of their memories for novel events occurring in their first week at Cambridge. The students rated their memories on a number of scales similar to those employed in the Pillemer study two weeks after the events had occurred and again four months later. As in the Pillemer study, none of the various measures were good predictors of memory vividness after two weeks, but four months later emotional reaction and surprise emerged as predictors of vividness. Conway suggested that initially most memories are vivid and that this is independent of encoding factors. Perhaps memories lose their vividness as other, similar, events are experienced and the original event becomes less accessible in memory. For memories of events which can be coded into an organizing knowledge structure in memory, then vividness may be maintained over a longer period. Conway suggested that the students' vivid memories were associated with knowledge structures representing the period 'my first term at university' (see Chapter 6). More recently Pillemer, Goldsmith, Panter, and White (1988) found that students' recall of events occurring in their first year at college are highly related to the emotional quality of the original events, high levels of emotion being associated with high levels of memory vividness up to 22 years after an event.

Emotional reaction at the time of an event may predispose a person to encode their memory of the event in terms of knowledge structures in long-term memory and this integration of the memory with memory in general may help to maintain the vividness or flashbulb quality of a memory. However, not all repeated recall studies have reached this conclusion (or indeed anything like it!) and in a recent paper McCloskey, Wible, and Cohen (1988) question the veridicality, consistency, and determinants of flashbulb memories.

In the McCloskey *et al.* study subjects were asked to remember their circumstances when they heard the news of the space-shuttle disaster – the explosion shortly after take-off of the space shuttle *Challenger* on 28 January 1986. Subjects recalled their memories a few days after the event and a subset of these subjects repeated their recall nine months later. In addition, a further group of subjects who had not been tested originally also recalled their memories of the event after a nine-month delay. Unlike the previous studies, the subjects in the McCloskey *et al.* experiment did not write descriptions of their memories nor did they complete ratings about emotion, consequentiality, surprise, etc. Instead McCloskey *et al.* required their subjects to answer the following four questions.

1 Where were you when you first learned of the explosion?
2 What were you doing when you first learned of the explosion?
3 Did you see the event at the time it was actually happening, or did you learn about it later? If later, how did you learn about it?
4 What were your first thoughts upon hearing the news?

These questions were selected because they corresponded to some of Brown and Kulik's canonical categories and, so the authors claim, question 4 approximates Pillemer's measure of emotion. In addition to answering these questions subjects also rated their confidence in their answers – that is, how certain they were that the answers they had provided were correct.

McCloskey *et al.* were primarily interested in what they called the 'strong' version of the flashbulb-memory hypothesis. This states that a special encoding mechanism operates to record the event into memory and that the event, because it was encoded in this way, is immune to forgetting. Thus McCloskey *et al.* argue that, if this view is correct, there should be no evidence of forgetting in their repeated testing study. Subjects' responses to each question were scored '1' if an answer was provided and '0' if no answer was provided. Averaging over questions, McCloskey *et al.* found that all the questions were answered substantively by the immediate testing group with the exception of question 4 which was answered by only 96 per cent of the subjects. For the repeated testing sample the results were: question 1, 96 per cent, question 2, 89 per cent, question 3, 100 per cent, and question 4, 89 per cent. The percentages of subjects who only answered the questions after nine months had a similar distribution to the repeated testing sample. By Brown and Kulik's measure of flashbulb memories, memory for one canonical category and a 'yes' response to the question 'Do you recall the circumstances in which you first learned about . . .?', all of McCloskey *et al.*'s subjects had flashbulb memories for the space-shuttle disaster.

There are two remarkable aspects to McCloskey *et al.*'s findings, first, the very low forgetting rate and, second McCloskey *et al.*'s interpretation of this finding. McCloskey *et al.* argue that, because they observed some forgetting, then the strong version of the flashbulb-memory hypothesis cannot be correct. If flashbulb memories are indeed immune to forgetting – because of the operation of a special encoding device – then no details should be forgotten. As McCloskey *et al.* observed a forgetting rate of about 5.6 per cent, they conclude that the strong version of flashbulb-memory formation is incorrect. This is a remarkable conclusion, given the extremely low forgetting rate – there are no findings in the memory literature which show 94 per cent retention over a nine-month period. Indeed findings from laboratory studies typically show dramatic and almost complete forgetting over periods of hours and days. Studies which have shown some retention over a period of a year have used unusual stimuli and lengthy learning trials in the original encoding phase, and only indirectly assess retention – these studies do not require the conscious unguided recall of the previous learning episode. Thus the McCloskey *et al.* findings and the earlier Pillemer findings stand out in the memory literature as demonstrating remarkable levels of retention.

Moreover, problems with McCloskey *et al.*'s version of the strong version of flashbulb memories and the incompleteness of the measures they took also call their conclusions into question. It will be recalled that Brown and Kulik thought that, although flashbulb memories, once formed, might exist in some unchanging state, there would be variations in memory descriptions on different occasions. Indeed, it is only to be expected that the same knowledge will not always be retrieved – the conditions at recall might influence what knowledge is recalled, retrieval processes might access the memory in different ways on different occasions leading to slightly different memory descriptions, or a person may assume that, as the experimenter already has a record of his or her memory, then total completeness is not required on the second and subsequent recalls. These factors could easily account for the (very) low forgetting rate observed by McCloskey *et al.*, indeed most memory researchers would expect such factors to have a far larger effect on recall than a decrement of 6 per cent.

The most important problem with the McCloskey *et al.* study, however, was the failure to measure factors such as consequentiality, emotionality, and personal importance. If, following the reasoning outlined earlier, we assume that all memories are retained in some detail for a comparatively short period after the experience of the initiating event, then, of course, we would expect all of McCloskey *et al.*'s subjects to have comparatively good memories when first tested. However, these memories would be maintained in a vivid form only for subjects who had had some emotional response to the event – the conclusion of Pillemer's study. As memory consistency was so high in the McCloskey *et al.* study, we can assume that most of their subjects did in fact have some emotional reaction when they learned of the news of the Challenger disaster. We can assume this but we cannot know it because McCloskey *et al.* did not directly assess emotional reaction. Thus, if there were some subjects in McCloskey *et al.*'s sample for whom the disaster was of little interest, and who had no emotional response when they heard the news, then we would predict forgetting for these subjects because they did not have flashbulb memories. Although we cannot know the number of subjects in the McCloskey *et al.* study who did not have flashbulb memories, we might expect that there would be at least a few, and these few subjects would be enough to account for the low rate of forgetting observed in their study. In contrast, subjects who had emotional reactions to the news of the Shuttle disaster may have formed flashbulb memories and may have shown no forgetting over the nine-month period. Many of these issues are raised in a comment on the McCloskey *et al.* paper by Schmidt and

Bohannon (1988) and responded to by McCloskey, Wible, and Cohen (1988) and the reader can pursue the debate in these articles. Also for recent empirical support of the McCloskey *et al.* view, see Christianson (1989). The conclusion here is that the McCloskey *et al.* study does not effectively assess the claim that flashbulb memories are immune to forgetting – if anything, their findings tend to support this view and they certainly demonstrate a remarkable case of retention over a long period of time.

Despite the McCloskey study few memory researchers would subscribe to the view that there are memories which are immune to forgetting or to changes which alter the original memory. Indeed, Neisser's 'impossible' flashbulb memory of hearing the news of the Japanese attack on Pearl Harbor clearly shows that even very vivid memories can be inaccurate. But how inaccurate? For instance, is Neisser's memory a complete fabrication? Does it contain other gross inaccuracies? Or is it a basically accurate memory containing comparatively trivial 'errors'? Thompson and Cowan (1986) report a serendipitous finding which bears directly on these questions. Apparently these authors, while listening to a radio interview with the American sports broadcaster Red Barber, were surprised when Barber commented that it was ironic that the Army–Navy football game to be played that year (6 December 1985) should occur on the anniversary of the bombing of Pearl Harbor. Thompson and Cowan then cite Barber's account of his memory of hearing the news of the Pearl Harbor attack:

> I was at the Polo Grounds to scout the New York Giants who had already won the eastern division and were to play the Chicago Bears in two weeks for the championship. I was to broadcast that game. The Giants were playing the old NFL football Dodgers. At halftime, Lou Effrat of the *New York Times* came down from the press box and said Pearl Harbor had been bombed by Japan. I got up and went home. I was sick.

Thompson and Cowan point out that in this football game the two teams bore the same names as rather famous baseball teams and, moreover, the football game was actually played at a famous baseball ground. It seems likely then that Neisser's flashbulb memory was not grossly inaccurate but rather contained a fairly commonplace reconstructive error (similar sorts of reconstructive errors are common in laboratory studies of memory). Thompson and Cowan conclude that Neisser's flashbulb memory may in fact have been a basically accurate, more or less, veridical record of the circumstances in which he learned of the Japanese attack upon Pearl Harbor.

Neisser (1982), in a reply to Thompson and Cowan, makes a rather different point. Neisser agrees that he must indeed have been listening to the Giants–Dodgers football game and it was this broadcast which was interrupted by the news of the attack. However, Neisser does not agree that this fact makes his memory a basically correct recollection of the event. He goes on to reveal something of his own lifelong interest in baseball and his childhood indifference to football. He argues that, as a teenage boy of immigrant parents who was not skilled in athletics, knowledge of, and interest in, the truly all-American game of baseball provided his developing self-image with a firm ground in his adopted culture. Reconstructing his memory of a highly significant event in American culture so that, rather than listening to what he would have found a dull and uninteresting game, he heard a broadcast in which an exciting and significant baseball game was covered, fitted well with his self-image. In other words Neisser takes his 'reconstructive error' to be purposeful rather than random, and to demonstrate how flashbulb memories act to link our self-images into the image of our times. Nevertheless it seems reasonable to conclude that much in Neisser's flashbulb memory was in fact accurate and persisted over a long period of time.

Let's briefly recap on this developing story of flashbulb or vivid memories. First of all, it seems unlikely that any flashbulb memory will always lead to exactly the same memory description. But, if this is the case then, we cannot (and do not) know how stable flashbulb memories are. What we can conclude from the research considered above is that flashbulb memories are remarkably consistent across many years. Such memories may be customized to some small extent to fit one's self-image but the actual memory does not seem to change much over long periods of time. In this sense Brown and Kulik may have been basically right, although they perhaps overstate the case, to characterize flashbulb memories as 'slumbering Rhinegold'. On the other hand Brown and Kulik were clearly wrong in their suggestion of a special encoding mechanism – the 'Now print!' device. If flashbulb memories are customized to fit one's self-image, or for some other reason, it seems unlikely that they can be a product of such an encoding mechanism.

Brown and Kulik's focus on the 'Now Print!' mechanism seems to have distracted researchers from a critically important part of their thesis and that is that emotional reactions play a critical role in the genesis of vivid memories. The research of Pillemer and other research discussed later in this chapter clearly implicate emotional reaction as an important condition for vivid memories. Presumably, if Pearl Harbor and baseball had been of no emotional interest to Neisser, he would not have remembered the interrupted radio broadcast in the first place. But does this mean that flashbulb memories constitute a special class of memories, as Brown and Kulik argued? This question is the topic of the next section.

Flashbulb memories: a special class of memories?

Winograd and Killinger (1983) conducted a study to examine the development of flashbulb memories. They noted that in the Brown and Kulik study, and the Yarmey and Bull study, subjects who would only have been seven years old at the time of an event had as many flashbulb memories as subjects who were considerably older when the event occurred. But what about younger subjects? Would people who had been six years or younger when John F. Kennedy was assassinated also have flashbulb memories for their circumstances when they heard the shocking news? It would be remarkable if very young subjects did have flashbulb memories because this would contradict the long-established finding of 'childhood amnesia'.

In Chapter 2 we saw that Waldfogel's (1948) study found that few people could recall any memories below the age of three years and in Chapter 8 childhood amnesia is considered in detail. But perhaps flashbulb memories constitute an exception to this well-documented finding. Winograd and Killinger asked 338 people who were between one and seven years old in 1963 to recall the circumstances in which they heard about the assassination of John F. Kennedy. They also required subjects to attempt to recall memories of hearing about the bombing of Pearl Harbor in 1941, the assassinations of Martin Luther King and Robert Kennedy, both in 1968, the moon landing in 1969, the shooting of George Wallace in 1972, and the resignation of Richard Nixon in 1974. Obviously the Pearl Harbor event was included as a control and subjects could not *remember* how they heard this news when the event occurred. Each subject completed a memory questionnaire similar to that used by Brown and Kulik in which they first indicated whether they remembered their circumstances when they heard the news and, if the answer was 'Yes', they then answered a series of questions. The questions probed subject's memories for location, ongoing activity, source of the news, the effect on the rememberer, the effects on others, what they did immediately after hearing the news, how often they had talked about their memory, and any additional details which came to mind.

Winograd and Killinger found that memory for the John F. Kennedy assassination steadily increased as age at encoding rose. Subjects who were seven to eight years or older when the event occurred all had flashbulb memories by Brown and Kulik's scoring method (see above). Of the subjects who were four-and-a-half years old at encoding only 50 per cent had flashbulb memories. They also found that, for subjects who varied in age of encoding and flashbulb memories, the subjects who were older at encoding had more elaborate and detailed memories. In their ratings of rehearsal Winograd and Killinger found only a small relation between flashbulb detail and overt rehearsal. Importantly, they conclude that 'the case is not strong for attributing a causative role to overt rehearsal in determining the richness of early memories' (p. 418).

Flashbulb memories for the assassination of John F. Kennedy appear to fit rather than contradict the findings for childhood amnesia and these flashbulb memories become more frequent and elaborate as the age at encoding of the child increases. Interestingly, rehearsal was not found to be a critical factor in determining memory detail and this does contradict the view of Neisser outlined earlier. But so far we have only considered Winograd and Killinger's findings for the Kennedy assassination; what about the other events they sampled? As the other events employed in the Winograd and Killinger study were more recent, we would expect a larger proportion of their subjects to have flashbulb memories for these events – but only when the events themselves fit Brown and Kulik's criteria of being surprising and consequential.

Winograd and Killinger found that many of their subjects had flashbulb memories for the assassination of Robert Kennedy but that few of their predominantly white sample had flashbulb memories for the assassination of Martin Luther King. This, of course, parallels the findings of Brown and Kulik for these two events for white Americans. More interesting were the distributions of flashbulb memories for the moon landing and resignation of Richard Nixon. Winograd and Killinger had selected these events because they were famous – even consequential – but were hardly surprising. In scoring the memories for the moon landing they report that they became suspicious because subject's responses often suggested that they were recalling hearing about other space flights rather than the moon landing itself. Scoring memories of Nixon's resignation was not subject to these problems and a high incidence of flashbulb memories to this non-surprising event were observed.

The focus of the Winograd and Killinger study was on developmental aspects of memory and we shall consider this further in Chapter 8. Here let's concentrate on their findings for flashbulb memory theories generally. First of all, they found that rehearsal was only peripherally related to memory detail. This, of course, is a problem for the Neisser view in which rehearsal and assignment of consequentiality are seen as occurring primarily *after* an event has occurred. One criticism is that Winograd and Killinger only collected ratings of overt rehearsal, i.e. how often people had talked about their memory. Obviously rehearsal might take the form of covert rehearsal in the form of thinking about, or even ruminating over, an event. As covert rehearsal was not assessed by Winograd and Killinger, we cannot conclude that rehearsal *per se* plays only a minor role in flashbulb memory formation. Perhaps covert rehearsal is more important than overt rehearsal and so Winograd and Killinger may have under-estimated the causative role of rehearsal in flashbulb memory formation. More generally we might want to ask, 'How accurate are such ratings anyway?' How can a person judge how often they talked about an event that occurred ten or more years ago? We will return to these questions later in this chapter.

Another important finding of Winograd and Killinger was the high incidence of flashbulb memories for the resignation of Richard Nixon – an event which they *assume* was not surprising. But how warranted is this assumption? One reason why an event may be surprising is because it occurred at all, because it was unexpected, because it 'came out of the blue'. Another reason, however, is that an event may be surprising because of the way it transpired, because of the way it unfolded in time. Thus the resignation of the President may have been 'on the cards' for some time but nevertheless Nixon's final television address may have been surprising and unusual. Surprise is not a simple all or none phenomenon as so many flashbulb-memory researchers seem to have assumed. Theoretical points aside, we also have to ask how surprising would this event have been for a child? Most of Winograd and Killinger's subjects would have been in their early to late teens when Nixon resigned; perhaps for this group the event was surprising. Whatever the case, because Winograd and Killinger did not take any measurements of surprise, their claim that the Nixon resigna-tion was not surprising is open to criticism. Similarly the inference they wish to make on the basis of this finding – that flashbulb memories may be formed in response to unsurprising events – is equally questionable.

The status of surprise and rehearsal as critical factors in the genesis of flashbulb memories remains equivocal. But what about the claim that flashbulb memories constitute a 'special' class of memories? In order to examine this Rubin and Kozin (1984) asked 58 undergraduates to recall their three clearest autobiographical memories. If flashbulb memories are the most vivid of memories and typically occur in response to events of national and international importance, then we would expect the student's memories to be comprised of memories of learning about such events. If the public nature of the precipitating event is irrelevant and simply focused on by previous researchers as a convenience, then, of course, we would not expect to observe many memories for such events in the corpus of 'clearest' memories. We would, of course, expect to find that surprise, consequentiality, and emotion were characteristics of the precipitating events – if the Brown and Kulik view of flashbulb or vivid memories is correct. On the other hand, only rehearsal might be characteristic of these memories, lending some support to Neisser's view of vivid-memory formation.

In order to investigate these different predictions Rubin and Kozin adopted the following procedure. Subjects were provided with descriptions and examples of flashbulb memories and asked to generate three of their own flashbulb memories. In order to avoid biases occurring in response to these instructions, the examples were varied so that one described a memory of hearing of the bombing of Pearl Harbor, one described an incident in which a girl spilled a drink on herself while on a class trip, and one described a person's memory for witnessing his dog being run over. The subjects recalled their three most vivid memories and wrote descriptions of these. Subjects then turned to a questionnaire and rated their memories on a series of rating scales. The rating scales were as follows:

1 How nationally important was this event? (1 means no importance to the nation at the time and 7 means tremendous importance to the nation at the time.)
2 How personally important was this event? (1 means no importance to you at the time and 7 means tremendous importance to you at the time.)
3 How surprised were you when this event occurred? (1 means not at all surprised and 7 means as surprised as you have ever been.)
4 How consequential has this event been to the rest of your life? (1 means no great consequences and 7 means consequences as great as any single event in your life.)
5 How vivid is your memory of this event? (1 means no image at all and 7 means as vivid as normal vision.)
6 Was there a change in the ongoing activity? (1 means no, the activity stayed the same, and 7 means totally, as large a change as ever occurs from one event to another.)
7 Did this event cause an emotional change in you? (1 means no, you felt exactly the same afterwards, and 7 means as large an emotional change as ever occurs from one event to another.)

Two other questions assessed how often the event had been talked about and how long ago the event occurred. A final question required subjects to rate how likely the event had been to occur. Figure 4.1 shows the distribution of ratings for all the 174 memories.

The first point to note about Rubin and Kozin's findings is that virtually none of their subjects recalled events of national importance; events such as the murder of presidents, the untimely death of popular figures, national disasters, and so on just did not feature among subjects' most clear and vivid memories. This suggests that sampling flashbulb or vivid memories with cues naming nationally important events is probably not the most effective way to investigate such memories. Second, it is clear from Figure 4.1 that, although nearly all the memories were rated as being of major personal importance and as being highly vivid, the same memories were associated with only modest levels of surprise, change in emotions, change in ongoing activities, and had low consequentiality. Also noteworthy is the finding that many of the memories were comparatively recent and that few memories were recalled from older time periods. In fact, age of memory did not correlate with any of the other measures, with the exception of vividness where the correlation was $r = -0.31$, demonstrating that, as memory vividness rose, age of memory decreased.

Rubin and Kozin also included one other manipulation in their study. They cued subjects with short descriptions of a range of events designed to sample flashbulb

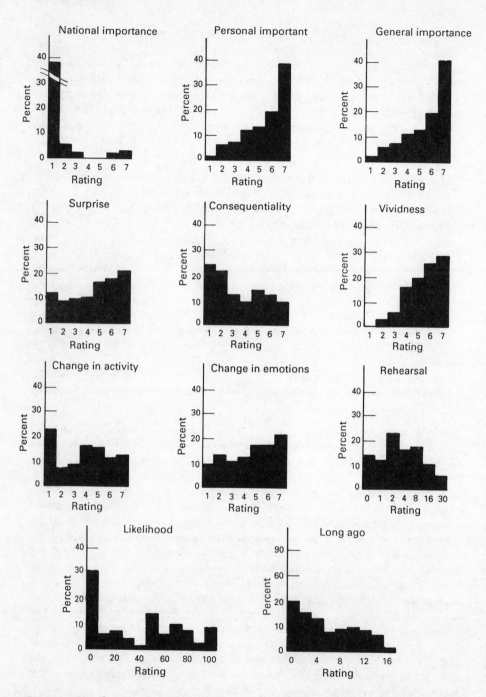

Figure 4.1 Distributions of vivid-memory ratings (reproduced by permission of the authors and publisher from Rubin and Kozin 1984, figure 1, p. 68. ©Elsevier Science Publications B.V.)

memories selectively. In this part of the study they found that those event descriptions which gave rise to flashbulb memories were rated as being more consequential, surprising, involved more emotional change, and were rehearsed more frequently than non-flashbulb memories. Taken together, these findings suggest that surprise and consequentiality may be a characteristic of flashbulb memories but they are clearly not necessary for the formation of vivid memories – as the earlier part of the study indicates. In fact, the single most important factor observed by Rubin and Kozin was personal importance. Events rated as being high in personal importance were reliably associated with high levels of memory vividness. Rubin and Kozin conclude that personal importance, and not consequentiality and surprise, is the critical factor in determining memory vividness and so favour Neisser's view of flashbulb-memory formation over the Brown and Kulik 'Now print!' proposal.

It seems clear that the Rubin and Kozin study is indeed an advance over previous studies. They sampled a broader range of memories and, for the first time in this type of study, compared flashbulb against non-flashbulb memories. Nevertheless there are some problems with their study. One problem relates to the troublesome correlation between memory age and vividness. Suppose that you are a subject in Rubin and Kozin's study. Would you be willing to write a lengthy public description of your three most vivid memories? No? Then how would you complete the task? Perhaps one way to go about this is to search memory for events which you are willing to disclose publicly but, remember, these memories must be detailed and vivid – they must have a flashbulb quality. Maybe you interpret 'flashbulb' to mean a memory of something important. Maybe, like me, you believe that you'd only have a flashbulb memory of an event if that event were personally important. Let's say that you can find one or, maybe, two memories which fit the bill. What about the third memory? Well, events which most people can remember in great detail are events which happened very recently. For instance, I can recall *ad nauseam* what I had for breakfast this morning, the trip we took last weekend, the conversation I had with a colleague a couple of hours ago, and I imagine that you can similarly recall such recent events. In the Rubin and Kozin study let's imagine that you solve the problem of finding a vivid memory by selecting virtually at random some very recent occurrence – even though this might not quite fit your belief that you have to recall memories of personally important events. What would the effect of these strategies be on the nature of the recalled memories?

The recall of 'sanitized' memories might involve recalling events which were memorable but predictable – for example, achieving an important goal one had worked hard for. Predictable events might be recalled because they are after all 'understandable' and justifiable and therefore ideal for public consumption. Recalling some memories from recent time periods (20 per cent of the memories sampled by Rubin and Kozin were less than two years old – see Table 4.3) might involve a positive bias towards selecting memories which are low in consequentiality and surprise. Intuitively, it would seem that few people, when randomly sampling their recent memories would recall events high in consequentiality and surprise except, possibly, for those of us who lead generally consequential and surprising lives. Finally, we should note that Rubin and Kozin assessed changes in experienced emotions rather than intensity of experienced emotions. Thus the relation of experienced emotion to memory vividness was not accurately assessed.

Despite these shortcomings in the Rubin and Kozin study and the possibility that their memory task led to a biased sample of memories, the fact remains that events of national importance simply were not retrieved by their subjects, indicating that our most vivid memories are of our most personally important experiences. This would make sense from the Brown and Kulik perspective, if the function of vivid or flashbulb memories is to record events of 'biological meaning' for a specific organism, although, of course, the findings do not support the operation of any special encoding mechanism and so do not support one of the major claims of the Brown and Kulik paper.

Clearly the Rubin and Kozin findings do not bear upon Neisser's conjecture that the function of flashbulb or vivid memories is to tie one's personal history into the public history of one's times. Indeed, Rubin and Kozin argue that the term 'flashbulb memories' might be constrained to refer to memories for learning about such public events, whereas the term 'vivid memories' might be reserved for memories of personally important events. The principal difference between the two classes of memory is that flashbulb memories appear to be associated with events which are comparatively high in consequentiality, surprise, and emotion, whereas vivid memories are not necessarily associated with high values on these parameters. Rubin and Kozin argue, however, that on grounds of parsimony the two classes of memory should not be separated. But this is a weak argument and there is little in their study to warrant this conclusion. Rather, their findings suggest that flashbulb memories just might be a separate class of memories which can be distinguished on the basis of their characteristic encoding conditions: high consequentiality and surprise.

Consider for a moment the class of vivid memories. These memories are not distinguished by consequentiality and surprise but rather by personal importance. But could this class also be subdivided? Conway and Bekerian (1988) thought so and conducted a study in which subjects were asked to recall two memories of events which were highly personally important and two memories of events which were of little personal importance. Subjects wrote descriptions of their memories and, for each memory, completed a questionnaire similar to that used by Rubin and Kozin. Conway and Bekerian found that events which were of high personal importance gave rise to memories which were significantly more vivid than memories of events low in personal importance. Memories of events which were of low personal importance were not, however, judged to be low in memory vividness, rather these memories were of moderate vividness having an average value of 5.1 on the 7-point rating scale compared to an average value of 5.7 for memories of personally important events. Thus memories of personally important events were highly vivid and memories of events low in personal importance were of above average to highly vivid.

For memories of personally important events ratings of consequentiality, surprise, and emotionality, at the time event occurred, were reliable predictors of vividness. Ratings of rehearsal were also good predictors of the vividness of these memories. In contrast, none of these parameters were predictors of the vividness of memories of personally unimportant events. In this case only ratings of changes in ongoing activities were found to predict memory vividness reliably. The Conway and Bekerian study is, of course, open to many of the criticisms mentioned earlier in connection with the Rubin and Kozin study. For instance, how does a person comply with the experimental demand to recall unimportant events? Presumably this is a difficult task and the 'naïve' subject must adopt some strategy. Maybe a subject uses changes in routine as a general cue to probe memory. Thus there may be other memories high in vividness which are not personally important which were not sampled in this study. Moreover, if we wished to take a Freudian perspective (see Chapter 2), then we might argue that these memories for so-called unimportant events were in fact classic screen memories hiding, as it were, memories of events of psychodynamic significance (see also Chapter 8).

The Rubin and Kozin and Conway and Bekerian studies, despite their shortcomings, all seem to point to the following account. Memory vividness is sometimes determined by factors in the encoding environment such as surprise, consequentiality, emotion, and changes in activities. At other times memory vividness may be determined by the nature of the encoding memory system (i.e. on the basis of a personal interpretation rather than in response to perceived event characteristics) and in this case vividness is a product of the perceived personal importance for the individual of the precipitating event.

Finally, as Neisser has suggested, memory vividness might be related to the encoding of events which represent an intersection of personal and public history. Given these multiple causes of vivid memories it could not be maintained that vivid memories constitute a single, unique, and special class of memories. Vivid memories it would seem have a complex history and arise in different ways from different events. A single encoding mechanism cannot encompass this complex history.

The role of emotion in vivid-memory formation

We have already seen that emotion may play a central role in flashbulb memory and vivid-memory formation. One criticism of this view was offered by Neisser who asserted that intense emotional experiences lead to a narrowing of attention and so could not give rise to detailed memories. But can we accept this claim uncritically? Do intense serenity and intense embarrassment both lead to a narrowing of attention? To the same narrowing of attention? Is it likely that irritation leads to a more detailed memory than anger? Or that a feeling of pleasure gives rise to memories containing more details than a feeling of elation and joy? Clearly Neisser's blanket condemnation of the role of emotion in vivid memory formation is in need of clarification and cannot be accepted at face value. It has already been suggested that emotions may reflect the involvement of central components of a person's cognitive system – components concerned with the self, with life-goals, and with personally significant plans – and this engagement of the cognitive system reflected in emotional experience may lead to the preferential encoding of experienced events.

A study which demonstrates the role of emotions in mediating the encoding of detailed memories was reported by Pillemer, Rinehart, and White (1986). In their first experiment Pillemer *et al.* asked first- and second-year undergraduates to recall four distinct memories from their first year at college. A further group of senior students recalled memories from their second year. Subjects wrote descriptions of their memories and answered a questionnaire similar to those described previously and featuring questions which directly probed the nature and intensity of emotional experience associated with the remembered event. Subjects also indicated why they thought the event was memorable.

In classifying the memory descriptions supplied by their subjects, Pillemer *et al.* found that 87 per cent of the descriptions described specific episodes or a one-moment-in-time memory. The authors provide the following example of a memory description.

> My first memory is of a woman I dated who lived in my dorm (she graduated). I met her in a show we both did, and the distinct picture I have is the two of us alone in the dining room, about 8 pm, really talking for the first time. I was wearing a yellow sweatshirt and red shorts, she a lavender/white striped blouse and a lavender skirt. She always wore skirts and I always wore shorts or jeans. We compared backgrounds – though we live within 1 hr. from each other, our childhoods were incredibly different. The scene seems to symbolize our relationship.

These memories were classified into four categories, academic memories relating to educational activities, romance memories describing romantic interactions, housing memories describing activities relating to student accommodation, and recreation and leisure memories. Only 19 per cent of all memory descriptions were classified as academic memories; the rest were comprised of the remaining three categories with recreation and leisure memories forming the largest class. Of these memories the vast majority were concerned with interactions with other people and memories which featured only the rememberer were comparatively rare. The same distributions of memories were found for both sexes and all years of college students.

As regards emotion, 84 per cent of the memories contained reference to the rememberer's feeling and 47 per cent also included mention of the emotional reactions of other people associated with the remembered event. Interestingly, no particular type of emotion dominated recall and events featuring negative emotions were as likely to be recalled as events featuring positive emotions.

Pillemer *et al.* also found that most memories were recalled from the early part of the first term, and this was the case regardless of how 'prepared' the student felt for university life. In terms of the other measures, rated emotionality of the remembered events was higher than rated surprise and life impact. Also of interest were that ratings of overt rehearsal were low and that 26 per cent of the memories were rated as never having been talked about previously. Pillemer *et al.* comment that the pattern of these ratings indicates that emotions have special relevance to the formation of distinctive memories. Even in cases where the memory description was apparently mundane, a subject might judge the event to have been of high emotion and to be highly memorable as a consequence. Indeed Pillemer *et al.* found that a cluster of factors relating to experienced emotion was the best predictor of ratings of clarify of memory.

In two subsequent experiments Pillemer *et al.* replicated these findings using slightly different procedures and different samples of college undergraduates. In summary then, distinct memories were found to cluster around the initial period of college life, the memories nearly all featured emotional reactions, and factors such as emotional intensity were reliable predictors of clarity of memory. Pillemer *et al.* propose two interrelated explanations for these findings. First of all, people remember distinctive events. Events occurring at the start of a transitional period in life, such as starting university, will initially be distinctive; as a person continues as a student many events which were initially novel and unusual become routine and mundane. Perhaps memories for such repeated events are represented in memory by some form of general memory such as a script for an often experienced routine (see Schank and Abelson 1977; Schank 1982; and Chapter 6). A second possibility is that, during transitional periods in life, emotional reactions are stronger and/or more frequent. Perhaps a 'spirit of adventure' elates the new student or a period of homesickness and loneliness ensues. Whatever the case, the findings of Pillemer *et al.* quite clearly demonstrates a close association between high levels of emotion and highly detailed memories. Other factors such as surprise and rehearsal were found to play a much less central role in these memories.

The Pillemer *et al.* study focused on vivid memories of early student life but what role, if any, do emotions play in the more frequently studied area of flashbulb memories? Brown and Kulik proposed that emotions play a critical role when they suggested that activity occurring in the limbic system – a brain area heavily implicated in emotional experience – initiated a sequence of neural events leading to the firing of the 'Now print!' mechanism. Even though it looks increasingly unlikely that there can be a single mechanism which accounts for flashbulb memories, the possibility of an initiating role for emotions remains open. One of the only studies to have directly examined the role of emotions in flashbulb-memory formation was reported by Bohannon (1988). In Bohannon's study, 686 subjects recalled the circumstances in which they learned about the space-shuttle disaster two weeks after the event occurred. Eight months later 262 different subjects recalled their space-shuttle flashbulb memories.

Apart from the vast numbers of subjects, Bohannon's study differed in a number of respects from previous studies. First of all, subjects were separated into groups according to whether they had heard the news from a person or from the media. The reasoning behind this manipulation was that the media distort presentation of news by training presenters to be unemotional in their coverage and, of course, by following a fairly rigid presentation of each news item – in Neisser's terms the news presenter somewhat slavishly follows a prescribed set of narrative conventions. In contrast, hearing the news from another person might provide more opportunity for emotional expression and experience and may involve rather different narrative conventions. The second unusual aspect of Bohannon's study was that subjects were also required to answer questions which probed their knowledge of the event itself rather than their memory of their circumstances when they learned about the event. Apart from these novel manipulations the study employed the type of questionnaire similar to that described previously, in which emotional reactions to the event are probed, rehearsal assessed, and knowledge of canonical categories collected.

In fact, Bohannon found that subjects who had learned of the news from the media – especially the television – tended to have less clearly defined, more 'fuzzy' flashbulb memories than subjects who had learned of the news from another person. Also, due to the nature of the design, some of the questions appropriate for people who had heard the news from another person were inappropriate for people who had learned the news from the media. Because of these differences between the two groups Bohannon decided to focus on the data supplied by people who had heard the news from another person, and there were 279 of these in his two-week delay group and 142 in the eight-month delay group. A further categorization of subjects was then undertaken. Subjects who had rated their emotional reaction as a three or less were classed as 'calm' and subjects who provided higher ratings were classed as 'upset'. These two groups were further subdivided on the basis of frequency of rehearsal: subjects who had recounted the shuttle story three times or less were put in a 'few' group and those recounting the story more frequently were consigned to a 'many' group. As regards emotion, Bohannon found that subjects who rated themselves as more shocked by the news of the shuttle disaster were more likely to remember details of their circumstances when they heard about the event and were more confident about their answers than subjects who had been unaffected by the news of the disaster. A clear demonstration that emotion may play a central role in flashbulb-memory formation and a finding which emphasizes the problems of the McCloskey, Wible, and Cohen (1988) study discussed earlier. However, rehearsal was also found to play a role in maintaining flashbulb-memory vividness over time and all Bohannon's measures of flashbulb memories were influenced by rehearsal: the more rehearsals the longer lasting the detail. Interestingly this was not the case for memory for facts about the Challenger disaster, which steadily declined regardless of rehearsal and emotion.

The general picture from Bohannon's study is that both emotional reaction and rehearsal play fairly critical roles in flashbulb memories. More detailed analysis suggested that either emotion or rehearsal would in the short term be sufficient to maintain a flashbulb memory of an event. In the long term, however, Bohannon found that both strong emotional reaction and frequent rehearsal were required to maintain memory vividness, suggesting a rapprochement between Brown and Kulik and Neisser. Before evaluating whether such a resolution is possible – or desirable – consider, finally, one last vivid-memory study.

Harvey, Flannary, and Morgan (1986) asked subjects to recall a past relationship and then to answer a series of questions, one of which included the recall of their five most vivid memories of the relationship. The questionnaire also included questions of a factual nature relating to the relationship and questions similar to those used on previous vivid-memory questionnaires. Note that the subjects were all adults, about half of whom had been married; the age of the recalled relationships varied and length of the relationships was slightly longer for divorced than single subjects. Subjects also completed a clinical questionnaire designed to assess their mood state at the time of recall. Administration of this questionnaire allowed Harvey *et al.* to subdivide the subjects into depressed and non-depressed groups.

Their central findings were that people who were depressed had more vivid memories than non-depressed subjects and that females had more vivid memories than males. Interestingly there was no effect of whether or not a person had been married. Other correlational evidence indicated that memory vividness was highly related to depression as was the flashbulb quality of the memories. The authors concluded that many of their 'depressed' patients were still grieving over the past relationships and this process may be closely involved with memory availability. Although Harvey *et al.* did not take any measures of rehearsal, it seems clear from the anecdotal evidence they cite that more depressed subjects thought more about the past relationship. For instance, one subject commented on a relationship which had ended some ten years previously, 'I think of him all the time even after all of these years. It is as if he is always there.'

A further interesting point raised by the authors is that many of the recalled incidents appeared to take on significance only after the relationship had ended. This finding, of course, fits very well with Neisser's view that consequentiality is assigned after an event has occurred. Perhaps personal relationships constitute a paradigm case of an experience which is extensively reprocessed after the experience itself is over. Yet it would seem impossible to judge on the basis of Harvey *et al.*'s data which factors are essential for vivid-memory formation and which are merely characteristic.

In summary then the studies reported in this section demonstrate that emotion plays some role in vivid- and flashbulb-memory formation and maintenance. But what role? Unfortunately the findings considered above do not directly tell us how emotions affect vivid and flashbulb memories; rather they simply indicate that emotions and vivid memories are closely related. Perhaps intense emotions lead to preferential encoding or, equally plausibly, perhaps emotions lead to deeper levels of processing and to increased rehearsals after an event, and in this way mediate vivid-memory formation. These issues are taken up in the following section.

Conclusions: characteristics of flashbulb and vivid memories

Before assessing theory let's summarize the main findings to emerge from the series of studies discussed in this chapter.

1 Vivid/flashbulb memories are more detailed and vivid than other types of memories.
2 Vivid/flashbulb memories have always been found (in the studies that looked!) to be associated with high levels of emotional reaction.
3 Flashbulb memories are often, but by no means always, associated with high levels of overt rehearsal.
4 Flashbulb memories are usually higher in attributes such as surprise and consequentiality than non-flashbulb memories.
5 Vivid memories appear to be closely related to high levels of personal importance.
6 Some vivid memories may be primarily related to factors such as change in ongoing activities rather than emotion or rehearsal.
7 Finally, and by no means least, descriptions of vivid/flashbulb memories are remarkably consistent over time, suggesting that vivid/flashbulb memories really do have, some immunity to forgetting.

The two principal 'theories' in this area are the Brown and Kulik 'Now print!' model and Neisser 'benchmark' model. The data do not support Brown and Kulik's detailed proposal of a 'Now print!' mechanism. The data do, however, clearly implicate emotional reactions in flashbulb- and vivid-memory formation and this aspect of the findings lends support to some of Brown and Kulik's proposals. Neisser's view critically depends upon the predominant role of rehearsal in flashbulb- and vivid-memory formation. The findings are mixed in this regard and it can only be concluded that, although rehearsal is a characteristic feature of these memories, it has not been found to be an essential feature.

What conclusions can be reached? From the research reviewed in this chapter it seems highly likely that events which directly engage a person's self-system are highly likely to lead to vivid or flashbulb memories. As a consequence, such events would provoke some type of emotional response and might involve frequent overt and covert rehearsals. In this way then we can agree with both Brown and Kulik and Neisser: emotions play an important role, as do rehearsal and the self. Presumably we could even (re)interpret Brown and Kulik's use of the phrase 'biological meaning' to refer to events which engage a person's self-system in some direct way. As we shall see in the next chapter, however, the self may act to create memories which are self-consistent rather than veridical – the person remembers the interrupted baseball, rather than the football, game. Quite often in psychology, psychologists take opposed views and this has the benefit of stimulating debate within an area. Usually opposed psychologists either resolve their differences or, as the debate itself becomes sterile and uninteresting, it is quietly abandoned. Rather than abandon the flashbulb vs. benchmark debate it is probably time to acknowledge that the extant data do not offer unequivocal – or even obvious! – support for either view. A common view can be developed and perhaps this is what researchers in this area should now attempt.

Finally, we should briefly consider one aspect of flashbulb- and vivid-memory research which was touched upon earlier. In this type of research the status of the measures which are used, memory descriptions and ratings, is unknown. That is, we do not have any idea of whether these are measuring properties of memories or something else. Now it might be objected that this criticism is true of most measures used by psychologists, but this would be wrong. Usually psychologists have some idea of what their measures are – albeit imprecisely – measuring. In the present case it seems equally possible that the ratings are completed on the basis of beliefs about memory in general and specific memories, rather than actual properties of a retrieved memory. Even a memory description may reflect what a person believes they should know about an event. Such beliefs do not have to be employed consciously and indeed they may be wholly implicit and the person totally unaware of their operation. In other words, the subjects in the studies considered above may believe that they are in fact rating properties of recalled memories, when in fact they are really reflecting their beliefs about what is required of them in this experimental situation.

It seems unlikely, in each study described above, that no memories were recalled and that all ratings were completed on the basis of implicit beliefs. What is more likely is that some ratings are highly sensitive to beliefs whereas others are not – some events engage beliefs and belief systems directly, others do not. For instance, is there a white American over the age of 40 who cannot 'remember' the circumstances in which he heard of the assassination of John F. Kennedy? Would anyone be prepared to admit it if they honestly did not 'remember'? Moreover, for those people who do 'remember', who among them does not have a 'vivid' or 'flashbulb' memory?

In conclusion, this chapter has shown that the study of vivid memories has raised important issues and generated interesting research. The problems now facing the area are, first, the development of a coherent theoretical position based on the principal findings in the area and, second, the development and deployment of procedures which either assess beliefs directly and/or which circumvent the influence of beliefs. Without progress on these fronts it seems unlikely that the study of vivid and flashbulb memories will make any further significant advances.

5 • EMOTIONS AND THE 'SELF'

In the preceding chapter we saw that emotions play a role in the formation and/or maintenance of vivid memories. It was suggested that emotions may have an effect upon autobiographical memory because when we experience an emotion the cognitive system is more fully engaged in processing that event, in comparison to the processing of events which are not associated with emotional experience. But what does it mean to say that the 'cognitive system is more fully engaged'? The basic idea is that the processing of events varies in terms of the nature of the pre-existing knowledge structures used by a person in comprehending and encoding different events. Consider, for example, the event of receiving and reading a letter. If the letter turns out to be your monthly bank statement (and you're in no more financial trouble than usual!), then it will probably be read with some indifference. In contrast, if the letter turns out to be something more significant, say good news about your recent job application or an intimate note from a close friend, then this letter event will be processed in a rather different way from the bank-statement event. In the case of a personally significant event, emotions may be experienced and knowledge structures representing significant life-themes and the self-system may be actively employed in processing that event. High levels of emotion then might signal to the autobiographical-memory researcher that an event has been encoded in terms of complex and personally significant knowledge structures. Lower levels of emotion may indicate that these knowledge structures were not centrally involved in processing a particular event. Of course, it could logically be the case that an event does not involve emotion but is highly self-relevant. Unfortunately, however, the concepts of 'emotion' and the 'self' are not sufficiently well developed within psychology to allow us to separate out the differential effects of emotion and the self on memory. The research reviewed in this chapter has attempted to focus on either emotion or the self, although inevitably the two blend into each other, and in some of the studies we will examine the effects of emotion and the self are so intertwined that the two cannot be even roughly differentiated.

One further problem is that there are no generally agreed models of either emotion or the self. In fact both these areas, although currently undergoing something of a research revival, are characterized by polarized theoretical positions and incomplete models. The terms 'emotion' and 'self' will, however, be used throughout this chapter. The term emotion will be used as it is used in ordinary everyday language, to mean experiences of love, anger, happiness, depression, and so on. The term 'self' will mainly be used to refer to a set of memory structures which represent specific self-knowledge, i.e. knowledge which refers to a specific single self. Towards the end of the chapter we will briefly consider some recent theoretical thinking about the self.

Emotion and autobiographical memory

A particularly interesting study of the relationship of emotion to autobiographical memory was reported by Robinson (1980). Robinson was interested in the effects of intensity of emotional experience versus pleasantness of emotional experience upon memory availability. The availability of memories of emotional experiences was assessed by recording memory retrieval times to cue words. In this methodology a subject recalls a memory to a cue word, such as *anger*, and the time taken to retrieve the memory is recorded. A fast retrieval time indicates that the memory was highly available to retrieval processes, whereas a slow retrieval time indicates that the memory was less available to retrieval processes. Obviously memories of emotional experiences will vary in intensity and pleasantness, some being high in intensity and some low, and some being pleasant and some unpleasant. The question is, which property, intensity or pleasantness, determines memory availability?

In Robinson's study subjects recalled memories to the cue words, *angry, amused, ashamed, curious, disappointed, excited, frightened, happy, jealous, lonely, pleased, proud, sad, sorry,* and *surprised.* Subjects were required to recall a memory of an event in which they had experienced the named emotion. Retrieval time was recorded, as were a number of other measures such as various ratings of intensity and pleasantness. In this and two subsequent experiments, Robinson found that intensity ratings were good predictors of retrieval time but other measures, including measures of pleasantness, were unrelated to retrieval time. Thus intense emotional experiences are associated with autobiographical memories which are readily available for retrieval. Robinson proposes that intense emotions lead to an increase in attention and more extensive processing of the associated event compared to attention levels and extent of processing for emotionally neutral events. The implication being that these factors act to make the memory of the intense event more available in memory. Indeed emotionally intense events may also be associated with high levels of rehearsal – although this is not always the case as we saw in Chapter 4 – and frequent rehearsal may also act to render a memory more generally available for retrieval.

This type of explanation for the effect of intense emotion on autobiographical memory is, however, unsatisfactory. Attention, level of processing, and rehearsal may well be characteristic processes associated with highly available memories, but the question is *how* do these processes make a memory more available? In Chapter 4 we reviewed the work of Pillemer, Rinehart and White (1986) which demonstrated that emotional memories from transitional periods in life (i.e. starting college) were highly available to college students when they were asked to recall memories of events from their first year in college. It was suggested that these types of memories might be highly available because the events they represent were processed in terms of personally significant pre-existing knowledge structures, perhaps directly involved in the self-system. These knowledge structures provide a means for representing an event in memory in a structured fashion and so facilitate subsequent access to the memory.

Recently, Pillemer, Goldsmith, Panter, and White (1988) have extended their work on emotional memories. In this study Pillemer *et al.* asked college alumnae who had graduated 2, 12, and 22 years previously to recall four memories from their first year at college. After they had recalled their memories, the subjects rated how intense their emotions had been when the event occurred, how surprised they had felt, the impact of the remembered events on their lives, and the clarity of their memories. In addition, subjects also dated the events, described the emotions they had felt, indicated how often they had talked about the memory, and suggested why they thought any of the events were memorable. We have already seen in Chapter 3 that subjects' memories from this study clustered in the first couple of months of the first year at college and only a few subjects recalled memories from later in the first year. In general, subjects' memories were of events which featured interpersonal interactions with others and most of the events were associated with emotional experiences. Although increased emotional experience was characteristic of these memories, high levels of rehearsal and of life impact were not. In fact, rehearsal and life impact were, on average, rated as being at below moderate levels. However, the two best predictors of clarity of memory were emotional intensity at the time of experience and perceived life impact at the time of experience. Other factors were also related to memory clarity but not as strongly as emotion and impact. What is surprising about these findings is that they were the same for all three groups.

Pillemer *et al.*'s explanation of these findings is as follows. Many of the events recalled by the alumnae dated from their first day at college and other events, not occurring on the first day, referred to first-time experiences, e.g. first lecture. These first-time events were, of course, succeeded by many similar events, which we might assume were not memorable simply because of their similarity. Perhaps only the first experience in a sequence of similar events is preserved in memory and the rest merge into a schematic representation. Indeed, Linton (1982) in her study of her own memory made a similar observation. Describing her own memory for board meetings she comments 'Some years later, after many meetings, I have lost my capacity to reliably pinpoint particular board meetings and I could not describe proceedings of most meetings – except perhaps the first, and (if it were recent) the last.' But Linton did not forget the usual procedure and protocol for board meetings abstracted from the many such meetings she had attended. The clarity of the memories of the alumnae in the Pillemer *et al.*'s study may therefore be related to some type of privileged encoding for first-time experiences. Perhaps, memories of first-time experiences from the basis of more complex schematic knowledge structures which will eventually be constructed in memory as similar events are experienced (see Chapter 8 for a developmental perspective on this suggestion). As such first time-events are enshrined in a knowledge structure and so are highly accessible, other memories, less directly associated with organizing knowledge structures, may be less available or only retrievable under special circumstances.

Privileged encoding of first-time experiences cannot, however, explain why emotion correlated with memory clarity and why ratings of experienced emotion were higher than all other measures. Yet it may be the case that the emotional quality of the alumnae's memories was purely incidental and had nothing to do with memory clarity. How could this be? When a person undergoes a period of life transition it seems likely that more events than usual might be reacted to emotionally. For instance, in a transitional phase a person might have a long-lasting heightened mood state such as anxiety, elation, or depression and it is this mood-state which causes emotional reactions to a wider range of events. It follows then that, when memories are retrieved from a transitional period, the probability of an intense emotional experience being recalled is increased – there are simply more emotional events available for retrieval. Thus emotion *per se* may not be a critical determinant of memory clarity.

But Pillemer *et al.* also found that intensity of emotional reaction and degree of life impact were positively correlated with memory clarity. Similarly Robinson found that intensity of emotional experience is positively correlated with memory vividness – as intensity goes up so does vividness. It seems possible then that increased emotional intensity and life impact are, in fact, important determinants of memory clarity and availability. The suggestion here is that these factors are important because they indicate that central knowledge structures relating to the self have been employed in representing the memory. We will return to this theme later in this chapter.

If first-time experiences and other novel, distinctive, or somehow unusual events are represented in memory as central parts of more complex knowledge structures, then we might expect such memories to be highly available when the knowledge structure is activated in a processing episode. For example, when processing a concept such as *board meetings*, we would expect Linton either consciously to remember her first and latest board meetings or to be able to retrieve these memories very quickly, if required. In fact something like this happens in everyday conversation. A conversation between two people about, say, a recent meeting which both people had attended, although not requiring any autobiographical memory retrieval, may none the less feature reminiscences about previous meetings. The circumstances under which this typically occurs are unknown but intuition and our own everyday experiences support the notion that autobiographical memories quite often feature in discourses of which they do not seem to be a necessary part. One obvious candidate set of concepts for which we might expect autobiographical memories to 'pop' into mind spontaneously are concepts which refer to emotions. On the assumption that emotions are centrally involved in vivid memory formation then we might expect that knowledge about emotions would be structured in memory around autobiographical memories. For instance, a concept such as *love* might be represented by memories of events in which the emotion was experienced particularly intensely or when the emotion was experienced for the first time. Thus, when we process such concepts, even though the processing may not require memory retrieval, it might be expected that related autobiographical memories would become highly available. Memories might even spontaneously come to mind and 'surprise' us by their involuntary recall.

In order to explore this possibility Conway (1989) conducted a series of experiments in which subjects generated images of whatever they took various emotion words to refer to. After generating an image individual subjects then judged whether their image was a specific datable memory, a generic image which was based on experience but could not be exactly dated, or a semantic image which could not in principle be dated. Subjects also provided various ratings of their images, e.g. vividness, frequency of past imagining and so on. The logic of these experiments was as follows: if autobiographical memories are associated with emotions, then subjects' images should be dominated by memories and only a few generic and semantic images should be present. For other classes of concepts, such as 'furniture' and 'weapons', autobiographical memories should not dominate type of image.

In the first experiment reported by Conway (1989) subjects generated images to concepts naming emotions, goal-derived categories (e.g. *birthday presents, farm animals, things to do at the seaside*, etc.), taxonomic categories (e.g. *furniture, sports, weapons, vegetables*, etc.), and to concepts naming groups of people (e.g. *hospital workers, politicians, manual worker*, etc.). Table 5.1 shows the distribution of types of images to each of these classes on concepts.

It can be seen from Table 5.1 that emotions gave rise to the highest level of spontaneous autobiographical-memory retrieval. Goal-derived categories also gave rise to high levels of spontaneous autobiographical-memory retrieval but this finding is discussed in detail in Chapter 10. In a second experiment Conway found that abstract concepts, some of which were associated with emotions and some of which were not, gave rise to high levels of semantic images, although abstract concepts which referred to the self (e.g. *honesty*) appeared to be at least partly associated with autobiographical memories. In a final study Conway compared type of images generated to words naming emotions and words naming personality traits. The personality traits were prerated by the subjects for self-relevancy and subjects then generated images of traits which were highly self-characteristic, marginally self-characteristic, or self-neutral. In this experiment emotion concepts were once again found to be dominated by autobiographical memories, but personality traits, regardless of their self-relevance, produced equal emounts of autobiographical memories, generic images, and semantic images. These findings indicate that autobiographical memories are closely associated with knowledge of emotions but not necessarily with knowledge of other types of concepts.

Table 5.1 Percentages of types of images retrieved to different classes of concepts

Category	Autobiographical memories	Generic images	Semantic images
Taxonomic	33.8	36.8	29.4
Goal-derived	53.0	23.5	23.5
Emotions	59.5	27.2	13.3
Persons	26.4	52.3	21.3
Means	43.2	34.9	21.9

(From Conway 1989, figure 9.1, p. 136)

Autobiographical memories may, then, become more available for retrieval when we process concepts which are structured in memory around records of specific experiences. But are there other ways in which emotions can act to raise the availability of memories? Research into mood-memory effects indicates that the experience of some emotions is associated with the increased recall of emotionally congruent memories. For example, a person in a sad mood may recall more negative events from their past than a person in a happy mood. Research by Teasdale and Fogarty (1979), Snyder and White (1982), and Gilligan and Bower (1984) has demonstrated that such mood-memory effects do occur. In this type of research a mood is induced in a subject and the subject then recalls memories from their recent or remote past. The typical finding is that, when a depressed mood is induced, then more memories of negative events are recalled in comparison to the recall rate of negative memories for subjects in happy or neutral moods. This effect is usually explained as a 'context' effect in which the induced mood reinstates a mood the subject experienced when some earlier event was encoded. It is unclear how context effects actually have an effect but one possibility, which is compatible with the view developed in this chapter, is that the experience of an emotion will activate certain knowledge structures in memory and these knowledge structures may have been employed on previous occasions when a congruent mood was experienced and an event encoded into memory (see Chapter 9 for further accounts of mood-memory effects).

One final effect of emotion and of the self upon autobiographical memories will be considered in this section. Nigro and Neisser (1983) observed that, when an autobiographical memory is recalled, the memory may maintain the perspective the rememberers had at the time of experience (a 'field' memory – the memory preserves the original field of view) or the rememberers may 'see' themselves in the memory (an 'observer' memory – the memory depicts oneself performing some action). Nigro and Neisser hypothesized that field memories might be more frequent for recent events and observer memories more characteristic of older memories. If all events are experienced from one's own perspective, then all memories should initially preserve one's field of view and only become observer memories as the initial field memory is recoded. Perhaps frequent rehearsals lead people to recode or reconstruct their memories in the form of observer memories. However, not all events are experienced solely from one's own perspective; sometimes we have a heightened sense of self-awareness and we observe ourselves as an experience unfolds. A good example of this is when one gives one's first public talk. In this situation many people report being highly self-aware. Nigro and Neisser argue that self-awareness at the time of experience might lead to an event being initially encoded as an observer memory.

In order to explore field and observer memories Nigro and Neisser conducted a pilot study in which subjects recalled memories to cues which named common experiences. After recalling a memory a subject then judged its field, observer or other perspective. The actual cues used by Nigro and Neisser and the frequency of the two different types of memories reported by their subjects are shown in Table 5.2.

This pilot study shows that people can meaningfully judge the perspective of their memories and that perspective varies with type of situation. In order to determine how a situation influences memory perspective Nigro and Neisser conducted a second experiment in which subjects made judgements about the similarity of pairs of events

Table 5.2 Number of different types of memories retrieved across a range of situational cues

Situation	Observer	Field	Neither
Having a conversation	4	13	3
Being embarrassed	4	11	2
Being elated	5	12	3
Being angry	6	13	1
Being frightened	7	9	2
Studying	7	11	2
Watching television	8	11	1
Swimming	9	8	3
Running	10	6	4
Giving a public presentation	11	6	3
Total	71	100	24

(Reproduced by permission of the authors and publisher, from Nigro and Neisser 1983, table 1, p. 471. ©Cognitive Psychology)

such as those used in the pilot study. The principal finding from the similarity experiment was that subjects' similarity judgements could be explained in terms of two dimensions, emotionality and self-awareness. In a third experiment subjects recalled memories and judged memory perspective to the cues used in the similarity study. The distribution of field and observer memories was related to the dimensions of emotionality and self-awareness. Observer memories were found to be characterized by high degrees of emotionality and self-awareness associated with the original experience. Field memories, on the other hand, were primarily related to how recent the remembered event was rather than any intrinsic properties of the event.

In their final experiment Nigro and Neisser manipulated the way in which subjects recalled memories. In this experiment some of the subjects were instructed to focus on the feelings they had experienced when the event occurred, other subjects were required to focus on objective aspects of the events, and a final group were given neutral instructions. In their previous studies Nigro and Neisser had found that feelings were frequently reported when subjects recalled field memories, but not when they recalled observer memories, and so they expected that the instructional manipulation would exacerbate this effect. In fact, they found that, when subjects focused on feelings at recall, more field than observer memories were recalled; when subjects focused on circumstances this difference diminished and subjects recalled approximately similar amounts of field and observer memories. In the case of neutral instructions more field than observer memories were recalled. The preponderance of field memories generally was due to filed memories being more recent – subjects tend to recall more recent than remote memories in these sorts of tasks (see Chapter 3).

These findings suggest that more recent memories have a higher probability of preserving the original perspective of the rememberer. This conclusion is, however, qualified by the finding that self-awareness and emotion at encoding may give rise to observer memories. Finally, Nigro and Neisser suggest that their findings, at least in part, support Freud's claim (see Chapter 2) that emotional memories are reconstructed over time from field to observer memories. Perhaps observer memories reduce the possibility of an emotion being re-experienced in its original intensity – an obvious advantage because if we re-experienced strong emotions each time we recalled a memory of an emotional event, then behaviour would be very frequently interrupted.

Although there have been comparatively few studies of the interrelations of emotion and autobiographical memory, the research reviewed in this section suggests some tentative conclusions: intensity of emotional experience is closely related to memory availability; memories of initial events which occurred in transitional life periods are also highly available in memory; these memories tend to be of emotional events and clarity of memory is closely related to emotionality and the impact of the event upon a person's life. In addition, the type of self-awareness, perhaps in turn dependent on the nature of experienced emotion, may determine the content of a recalled memory. Finally, more recent memories which have not been subjected to reconstruction tend to represent more literally the actual experience.

The self and autobiographical memory

In a remarkable paper Neisser (1981) reported what is probably one of the best 'real world' studies of autobiographical memory. Neisser compared John Dean's testimony to the Senate Watergate Investigating Committee with tape recordings made at the time the conversations had taken place. John Dean acted as counsel to President Richard M. Nixon in the lead-up to the Watergate scandal and was one of the Whitehouse aides whose testimony was instrumental in leading to Nixon's resignation. In his role as counsel to Nixon, Dean had frequent meetings with the president in which they discussed the unravelling scandal at some length. Unknown to Dean their conversations were tape-recorded and Nixon later released transcripts of the tapes in order to discredit Dean's testimony.

John Dean had, by all accounts, a remarkable memory. For instance, his testimony to the Watergate Committee commenced with a 245-page statement in which he recalled the details of literally dozens of meetings, some of which took place with the president. During his testimony his amazing ability to recall the minutiae of past events earned him the name 'the human tape recorder'. In fact, however, the comparison between the human and mechanical tape recorder favoured the latter for accurate preservation of detail. Dean, it turned out, was remarkably inaccurate in his recollections of conversations between himself and the president; even worse, his recall of specific episodes was shown to be incorrect – many of these errors are detailed by Neisser. Just as remarkably, however, Dean was basically correct about what had been going on, as Neisser comments: 'Nixon wanted the cover-up to succeed; he was pleased when it went well; he was troubled when it began to unravel; he was perfectly willing to consider illegal activities if they would extend his power or confound his enemies.' Dean's testimony quite clearly supports these 'themes' evident from his interactions with Nixon.

Dean's testimony is also clearly distorted in terms of his own role in the Watergate cover-up. In his testimony he repeatedly emphasizes his own role, particularly as a kind of moral counsel and detector of coming disaster. It seems then that Dean's testimony was basically correct in as much as it accurately reflected the tenor of the Nixon administration and Nixon's own attitude to Watergate. It was distorted in that the claimed recall of specific episodes was incorrect and probably provided Dean with a role which, in reality, he did not have or fulfil.

The case of John Dean's memory is, however, unusual in a number of respects. First of all, much was at stake for Dean and he could not know, while giving his testimony, that the tapes had been made and would later be released. Quite probably his testimony would have been radically different had he been aware of the existence of the tapes. Perhaps he would not have claimed to have remembered so much and been more circumspect in his testimony, reflecting more accurately what he actually recalled. Moreover, Dean's testimony is largely concerned with conversations between himself and the president and in most cases these were conversations which, with minor variations, had been repeated across a number of occasions. Thus it is not too surprising that he only recalled the meaning of the conversations and even then this was the meaning to emerge from repeated rather than single conversations. It seems unlikely that memory for episodes from one's life would always, or even frequently, fit this pattern of recall of themes only. Nevertheless the case of John Dean's memory provides good evidence that memory can be, and is, distorted by the influence of the self.

In a series of studies Barclay and his colleagues (Barclay and Wellman 1986; Barclay 1986; Barclay and Subramaniam 1987; Barclay and DeCooke 1988) have demonstrated how distortions of memory can arise under the influence of the self. Barclay and Wellman (1986) instructed a small group of subjects to keep records of memorable everyday activities over a period of four months. The subjects' memories for the recorded events were tested in five sessions spread out over a period of two and a half years. The memories used by Barclay and Wellman were particularly interesting as they assessed recognition memory. In recognition-memory testing the usual procedure is to present subjects with previously learned material mixed in with new material and the subject's task is to discriminate 'old' from 'new' items. Of course, the interesting problem from Barclay and Wellman's point of view is how to create 'new' items or *foils*, as they are usually called. For instance, let's say that one of Barclay and Wellman's subjects records in his or her diary the following event 'Went and saw the movie *2001* (again)'. Clearly radically changing such a record will not necessarily lead to an effective test of memory. For instance, if a foil were created such as 'Went and saw the movie *Apocalypse Now* (again)', then there may be many ways in which a person can classify this item as a foil – perhaps they are interested only in science-fiction movies and do not usually watch other movies, maybe they do not usually watch any movies and only went to *2001* as an indulgence to a friend. To obviate these problems Barclay and Wellman had subjects record descriptions of events and their evaluation of each event. They then created foils which altered the description or the evaluation. In addition they created a further group of foils – called 'other foils'– which changed both description, evaluation, and event. In addition to making recognition judgements the subjects also rated how confident they were about the accuracy of their judgements.

The principal finding was that subjects incorrectly classified many description and evaluation foils as actual events. In fact 50 per cent of these foils were judged to be actual events. Even more surprising was the finding that 23 per cent of other foils were also classified as actual events. Somewhat more reassuringly, accuracy rates for events that had been experienced were high, 93 per cent, falling to 75 per cent after a two-and-a-half-year retention interval. Confidence ratings were uniformly high and stayed that way over the whole retention interval, demonstrating an inaccurate belief in the accuracy of memory. In order to explore these effects further Barclay and Wellman had a separate group of subjects judge how semantically or conceptually similar the foils were to the event records. They found that foils which were high in semantic similarity were associated with high rates of false recognition judgements, whereas foils low in semantic similarity were associated with lower rates of false recognitions. Barclay and Wellman conclude that autobiographical memory is typically inaccurate and that memories are reconstructed in terms of schemas so that any plausible event description which does not violate a schema expectancy might be erroneously judged to have been experienced.

If it is the case that autobiographical memories are reconstructions based, at least in part, on schema knowledge, then we might expect that as the retention interval increases, less information about the actual event will be available and more reconstruction will take place. If this is the case then subjects' abilities to discriminate between semantically similar foils and actual event descriptions should diminish as the retention interval increases. This was exactly the finding of Barclay (1986) and the distribution of the false alarm rate (the frequency with which a person classifies a foil as 'old') by retention interval is shown in Figure 5.1.

Barclay and Subramaniam (1987) directly investigated the influence of the self upon memory reconstruction. In this study they focused on Markus's (1977) proposal that self-schemas might subdivide into personality dimensions and, in particular, into the dimensions of dependence and independence. According to Markus people who are

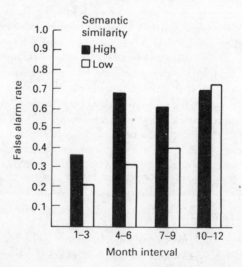

Figure 5.1 False-alarm rate over a 1-year delay for foil items high and low in semantic similarity (reproduced by permission of the author and publisher, from Barclay 1986, figure 6.1, p. 94. ©Cambridge University Press)

dependent-schematic characteristically respond to adjectives such as 'co-operative' and 'conforming', whereas independent-schematics respond to adjectives such as 'individualistic' and 'unconventional'. Barclay and Subramaniam in a pre-test classified a group of subjects into dependents and independents. All subjects kept a diary for three weeks and after a delay of five and a half weeks their memories were tested. In the memory-test phase of this study subjects free-recalled events they had recorded in their diaries and also recalled events to cues taken from their diary entries. The principal findings were that the type of schematicity, dependent/independent, influenced recall in that subjects recalled information which was schema dependent. This finding was not present in cued recall and Barclay and Subramaniam conclude that, in the absence of memory cues, schematic aspects of the self-system will influence memory retrieval – this effect appears to be overridden when direct memory cues are available.

Barclay and DeCooke (1988) further investigated people's abilities to discriminate between memory for everyday events which they had experienced and plausible foils. In this experiment four women recorded events in diaries over a two-week period and recognition memory was then assessed at one and a half and three weeks. These subjects also provided a number of ratings of the events and in a final post-test session grouped the events they had recorded into meaningful categories of their own choosing. One of the dimensions subjects rated the recorded events upon was a dimension of typicality which reflected how typical/atypical each event was in the context of their own lives. A particularly interesting finding here was that events which were highly typical were associated with different properties for different subjects. For example, for some subjects typical events were characterized by high values of emotion, whereas for others typical events were characterized by high values of satisfaction. In contrast, atypical events tended to share common features across subjects and were characterized by high levels of emotionality, personal importance, satisfaction and surprise. Thus what is typical for one person is not typical for another person and this may reflect differences in event parameters which correspond to processing differences initiated by the self-system. Atypical events, however, may be atypical on the basis of some external criteria which are perhaps specified within a culture, e.g. unexpected events are atypical.

A finding which further illustrates individual differences in autobiographical memory was that different subjects sorted their memories into markedly different numbers of groups. For instance, one subject employed 3 groups only, whereas another subject used 13 groups. On the assumption that these groupings reflect something of the underlying nature of organization in autobiographical memory it seems reasonable to conclude that autobiographical memory differs radically from subject to subject (but see Chapter 6 for a different view). For the recognition test Barclay and DeCooke created three types of foils: foils in which the style of the memory reports had been altered but meaning preserved; foils in which the style was similar but the meaning changed; and foils which were memory descriptions written by a person who had not taken part in the study. The principal findings were that subjects were at ceiling for recognition of true event descriptions with performance at 100 per cent at two- and three-and-a-half-week testing periods. Performance on meaning-changed foils was about 90 per cent and on other foils was over 90 per cent, and so subjects correctly rejected nearly all of these foils. For foils in which only the style had been changed, recognition performance was comparatively poor with 82 per cent of these memory descriptions being incorrectly judged as 'old'. Thus memory descriptions created by an experimenter which closely correspond to memory descriptions reported by subjects are frequently confused with actual memory reports. In contrast, memory descriptions created by an experimenter which violate the *meaning* of memory reports of a subject are rarely confused with actual memories.

In the Barclay and DeCooke study a tragic event occurred when the mother of one of their subjects was suddenly hospitalized and subsequently died. This occurred during the diary period of the study and, although the subject abandoned the project as her mother's condition deteriorated, about half the diary was none the less completed. After a delay of some months this subject agreed to take part in a cued recall test for events from this traumatic and personally significant phase of her life and her memory performance was compared with that of another subject with whom she had originally been paired (of course, the control subject had not experienced events of such high personal significance during the diary period). The principal finding was that the subject who experienced the traumatic event recalled many memories in great detail and these memories related to events both before and after the hospitalization of her mother. This finding is of some interest because it is often argued that events which are associated with high emotionality lead to a narrowing of attention at the time of encoding and hence to impoverished memories (see, for example, the discussion of Neisser's view of the impact of emotion on memory discussed in Chapter 4).

What conclusions can we reach on the basis of Barclay's findings? It seems clear that memory for everyday events is not exact and detailed; such memories are frequently confused with descriptions of foil events which are similar in meaning. The events which subjects recorded in their diaries were not, however, judged to be memorable at the time they were recorded. Indeed, Barclay and DeCooke comment that 'Almost all subjects in this and previous studies stated that formerly they had thought of their lives as really interesting until they had to keep records of what they did every day!' Perhaps John Dean's memory was subject to a similar bias – a belief that the events he experienced were important and memorable when in fact they were routine, often repeated, comparatively mundane events, only the meaning of which was accurately preserved in his memory. In contrast, events which are high in personal significance and emotionality appear to be represented in memory in great detail and events which are not themselves high in these values but which are associated chronologically with an emotional and personally important event may also be represented in memory in some detail. In conclusion then, it seems that memories of unremarkable routine events are in fact largely reconstructed at recall in terms of schema knowledge and in terms of properties which are of concern to a specific person – to a self. Other events which are emotional and personally significant appear to be represented in memory in some detail and may be less subject to reconstruction.

Although not directly concerned with autobiographical memories, a related line of research which directly concerns the role of the self in memory has been reported by Ross and his colleague (Ross and Michael Conway 1986; Ross 1989). The main focus of research in this area has been on how accurately people can remember past opinions and attitudes. For example, what was your attitude to nuclear disarmament ten years ago? Ross proposes that answers to such questions are made with reference to one's current self. For instance, a person might consider their present attitude and then assess how likely it is that their attitude would have been different at some time in the past. This process, however, requires the utilization of beliefs about stability and change. If people believe that they have markedly changed over a 15-year period, then they might conclude that their attitude was quite likely to have been different in the past. On the basis of other personal knowledge they might then infer what their attitude would most probably have been. In contrast, a person who believes that they are pretty much the same now as they were 15 years ago might infer that their attitude was probably the same in the past. One can readily imagine how the former 'change' belief might be employed by a 30-year-old and the latter 'stability' belief by a 55-year-old. Ross's point is that beliefs about stability and change vary for different types of characteristics and interact to reconstruct the past.

Certainly it seems likely that one's impression of how one was in the past, in the absence of distinctive and vivid memories, will be determined in large part on the basis of one's current self-image and beliefs about change and stability. Indeed, Ross (1989) reviews empirical research which clearly supports this view. In this research subjects might be asked to assess their attitudes on a questionnaire and then, days or months later, to re-rate their attitudes and then to recall their earlier attitudes. The typical finding is that recall correlates more positively with current, than with past, attitudes. If a manipulation is introduced so that subjects are exposed to some form of attitude change, then recall of previous attitudes once again corresponds more closely to current than past attitudes, even though a person may be unaware that his or her attitudes have changed. However, it appears that subjects can be more accurate about their past attitudes under certain circumstances, e.g. if rewarded for being accurate. This suggests that, on at least some occasions, memories can be retrieved and will improve accuracy of recall. Recall biases in terms of the current self may more typically occur when an extensive memory search is not undertaken. Moreover, a further problem with research in this area is that no attempts have been made to assess the personal importance of past attitudes to the individual. It is after all possible that an attitude or set of beliefs which were of high personal importance to an individual at some point in the past might well be recalled, even though those attitudes have changed or been abandoned.

Research into the effects of the self on memory indicates that events and beliefs which are of little personal importance and/or are mundane and routine are not well remembered. It seems that these events may not be represented in memory in any great detail and, as a consequence, are subject to much reconstruction when 'remembered'. Reconstruction may involve the use of schematic knowledge structures in long-term memory to 'fill in' what would most probably have been the case. Other knowledge structures which represent beliefs about the self and the current version of the self may act to reconstruct the past so that it is compatible with the present. Yet events which are important and emotional, or attempts at remembering which are highly motivated, indicate that at least some memories represent, in detail, both events and beliefs. It seems that the inescapable conclusion is that autobiographical memory is partly constructed and partly remembered – as, indeed, Brewer argued (1986, see Chapter 2).

Self-knowledge

So far we have avoided the issue of just what the self or self-system may be and, as there are few satisfying models of the self (although there are a lot of interesting ones), the issue of just what the self is cannot be resolved here. There have, however, been some recent theoretical advances which suggest interesting perspectives on the research reviewed in this chapter and two of these suggestions, one by Neisser and the other by Markus and Nurius, are considered in this section.

Neisser (1989) has outlined an approach to the self in which aspects of the self-system are differentiated on the basis of different types of self-knowledge. Neisser proposes that five kinds of self-knowledge can be identified. The ecological self refers to a self which is based on a person's physical perspective on the world. That is, a person has a sense of self which depends on the fact that the self is a central point in the optical array which impinges upon it – even the youngest babies respond to objects looming towards them in appropriate ways. The interpersonal self refers to species-specific behaviour in which people relate and communicate to members of their own species. Again very young babies appear to be born with, or develop within a very short time, appropriate responses (in the form of body language and non-linguistic verbal utterances) which they utilize in interactions with adults. The ecological and inter-personal selves comprise the basis of the present self and are directly experienced. Of course, it does not follow that these types of self-knowledge do not develop over time and Neisser's point is simply that these two types of self-knowledge are types which we all have and which are either innate or develop very rapidly. Interestingly Neisser points out that these types of self-knowledge may be associated with impairments of the self-system. For instance, autistic children may suffer from impairments of the interpersonal self.

Of more relevance to present concerns is the extended self. Between the ages of about two and four years most children show that they remember past events. These momories take two forms – specific autobiographical memories and schematic memories or memories of scripted activities. Young children describe some past events in detail and they can also describe what typically happens in routine activities such as 'baking cookies' (see Chapter 8). Most young children, however, are not particularly interested in the past, preferring to concentrate on upcoming events or to engage energetically in current activities. As the child matures, it seems that the potential of autobiographical memory as a means of extending and developing social relations becomes more apparent. Possibly this function of autobiographical memory is taught within a culture in the form of implicit instructions provided in, say, mother–child interactions (Edwards and Middleton 1988). Whatever the case, Neisser argues that 'The most important adaptive function of memory may be that it makes permanent interpersonal relations possible, and thus vastly strengthens the coherence of human groups.' This is perhaps overstating the role of autobiographical memory in human affairs but certainly such memories must support and foster social relations – a shared past which is remembered and discussed must surely increase group cohesiveness, although we shall see in later chapters that this is unlikely to be the sole function of autobiographical memory.

The private self develops when the growing child learns and/or realizes that certain of her experiences are uniquely hers – she has privileged access to her own experiences – the pain she experiences cannot be experienced by someone else, the dream she dreamt is hers alone. The private self is based on our own feelings and beliefs, our ultimately private thoughts which perhaps cannot be verbalized or expressed in a simple or direct way. In a sense this aspect of self-knowledge may correspond to Barclay and DeCooke's measures of 'events which were typical' for their subjects. The characteristics of these typical events differed from subject to subject and such characteristics might be a dim reflection of the feelings and thoughts which comprise one's private self-knowledge. The conceptual self is based on culture-specific belief systems concerning nature and the workings of our own minds. Presumably the knowledge base of the conceptual self is shared to some degree between members of a society. This aspect of self is clearly related to Ross's account of how beliefs about consistency and change might influence the reconstruction of a person's past.

Different types of self-knowledge might then relate to different uses and manifestations of autobiographical memory, although, at any one time an adult will experience an event as a unified self rather than as a collection of knowledge domains. Autobiographical memory may facilitate the development and maintenance of social relations and serve as an important base for the development of private introspections and the representation of belief-systems. What other roles might autobiographical memory play in the self-system? Markus and Nurius (1986) propose that the self is comprised of a number of possible selves – self as I am now, selves I could have been, selves I could be. Possible selves can be positive or negative but, most importantly, they 'derive from representations of the self in the past and they include representations of the self in the future' (p. 954). Markus and Nurius propose that the self-concept is represented by a set of cognitive–affective knowledge structures which are employed in the processing of self-relevant events. Autobiographical memories, to the extent that these are implicated in some past and/or future self will play a major role in determining the current self.

Possible selves might be represented by knowledge structures which encompass the types of knowledge classified by Neisser as extended, private, and conceptual self. Possible selves are obviously part of the current self and must draw upon the past, upon one's own knowledge of one's self, and upon knowledge about what is possible within the culture in which one lives. Markus and Nurius propose that at any one time the self is a dynamic structure comprised of specific possible (past and future) selves which help define and structure the current self-concept. Autobiographical memories may represent knowledge which is critical to the functioning of these processes and in this sense autobiographical memories may facilitate the maintenance of a dynamic self-concept.

Summary: emotion and personal significance

Research into emotion, the self, and autobiographical memory is at a preliminary stage. The studies reviewed in this chapter although tempting us with intriguing findings have yet to generate strong claims about the interrelationships between self, emotion, and memory. The new theoretical approaches being developed by researchers such as Neisser and Markus and Nurius indicate that exciting developments may yet take place in this area and it is to be hoped that such developments are realized – the intersection of self, emotion, and memory in cognition undoubtedly represents one of the key areas in which psychology must advance if the discipline as a whole is to progress.

The preliminary findings reviewed in this chapter suggest that the emotional intensity and personal significance of an event give rise to autobiographical memories which are detailed, highly available for recall, and comparatively resistant to forgetting. Such memories may serve many different functions in cognition providing the basis for extended social interactions, maintenance of a dynamic self-concept, and perhaps serve a wider function in the representation of the meaning of concepts. In contrast, autobiographical memories of routine, often repeated, low-emotion, everyday events do not appear to be represented in memory in any great detail. These events may be represented schematically in the form of knowledge structures which do not preserve details but do preserve regularities of events. Remembering these events is heavily dependent upon reconstruction and beliefs, theories about the mind, and the self, all of which may be drawn upon in the reconstructive process and lead to 'memories' which are consistent with the current state of the cognitive system at the expense of accurately representing the past.

6 • ORGANIZATION IN AUTOBIOGRAPHICAL MEMORY

The study of characteristics of autobiographical memories such as date, vividness, and emotion, has suggested interesting hypotheses concerning differences between sets of memories. In the present chapter and in the chapter which follows it, research with rather different aims is considered. The studies reviewed in this chapter are concerned with how memories for experienced events might be represented in long-term memory in some structured way. In Chapter 7 studies examining ways of retrieving auto-biographical memories are considered. Of course, organization and retrieval are closely interrelated issues, and studies of one always tells us something about the nature of the other. Thus Chapters 6 and 7 should be seen as slightly different treatments of the same topic and at various points in both chapters this will become self-evident. One further point is that in these investigations characteristics of auto-biographical memories (vividness, emotion, etc.) are only of secondary interest and measures of these characteristics are frequently not taken by researchers concerned with organization and/or retrieval strategies. Nevertheless we will see that some aspects of autobiographical memory, which were suggested by research into memory characteristics, receive further support from investigations of organization and retrieval.

There are two more or less distinct approaches to the study of organization of autobiographical memory. The first approach has evolved from attempts to construct computational models which can comprehend language. The aim here has been to suggest organizational structures and principles which, when embodied in a computer program, produce human-like language understanding. The problems confronted by artificial intelligence (AI) workers led to some researchers taking a direct interest in the nature of human memory and, latterly, in the possible structure of human-event memory. The second approach tackles the problem of organization in a more empirical way. The question here is not 'What possible structures could deliver this particular type of human behaviour?' but rather 'How do people actually organize their memories?' In this chapter we first consider the AI approach and then examine how investigations of human memory have given rise to rather different models.

Computational models of event knowledge

Schank (1982; 1986a; Schank and Abelson 1977) has been the key figure in this area. In their original work, Schank and Abelson proposed the concept of a 'script'. A script was meant to be a knowledge structure in long-term memory which represented knowledge about frequently repeated events or stereotypical action sequences. The classic example script provided by Schank and his co-workers is that of *going to a restaurant*. Many invariant action sequences, physical props, and settings, characterize this type of script, e.g. sitting at a table, reading the menu, ordering the meal, paying the bill, etc. Schank and Abelson's main point was that such knowledge structures can be used in language comprehension to make inferences. For instance, we have no problems in understanding the statement 'the service there is terrible' as a comment on either a specific type of restaurant or class of restaurant. We can comprehend this statement because we have a restaurant 'script' which, when activated, automatically makes available the knowledge that restaurants involve someone serving someone else a meal. It is, however, immensely problematic to devise a computer program which can make such inferences appropriately – something like a script-type knowledge structure offers one approach to tackling this problem.

The script concept is itself problematic. For instance, what would be the difference between a plan and a script? Schank (1982) discusses this problem at some length and concludes that it is difficult to differentiate scripts from any other high-level knowledge structures. Suppose I planned to go to a restaurant, suppose further that as the organizer of the departmental talks in the Psychology Department at Lancaster I planned dinners out one night every week in term time (about twenty visits to restaurants a year). Which is the plan and which the script? Does it make any sense to propose that I have a script for planning trips to restaurants with visiting speakers? Moreover, as Schank (1982) points out, scripts may involve so many other scripts that it would be impossible to say which script was guiding some action sequence or act of comprehension. Planning meals out with visiting speakers is a subpart of planning a talk sequence which may, in turn, be part of some larger plan. All these different levels of planning involve routine activities such as writing to speakers, telephoning restaurants, booking seminar rooms, arranging accommodation, introducing speakers, attending talks; the list, although not endless, is probably quite large. If most types of activity involve a multitude of scripts at different levels of abstraction and interconnected in a multitude of ways, then the concept of a script may not after all be that useful in understanding comprehension and memory because a script can be anything.

In order to obviate some of these problems Schank (1982) developed a dynamic model of human memory in which scripts served a specific role. Schank's general point is that scripts represent highly predictable action sequences which have been abstracted from often repeated experiences. As such they represent the most tedious and uninteresting stories we can tell; moreover, it is difficult to see how a representation of highly predictable actions could be employed more generally in under-standing. Schank proposes that other high-level knowledge structures are employed in generalizing from experiences and we shall see what these are shortly. The more far-reaching proposal is that 'scripts', as previously conceived by Schank and Abelson (1977), usually do not pre-exist in memory at all. That is, in processing an action sequence such as *a trip to the dentist* a person *constructs* a representation. The knowl-edge used in constructing a dynamic on-line model of the action sequence might be in the form of specific autobiographical memories and/or previously stored models of specific routine activities (e.g. checking in with the receptionist, sitting in the waiting room, etc.). Of course, for frequently repeated experiences we might expect that the model, which is habitually constructed on-line as it were, becomes prestored in memory. It would not make sense (or an efficient cognitive system) continually to keep constructing the same model. In this new formulation then, comprehension arises from the dynamic application of memory in constructing models of the to-be-compre-hended materials rather than in simply accessing prestored 'scripts'.

Schank proposes five types of knowledge structures. A *scene* he characterizes as 'a general description of a setting and activities in pursuit of a goal relevant to that setting'. A *script* is an instantiation of a scene, that is a specific realization of a scene. For example, a person who eats out at many different restaurants may have a restaurant scene represented in memory. Attached to this scene will be numerous scripts such as scripts for eating in French restaurants, Indian restaurants, McDonald's, and so on. *Autobiographical memories* in this scheme are represented along with scenes and scripts but not in a discrete way. Schank proposes that memories are broken up and represented along with the knowledge structures which were originally used to process them. According to this view my memory of the visit of speaker X to our department is fragmented and represented in my memory along with scenes and scripts such as *professional discussion with a colleague, attending talks, drinking with colleagues, eating at restaurants, catching taxis*, and so on. The whole episode of the visit of X might be retrievable, if I could construct some common theme with which to search the array of knowledge structures in which fragments or episodes from the visit are represented (see Chapter 10 for further discussion of these issues).

Schank's final two types of knowledge structures provide ways in which memory can be used dynamically and searched in complex ways. *Memory organization packets*, or MOPs as they are usually referred to, are used to organize scenes. Schank's definition of a MOP is that 'A MOP consists of a set of scenes directed towards the achievement of a goal. A MOP always has one major scene whose goal is the essence or purpose of the events organised by the MOP' (p. 97). For example, if one's goal is to organize a successful talk sequence, then the scene one might have in mind would be of a full seminar room, and interesting talk, followed by a lively discussion, and a pleasant evening in which the speaker is socially entertained. Specific scripts and scenes relating to this successful-talk-sequence MOP could be retrieved from memory and the resulting MOP used to guide behaviour. One interesting feature of MOPs is that they do not contain memories; rather these are indexed by the scenes and scripts organized by the MOP. Thus memories can be retrieved by reactivating or regenerating a MOP and searching the scenes and scripts it indexes or by accessing the scenes and scripts directly or via some other MOP. Such a scheme clearly predicts that memories relating to previous MOPs may come to mind when utilizing a completely different

MOP – such unexpected and 'surprising' remindings are part of our everyday experience (see Chapter 10).

Another way in which we might be reminded is by the operation of *thematic organization points* or TOPs. TOPs are knowledge structures which represent abstract, domain-independent knowledge drawn from one or more episodes. It is evident that people abstract high-level knowledge and rules from their experiences and can detect the emergence of similar meanings in other experiences. Schank describes a number of reports he collected in which this happens:

The Steak and the Haircut

X described how his wife would never make his steak as rare as he liked it. When this was told to Y, it reminded Y of a time, 30 years earlier, when he tried to get his hair cut in a short style in England, and the barber would not cut it as short as he wanted it.

Marijuana and the Oil Crisis

X was talking about how there was no marijuana around for a month or two. Then, all of a sudden, everyone was able to get as much as they wanted. But the price had gone up 25 per cent. This reminded X of the oil situation the previous year. We were made to wait on lines because of a shortage that cleared up as soon as the price had risen a significant amount.

Schank's proposal is that analogies between abstract aspects of events are possible because TOPs represent sets of memories which are thematically related to a goal. In the steak and haircut story the common theme is of a goal which is not achieved, and in the marijuana and oil crisis story the theme is commodity unavailability and the consequences of re-establishing supply. Thus TOPs are colonies of memories organized around a common high-level abstract theme.

Two final points about Schank's work. First of all, memories are stored in terms of scripts and scenes and Schank argues that memories of events in which script or scene expectations were violated are most likely to be preserved in memory. Such events are interesting and informative, events which simply fulfil schema expectations are of little or no interest and do not require storage in memory. Second, memory is organized in terms of goals – MOPs and TOPs are all structured around goals and memories are stored in terms of goal fulfilment. There are many other aspects to Schank's model of dynamic memory and the interested reader should consult Schank (1982) for further details. The important point is that in Schank's model, memories are represented in terms of knowledge structures at varying degrees of abstraction and at all levels correspondences between goals and experienced events are utilized in learning and structuring memory.

Kolodner (1983) in two major papers described a computer model of human-event memory based directly on Schank's earlier work. The model, which was called CYRUS, represented knowledge of diplomatic activities undertaken by the American politician Cyrus Vance, and a separate data base represented similar knowledge for the politician Edmund Muskie. Kolodner's major concerns were with the integration of new items into CYRUS and with the retrieval of old items already in CYRUS. Her starting assumption was that memory must be structured in some way and that in retrieval memory is not simply exhaustively searched. Kolodner proposed that memory was structured in terms of conceptual categories that represented normative information about similarities and differences between events. For example, knowledge about diplomatic meetings would contain normative information about features which were generally true of such meetings. Indices connecting the normative information to other norms and to specific episodes would mark differences between the various representations or nodes in the network. An example of this type of knowledge structure is shown in Figure 6.1.

The representation in Figure 6.1 is called an *event-memory organization packet* or E-MOP. E-MOPs are the general structure which Kolodner employs to organize similar episodes and to track differences between episodes. One important point about E-MOPs is that they represent 'locked' networks. That is, in order to get from one part of an E-MOP to another part, activation must traverse the appropriate indices but indices are labelled by differences. So, unless the retrieval process can locate the appropriate differences, a target memory cannot be accessed. For instance, if 'Dayan' cannot be located as the distinguishing feature of EV4 (event 4) in Figure 6.1, then the memory of a diplomatic meeting between Vance and Dayan cannot be accessed. (Note that MOPs in this scheme are generic forms of E-MOPs and appear to represent what Schank in his reformulation meant by the concept 'scripts'.) Thus indices represent salient features of events and salient features single out ways in which an event differs from other events and from normative information about a class of event. Kolodner proposes that people have E-MOPs for all the major event types they experience.

New knowledge is represented by pre-existing sets of E-MOPs and, as Schank proposed, episodes are fragmented and represented across the various E-MOPs originally used to process different aspects of the event. One criticism of this scheme which we might note here is that it is difficult to see how Kolodner's model of the structure of event memory can account for the common experience of someone remembering an episode but being unable to recall critical details about that episode, e.g. who was there?, what was discussed?. Kolodner's model of retrieval, however, goes some way to answering this criticism. Retrieval processes in CYRUS are fairly complex and it is not intended to describe them in detail here; rather we will consider some general aspects of the CYRUS retrieval mechanisms. The first point is that retrieval in CYRUS is reconstructive and reconstructions occur by inferring what must have happened, what must have been the case, and putting this together with any details which have been retrieved. Memories then are compilations of normative knowledge with some actual retrieved detail (see the discussion of Bartlett in Chapter 2). A memory of a diplomatic meeting between Vance and Dayan will perhaps contain knowledge about the location and some other distinctive features and will contain normative knowledge about what generally happened at meetings between the two statesmen. In other words, for the retrieval process to work at all

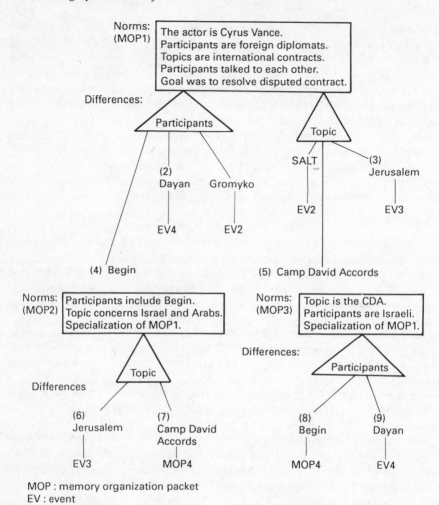

Figure 6.1 Knowledge structures in CYRUS (reproduced by permission of the author and publisher, from Kolodner 1983, figure 1, p. 248. © The Cognitive Science Society)

some contextual information must be specified. In CYRUS this is contained in the query a user puts to the data base. Contextually based search must, however, proceed by the retrieval process narrowing down the scope of the context until a specific memory is accessed (when the query requires a memory as a response). Thus retrieval processes operate on a context-to-instance basis.

Kolodner's model seems to capture and embody many of our intuitions about autobiographical memory. Memories do appear to be structured in some way and structure seems to capitalize on similarities in meanings between different events. Furthermore, events are often memorable because they differed in some distinctive way from similar events. Moreover, memory is imprecise and recall of apparently accurate knowledge often turns out to be partly reconstructed (see Chapter 4). Apart from these intuitions, is there any evidence that human memory actually works in ways similar to CYRUS?

Much of Schank and Kolodner's thinking about autobiographical memory is not directly testable – nor was it intended to be; their concern was with computer models of knowledge representation and not with modelling the human mind. Nevertheless some aspects of Kolodner's model are testable; in particular the claims about retrieval processes can be investigated by experimental methods. Just such an investigation was undertaken by Reiser, Black, and Abelson (1985). Reiser *et al.* were interested in the types of event-knowledge structures used in memory retrieval. They proposed that, typically, autobiographical-memory retrieval is an effortful process in which the query for retrieval is underspecified. As cues for retrieval are underspecified, retrieval processes must elaborate upon the cues and it is suggested that this elaboration takes place by utilizing the underlying structure of autobiographical memory. One implication of this view is that some cues will be more effective than others. Effective cues for memory retrieval will contain information which corresponds to the underlying structure of autobiographical memory, whereas less effective cues will require elaboration. To see this try retrieving a memory to the following cue: 'Recall a memory of a time you paid for something.' Now try retrieving a memory to this cue: 'Recall a memory of a time when you went to a post office and queued at the counter.' The latter cue should be more effective because it specifies a context in which a general action occurs, whereas the former cue specifies only a general action. Reiser *et al.* propose that memory is organized in terms of contexts which index memories – they call this the context-plus-index model. Contexts can be constrained by specification of features of the context (i.e. queuing) but features out of context are so general as to require elaboration (identification of a context) if they are to serve as effective retrieval cues.

In order to explore these proposals Reiser *et al.* conducted two experiments on cued retrieval from autobiographical memory. In their first experiment Reiser *et al.* required subjects to recall memories to cues which named general actions and activities. General actions denote activities which are part of many different types of action sequences, e.g. *finding a seat*. Activities, on the other hand, refer to action sequences occurring in specific contexts, e.g. *going to the cinema*. Reiser *et al.* postulated that, if autobiographical memories are organized in terms of activities (i.e. sets of actions in specific contexts), then presenting cues in the order activity–then–general action should lead to faster memory-retrieval times than presentation in the order general action–then–activity. Try retrieving a memory to the cue *went to the cinema – found a seat* versus *paid at a ticket booth – took a ride on a train*. In the Reiser *et al.* experiment the first cue in any pair of cues was presented singly for a period of five seconds and then the second cue was presented and subjects retrieved a memory to the event described by both cues. If the first cue corresponds to the underlying organization of autobiographical memory, then retrieval processes can come into operation almost immediately, leading to a fast retrieval time. If the first cue does not correspond to the underlying memory organization, then retrieval processes cannot be immediately activated and the cue must first be elaborated leading to a slower retrieval time.

In addition to these manipulations Reiser *et al.* included a further condition which featured *failure* actions, e.g. *did not find a seat*. The reasoning behind this manipulation was that Schank (1982) had suggested that memories of experiences in which script expectations were violated (the routine did not run as expected) would be stored in some distinctive way. Thus failure actions, in comparison to regular (general) actions, might lead to very fast memory-retrieval times once an appropriate context has been activated. Two further measures taken in this experiment were age of memory and ratings of how pleasant the original event had been – clearly failure actions might lead to the recall of unpleasant experiences and this negative emotion might in itself influence retrieval time (see Chapter 8).

The main finding was that activity–then–general action cues led to fastest memory retrieval times and this was the case for both regular and failure actions. Table 6.1 shows the mean retrieval times reported by Reiser *et al.*

In their analysis of the other measures, Reiser *et al.* found that failure actions reliably gave rise to memories of experiences which were rated as being less pleasant than memories of experiences retrieved to regular actions – a result which is hardly surprising. No other effects of pleasantness and age of memory were observed and presentation order of the cues was found to be the main determinant of retrieval time. Thus Reiser *et al.*'s first experiment quite clearly supports the proposal that auto-biographical memories are organized in terms of contexts, and cues which correspond to contexts represented in memory facilitate the retrieval of specific memories.

In a second experiment Reiser *et al.* replicated these findings and also found that activity cues on their own gave rise to faster memory-retrieval times than activity-plus-action cues and action cues only. Activity-plus-action cues, however, gave rise to faster memory retrieval times than action cues only. In a separate study Reiser, Black, and Kalamarides (1986) demonstrated that retrieval strategies which occur in response to action cues tend to take the form of a narrowing down or constraining of the context, whereas retrieval strategies to other types of cues take the form of an elaboration of the cue and usually involve mapping the cue on to other aspects of a person's history. For instance, in response to the cue 'think of a time you went to a birthday party', one subject recalled that s/he had attended a lot of birthday parties when at high school and subsequently recalled a memory from this period of her life. Reiser, Black, and Kalamarides call this the *select a time era* strategy.

Taken together these findings lend some support to the view that autobiographical memories are organized in terms of knowledge structures which are accessed by contextual information. Decontextualized general information does not facilitate memory retrieval and this must be because cues containing general information do not

Table 6.1 Mean retrieval times in seconds to retrieve memories to activity + action cues

Action type	Presentation order		Mean
	Activity first	Action first	
Activity + regular action	4.164	6.384	5.274
Activity + failure action	5.610	7.853	6.732
Mean	4.887	7.119	6.003

(Based on Reiser, Black, and Abelson 1985, table 2, p. 107)

map on to the underlying structure of autobiographical memory. Cues which do correspond to the underlying structure of memory only require the addition of one or two constraints to become effective cues, whereas cues which do not correspond to the organizational structure require much more extensive elaboration.

The structure of autobiographical memory

The computational approach to memory has postulated possible representational schemes for event knowledge and some evidence suggests that people may represent memories in terms of event structures. There are, of course, many other ways in which we might model the representation of autobiographical memories. The question addressed in this section is 'how, in fact, do people represent memories of experienced events?'

Robinson (1976) reported the first of contemporary retrieval time studies which directly investigated the representation of autobiographical memories. In this experiment Robinson adapted the cued-recall procedure originally employed by Galton (see Chapter 2) and subjects recalled memories to cue words. The cue words used by Robinson were words naming objects, activities, and affective states. There were sixteen words in each of these classes and subjects responded with the first memory of which the cue word reminded them. The subjects in Robinson's experiment were twelve men and twelve women, all undergraduates with an average age of 18.5 years. Four measures were taken: time to recall a memory (RT); age of memory backdated in months from time of recall; temporal specificity of the memory assessed by mention in subject's memory descriptions of temporal information; and type of experience in which memories were classified into larger groups. Robinson was essentially interested in whether different classes of cue word might give rise to memories of different ages and whether memories would be differentially available according to cue-word class. This later hypothesis would lead to differences in retrieval times if some cue-word classes (i.e. activities) corresponded more closely to the underlying structure of autobiographical than other cue-word classes.

Let us consider memory age and temporal specificity first. The age range of memories retrieved in Robinson's experiment was from 0 to 12 years, where zero represents the time of retrieval. Overall, words naming affect lead to the retrieval of more recent memories, although women reported more recent memories than men for object and activity words. About a week after the experiment subjects returned and again dated their memories and the correlation between original and re-dates was 0.94, indicating high consistency in memory dating. As regards temporal specificity, time signs such as 'morning', 'afternoon', 'evening', and 'night', were frequently mentioned in subjects' memory descriptions. Robinson found that memories retrieved to object and activity words were associated with more time signs, and so were more temporally specific than memories retrieved to emotion words.

The different classes of cue words gave rise to reliably different retrieval times and object and activity words gave rise to faster retrieval times than emotion words – these findings are shown in Table 6.2.

Object and activity cues did not, however, differ in retrieval times. Finally, Robinson

Table 6.2 Mean median response times in seconds to different classes of cue words

Prompt class		
Object words	Activity words	Affect words
10.47	10.85	14.01

(Based on Robinson 1976, table 4, p. 586)

was able to classify 27 per cent of the memory descriptions provided by his subjects. The most frequent class was that of accidents and injuries, followed by romantic episodes, and a smaller class of memories representing first-time experiences.

The finding that object and activity cue words did not lead to differences in retrieval times is a problem for models which claim that autobiographical memory is organized in terms of activities. According to these models activity cues should give rise to faster retrieval times than other types of cues. Yet Reiser *et al.*'s findings show that not all activity cues will lead to fast memory-retrieval times and actions which do not entail a context generally lead to slow retrieval times. The activity cues employed by Robinson – words such as *open, throw, cut,* etc. – constitute activities which may occur in many contexts and so, as Reisser *et al.* found, give rise to slow retrieval times. If Robinson had used activities which occurred in specific contexts, then it seems likely that activities would have led to fastest retrieval times, followed by objects, with affect words showing slowest retrieval times.

However, the finding that affect words gave rise to significantly slower retrieval times than the other cue words is a more difficult problem for activity-based models of auto-biographical memory organization. The problem is difficult because these models do not explicitly include emotions nor do they offer any indication of how events which vary in emotional intensity might be differentially encoded. This criticism, however, is not local to the activity class of models; in fact none of the models to be reviewed in the present chapter and in Chapter 7 have any way in which to accommodate this effect. One possibility, which relates to Robinson's own suggestion and to the Reiser *et al.* model, is that emotions are like general actions in that a context must be specified if a memory is to be directly accessed. Robinson originally suggested that all experiences may entail at least some emotion and so all memories represent some knowledge about affect, but to varying degrees. Thus, when a memory is retrieved to an affect cue, many (more) memories must be searched in order to find a memory which fits the cue. Presumably a number of retrieved memories will be rejected as not fitting the cue according to criteria set by the subject – hence the longer memory-retrieval times to affect words.

Robinson's study does not provide unequivocal support for the activity view of memory and it is only with additional assumptions that this model can be applied to Robinson's findings at all. Nevertheless the findings do indicate that organization in autobiographical memory supports more direct access of memories cued by objects and activities than memories cued by words naming affect. In order to explore this further Conway and Bekerian (1987) conducted a series of experiments which attempted to investigate directly the structure of autobiographical memory. Conway and Bekerian employed a priming procedure in their experiments. In this procedure a memory-cue word, such as *chair*, is preceded by a related or unrelated word, e.g. *furniture* or *ready*. The prime words used by Conway and Bekerian in their first experiment were the names of semantic categories from which the memory-cue words were taken and three semantic categories, *sports, furniture*, and *emotions*, paralleling those used by Robinson were employed. The reason for using primes and semantic categories was as follows: previous research has established that semantic knowledge may be organized in memory in terms of categories and that 'good' or 'clear' examples of a category become activated when the category name is processed, whereas poor or peripheral members of the category receive less activation (see, for example, Rosch 1975). If we assume that autobiographical memories are organized by the same knowledge structures (semantic categories), then it follows that primes should speed memory retrieval when the cue word is a good example of the category. (Note that in the Robinson study no attempt was made to control for typicality of the cue words.) For example, memory retrieval to the cue word *chair* should be faster when chair is preceded by the prime *furniture* than when it is preceded by the unrelated prime *ready*. One further manipulation employed by Conway and Bekerian was to vary the typicality of the cue word. For instance, *carpet* (an atypical cue for the category furniture) might be primed with the related prime *furniture*. If autobiographical memories are organized in terms of semantic categories, then not only should related primes speed memory retrieval but this effect should be selective and atypical members of the category, because they receive less activation from the prior processing of the prime, should lead to comparatively slower retrieval times.

In their first experiment Conway and Bekerian found no effects of priming and memories retrieved to related and unrelated primes, typical and atypical cue words, did not differ in speed of retrieval. In fact, memory-retrieval times were highly variable and no systematic patterns were evident in the data. Thus autobiographical memory does not appear to be organized in terms of semantic categories. In a second experiment Conway and Bekerian employed a wider range of semantic categories, arguing that the three semantic categories used in the first experiment may have underrepresented this class of knowledge structure. In this second experiment a further novel class of cues was introduced. Conway and Bekerian argued that in everyday life autobiographical-memory retrieval is often primed by mention of lifetime periods. For instance, a conversation featuring mention of 'when I was an undergraduate' or 'in my first job' often primes a person to recall memories of their own experiences from similar lifetime periods (note that lifetime periods appear to correspond to Reiser *et al.*'s (1986) concept of a 'time era'). In order to explore this effect Conway and Bekerian had subjects complete a personal memory questionnaire in which they listed ten lifetime periods. Lifetime periods were described as periods which, in retrospect, had marked beginnings and endings, and represented events which had some common theme. It was also pointed out that lifetime periods were not chronologically exclusive because a lifetime period such as 'when I lived with X' might partly or even wholly overlap with some other lifetime period such as 'When I worked in Y', the idea being that lifetime periods, although chronological in that they had beginnings and endings, represented themes in a person's life rather than exclusive time periods. Subjects had no difficulty in completing this part of the questionnaire, and most apparently enjoyed the exercise. Next, subjects went back over their lifetime periods and for each period recorded five general events occurring in that period. General events were described as events which happened over periods of days or weeks but which did not themselves directly refer to a single specific datable memory.

On the basis of the personal memory questionnaire Conway and Bekerian were able to create primes which named lifetime periods (e.g. 'when in sixth form') and pair these with related general events (e.g. 'holiday in Italy'), and require subjects to retrieve memories to general events. Thus in this second study subjects recalled memories to cues which named semantic-category members or general events which they them- selves had experienced, and these cues were primed with a related prime (semantic- category name or lifetime period) or with an unrelated prime. The principal finding was that lifetime periods primed memory retrieval but no prime effects were observed for semantic-category names. In a third, and final, experiment Conway and Bekerian replicated this effect and were able to show that the findings were unrelated to the prior completion of the personal memory questionnaire. Interestingly, this final experi- ment also included a condition in which subjects retrieved memories to general actions primed by activities (e.g. prime: 'going to the cinema'; cue: 'finding a seat'), paralleling the stimuli used by Reiser *et al.*, but no prime effects were observed. Conway and Bekerian, in interpreting this finding, focus on differences in presentation rates between the two studies. In the Reiser *et al.* experiment, primes (activities) were shown for five seconds prior to presentation of the memory cue, whereas in the Conway and Bekerian experiment primes were exposed for only 1.5 seconds prior to memory retrieval. Conway and Bekerian argue that the long prime exposure in the Reiser *et al.* experiment allowed subjects sufficient time to recall a lifetime period in which they had performed the activity and in this way to activate sets of memories which might include a general activity which would correspond to the to-be-presented memory cue. In the Conway and Bekerian experiment the short prime–target interval did not allow sufficient time for effective execution of this retrieval strategy and hence the lack of prime effects.

On the basis of their findings Conway and Bekerian propose that autobiographical memory is organized in terms of an abstracted personal history. One level in this abstract personal history corresponds to knowledge structures which represent life- time periods and these are referred to as autobiographical-memory organization packets or A-MOPs. The basic idea of A-MOPs is that they represent thematic aspects of a person's life and index general events. General events might, in Kolodner's terms, be conceptualized as E-MOPs and it is the E-MOPs which directly access specific auto- biographical memories. There are, however, a number of important ways in which E- MOPS and A-MOPS differ from the activity model of Reisser *et al.* Conway and Bekerian found that lifetime periods and general events listed by their subjects did not exclusively, or simply, name activities. Rather these cues included activities, locations, and temporal information in such a way that the separate components could not be easily separated out. Thus activities, in the Reiser *et al.* sense, did not appear to play a central role in memory organization as this was reflected in the Conway and Bekerian study. In addition to this, Conway and Bekerian posit that E-MOPs are typically accessed through A-MOPs in the process of retrieval and so a cue such as 'going to the cinema' will have to be elaborated prior to memory access. This elaboration, according to Conway and Bekerian, will take place by accessing appropriate A-MOP knowledge. For instance, a person may select an A-MOP because that was a period in which they frequently (or comparatively frequently) performed the activity – i.e. a person accesses 'when I was at university' in response to the activity cue 'going to the cinema'. One further point is that A-MOPs, because they represent personally significant themes from one's own life, should also be closely associated with the self-system. This aspect of A-MOPs has yet to be investigated.

The work of Robinson, and Conway and Bekerian indicates that autobiographical memory may not be simply organized in terms of contexts and actions. More recently, however, work by Barsalou (1988) and his colleagues has seriously questioned whether autobiographical memory is organized, at any level, solely by activities.

Barsalou (1988) refers to the models of Kolodner and Reiser *et al.* as the 'activity-dominance hypothesis' which emphasizes the main point of this class of models, namely their focus on activities as the principal organizing feature in autobiographical memory. According to the activity-dominance hypothesis, when people recall auto-biographical memories, it should be the case that memories of activities dominate retrieval and the retrieval process itself should be facilitated when cues in the retrieval environment name activities. Clearly this must be the case if autobiographical memories are organized in activity-based knowledge structures. A further claim of the activity-dominance hypothesis is that memory is dominated by generic knowledge structures which summarize similar events – as we have seen, in Kolodner's model these are called E-MOPs.

In a simple study Barsalou reports that people returning to university after the summer break were stopped and asked to recall specific events which they had been involved in that summer. The memory descriptions provided by subjects were classified into various groups and Table 6.3 shows the distribution of memories across the groups.

What is particularly interesting about this distribution of memories is that only 21 per cent of subjects' descriptions actually refer to specific datable autobiographical memories. The largest group of memory descriptions refer to repeated actions which occurred over extended periods of time and the second largest group refer to comments on aspects of extended events.

In a second study subjects retrieved memories to cues which named *people, activity, location* or *time*. In order to collect these types of cues subjects were initially led to believe that they were taking part in a categorization experiment, part of which was the generation of cues from one of the four classes. For instance, subjects would be asked to generate 'the names of as many *people* as you can think of whom you did things with this summer' (p. 202). Subjects returned one to two weeks later and retrieved memories to the cues they had previously generated. After a delay, subjects were supplied with the classification scheme employed by Barsalou in the earlier free-recall study, and asked to classify their own memories. The principal finding was that across all groups of cue words summarized events comprised about 60 per cent of memories, whereas specific events comprised only about 40 per cent of memories.

These findings lend some support to the claim of the activity-dominance hypothesis, that similar and/or repeated events are represented in memory by generic knowledge structures (E-MOPs). But what about the second claim of the activity-dominance

Table 6.3 Percentage of different types of 'memories' free-recalled from the summer period

Statement type and examples	Percentage
Summarized events we also went to movies while we were there I watched a lot of TV every day we would leave our house	32
Comments about aspects of events I did that for about four weeks the family is friends of ours . . . we had a lovely apartment	31
Specific events we saw a play we had a little picnic filled out an application at home	21
Extended events I worked there for two weeks I took a trip to Italy I went on a diet	9
Alternative events I had not taken a shower I'll probably go back to work at Christmas . . . they could have given me a job for a week . . .	3
Miscellaneous statements	4

(Reproduced by permission of the author and publisher, from Barsalou 1988, table 8.1, p. 200. ©Cambridge University Press)

hypothesis, that generic knowledge structures are based on activities and contexts? In a third study subjects retrieved memories to composite cues similar to those employed in the Reiser *et al.* experiment. The cues named either activities, persons, locations, or times, and were combined in pairs so that all pairwise combinations of cues were represented in the experimental stimuli (activity/person, activity/location, activity/time, person/location, person/time, location/time). For one group of subjects the cues were presented in the above order, two seconds apart, and for a second group of subjects cues were presented in the reverse order, representing the main manipulation of the Reiser *et al.* experiment. No differences in retrieval time were observed between different orders of cues or between different types of cue pairings. These findings demonstrate that activities do not play any privileged role in retrieving autobiographical memories; location, person, and time, cues are equally effective. Moreover, cue order does not affect retrieval time and this suggests that there is no special suborganization of autobiographical memories structured around contexts plus other knowledge.

Retrieval time is, however, not the only way in which to investigate underlying structure in memory. An alternative method is to examine the total amount of knowledge produced in response to different cues in a constrained period of time. If a particular set of cues lead to a marked increase in knowledge production, then it can be concluded that cues facilitate memory access because they correspond to the underlying organizational structure of knowledge in memory. The cued-recall experiment described previously, in which Barsalou's subjects recalled memories for a 60-second period to cues they had previously generated, provides evidence on rate of production. Table 6.4 shows the total number of cues, memories, and number of memories per cue produced in this experiment.

The first point about these data is that participant (person) cues were clearly more productive than all other cues – subjects found it easier to generate these cues and (as a consequence) had more to retrieve memories to. In terms of the number of memories retrieved per cue, location cues were most productive and reliably more productive than participant and time cues but did not differ significantly from activity cues. Finally, participants' cues provided fastest access to memories, location cues next fastest, followed by time cues, and activity cues were associated with slowest access times. All these differences were statistically reliable.

These findings then provide little support for the claim that activities are the central form of organization in autobiographical memory. Other types of knowledge such as knowledge of people and places may be equally effective in accessing specific memories and this suggests that the activity-dominance hypothesis must be modified if it is eventually to provide an account of autobiographical memory organization. Barsalou attempts such a modification and draws heavily on an analysis of subjects' protocols from the original free-recall study. In subjects' descriptions of events in which they participated in the summer vacation, descriptions of extended events dominated the protocols. Typically a subject would start out describing an extended event from beginning to end, perhaps dipping into specific memories along the way and providing comments on aspects of the event. For example, subjects might describe their holiday in a summarized way, picking out one of two specific events and passing comments on the quality of hotel rooms and their verdict on places they had visited. Recall might then switch to another extended event and this second extended event might chronologically parallel an extended event already described but focus on a different theme and pick out different memories.

Table 6.4 Mean frequency of recall across cue types

	Cue type			
Measure	*Participant*	*Activity*	*Location*	*Time*
Number of cues	19.54	11.79	11.50	5.13
Number of events	87.75	65.58	71.50	27.13
Number of events per cue	4.61	5.48	6.18	5.08
Number of events in first 5 sec	1.30	.62	1.05	.78

(Reproduced by permission of the author and publisher, from Barsalou 1988, table 8.4, p. 208. ©Cambridge University Press)

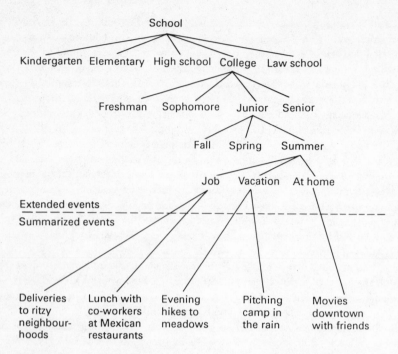

Figure 6.2 Nestings of summarized events in extended events (reproduced by permission of the author and publisher, from Barsalou 1988, figure 8.4, p. 225. ©Cambridge University Press)

Barsalou's model of autobiographical memory focuses on *extended-event time lines* which he argues are the primary organizers of autobiographical memory. Representations of extended events are indexed by extended-event time lines and nested within extended events are summarized events. This model is shown diagrammatically in Figure 6.2

Summarized events may, in turn, index specific autobiographical memories. Barsalou's model is virtually identical to the models of A-MOPs, E-MOPs, and autobiographical memories proposed by Conway and Bekerian, although the two lines of research were conducted and reported independently. Moreover, other researchers have converged on similar conclusions. For instance, Linton (1986) in her longitudinal study of her own memory proposed that memory is hierarchically structured with *mood tone*, forming the highest most abstract level of the hierarchy, followed by themes and sub-themes which either index or are part of *extendures*, which in turn index events and episodes. Extendures correspond to A-MOPs and extended-event time lines. Similarly Kolodner (1978) proposed a set of high-level knowledge structures called *eras* which represent extended-lifetime-period knowledge and we have already seen that a similar concept of *time eras* was introduced by Reiser *et al.* (1986).

Where then does this leave the activity-dominance hypothesis? The claim that activities constitute the primary form of organization in autobiographical memory must be rejected. Rather, activities like other types of knowledge support autobiographical memory organization but do not constitute the sole, or even the dominant, means of organization. The emerging consensus is that autobiographical memory is hierarchically organized and therefore must contain representations of knowledge at different levels of abstraction. Thus the claim of the activity-dominance hypothesis that autobiographical memories are indexed by generic knowledge structures appears to be supported. The nature of generic knowledge does not, however, appear to correspond closely to the proposals of Kolodner or Reiser *et al*. Extended-event time lines, A-MOPs, and extendures are idiosyncratic to individuals and represent thematic knowledge of a diverse kind. General events and E-MOPs also are idiosyncratic to individuals and may be dominated by knowledge of activities, people, places, and time. Possibly most E-MOP structures contain an equal mix of these types of knowledge; conversely it may be that some E-MOPs are wholly structured around a particular sort of knowledge. In conclusion, it seems that the research into human autobiographical memory has largely supported Schank's (1982) general (but not detailed) proposals that memories are organized around themes (TOPs) and event characteristics (MOPs).

Life themes

Barsalou (1988) suggested that extended-event time lines and general events might themselves be structured by representations of goal attainment. For instance, a lifetime period such as 'when I was at school' might include knowledge about various goals related to the general theme of the period, e.g. theme: 'had an unhappy time'; goal attainment: 'did not pass any exams'. Similarly, extended events within a lifetime period might represent goal-knowledge which is related to the lifetime-period theme, e.g. extended event: 'read a lot of science fiction'; goal attainment: 'got good marks in creative writing'. One problem here is that of how a person comes to have a goal or set of goals which characterize a lifetime period. One way in which this might occur is simply by the specification of goals within a culture and within sub-groupings of the culture. Thus goals may be externally specified. But perhaps the more important goals are those which are specified by the individual; certainly we might expect self-defined goals to be important structural elements in the organization of autobiographical memory.

In an important paper Csikszentmihalkyi and Beattie (1979) reported a study which attempted to examine the emergence of goals in the form of what they called 'life themes'. Csikszentmihalkyi and Beattie define a life theme as

the affective and cognitive representation of a problem or set of problems, perceived or experienced either consciously or unconsciously, which constituted a fundamental source of psychic stress for a person during childhood, for which that person wished resolution above all else, and which triggered adaptive efforts, resulting in attempted identification of the perceived problem, which in turn formed the basis for a fundamental interpretation of reality and ways of dealing with that reality (p. 48).

In their theoretical analysis Csikszentmihalkyi and Beattie identify four main stages to the development of a life theme. First, the family group or caretaker group in the child's environment labels some aspect of the environment as a problem or stressor and this, in some way, corresponds to the child's phenomenal experience of stress. For instance, poverty, inequality, or inability, might be labelled as major problems. Note that, as with all the stages in the development of a life theme, this does not have to happen in any conscious or explicit way. Second, the features of the problem must be identified by the child and this may take the form of some concrete and tangible quality of life such as 'where's my next meal coming from?', or may be generalized into some more abstract property such as 'What's the meaning in the order of the universe?' In a third stage the problem is conceptualized in terms of causality, for instance, poverty might be simply conceptualized as a problem arising from lack of money or, alternatively, it might be conceptualized as a problem arising from social inequality. Undoubtedly the conceptualization the child arrives at will determine the fourth stage which is identification of a solution. If poverty arises from lack of money, then ensuring one has a reliable and reasonably well-paid job later in life will solve the conceptualization of this problem. If, however, poverty is conceptualized as arising from social inequality, then a mundane but remunerative job will not constitute a solution to the definition of the problem, and we might expect the individual to pursue activities which more directly engage their conceptualization of the problem.

In order to investigate this model of life themes Csikszentmihalkyi and Beattie interviewed 30 white male subjects aged between 36 and 75 years. The subjects all had similar backgrounds in that they had all originated from poor, or very poor, lower socio-economic families. Half the group were, however, successful professionals and half were blue-collar workers. In the interviews subjects were asked to describe the kinds of influences which they judged had been critical in shaping their own lives. In particular they were asked to consider factors in their early life and work their way towards present influences. In addition to this they were asked direct questions about parental influence.

The principal findings were that two-thirds of the subjects in each group reported experiencing difficult events which had critically shaped their later life. In general members of both groups described events relating to poverty, death, divorce and alcoholism. Subjects who did not recall such events nevertheless recounted being troubled by a parent who 'pushed them too hard'. Interestingly, subjects who could recall particular events apparently had highly vivid memories of these events and described them in great detail and at some length. Needless to say, these were highly emotionally charged events for the individuals concerned (see Chapter 4). One way in which the two groups markedly differed was in their conceptualization of these problematic events. Nearly all the professionals abstracted the events into universal problems whereas the blue-collar workers tended to conceptualize the problems in more concrete, specific and personal ways.

Consider the following case reported by Csikszentmihalkyi and Beattie. John, who was part of the group of professionals, was the son of poor immigrant parents and at the age of 8 years was hit by a car driver while riding his bicycle. The driver of the car was a woman doctor and the accident was her fault as she had ignored a traffic signal. This doctor rushed John to hospital and cared for him but did not reveal that she had been responsible for the accident but rather portrayed it as a hit-and-run accident. So successful was her deception that she was able to force John's parents to pay all costs for the accidents including medical fees and the price of a new bicycle! John's comment on this traumatic event was as follows:

> My poor parents could hardly speak English and had no way to cope with the sophistication of the woman doctor. They had no idea how to do anything. They had no idea about insurance, liability, and so forth. So they ended up being taken in just like that – and paying and paying when they shouldn't have been paying at all. They ended up paying a woman who almost killed me. When I saw all these things happening, I didn't know what to do either, but I knew something was very wrong in the way things had worked out. So I vowed that I would know the law regarding what rights an accident victim had and so forth, as soon as I could ... I very early extended this to knowledge and curiosity regarding the law as it relates to minority groups. It was the immigrant status of my parents which put them at a disadvantage. So I knew that it was important for minority group members to have someone advise them of their rights before the law.

Of course, not all the professional respondents reported such clearly defined childhood problems nor did the majority report that problems of which they appeared to be fully aware had led to the development of a life theme. Yet all describe events and conditions to which they had responded in such a way as to formulate a life theme. In John's case he subsequently took a law degree, followed by a degree in economics and a career in government, where he was known for protecting the rights of minority groups.

Consider now the case of Harry, a blue-collar worker. Harry's father had died when Harry was only 8 years old. His subsequent childhood had been marked by near-starving poverty, many incidents of which he clearly recalled. He mentioned his mother's constant admonition during these years which was 'I hope you will find a way to have enough money when you're older ... and to have it in cash.' Not surprisingly Harry identified the problem of his childhood as one of poverty and the solution as one of thrift. Throughout the rest of his life Harry had been careful with money and had been able to accumulate fairly large sums so that at the age of 40 he owned five apartment blocks and at the age of 60 was estimated to be worth at least half a million dollars. Nevertheless, he worked in a steel mill, never married, and wore old clothes and owned an old car.

A third case involves George who recalled that his father had thought him a sissy when he was a child. Subsequently George became a policeman and one of the best shots in the county. A further tension in George's childhood had been his long blond hair which his mother had greatly admired. Later in life George's hair thinned and, in order to please his mother, who was then 55, George was saving up for a hair transplant.

Clearly both Harry's and George's responses contrast markedly with John's response to his childhood problems. Let us consider one more case, Max, a member of the professional group. Max, at the age of 4, had been boarded with a family in a distant town as his own parents had separated and his mother could not support him. In his childhood and teens Max had been a stateless person, travelling without a passport and spending various amounts of time in foster homes throughout Europe. At the age of 13 he read two history books which pointed him towards a solution to his problems of loneliness and disaffection. Max comments:

> When I was reading Van Loon and Burkhart, I knew that something important was happening to my life . . . because while reading them I was knowing that I had found a way to view the world. These two books . . . determined what questions I asked about life and from what perspective I viewed life thereafter.

Max then was able to conceptualize his existential problem in terms of history more generally – if he was stateless, lonely, alienated, and without a family, he could find a home and a state in the study of history. In later life Max became an eminent historian.

The essential difference between the professional and blue-collar workers was that the professionals discovered or created a solution to their childhood problems, whereas the blue-collar workers tended to accept a culturally specified solution. In both cases the solution formed a life theme. However, Csikszentmihalkyi and Beattie are careful to point out that life themes do not necessarily extend throughout a person's life. For many of their subjects the problems of childhood were resolved within a few years of reaching adulthood. In some cases the occupations chosen as part of the solution continued to provide intrinsic challenges to the person and so, although the choice of a particular profession might be traced to the resolution of childhood existential problems, further pursuit of a career may relate to other factors.

Csikszentmihalkyi and Beattie consider the problem of whether we can rely upon these accounts of life themes. After all, people may misremember, deliberately distort, or unconsciously rewrite their personal histories to fit their current self-image (see Chapters 4 and 5). Csikszentmihalkyi and Beattie argue that the memories recalled by their respondents were so vivid and detailed that it seems highly unlikely that these could have been intentionally or unintentionally fabricated. Moreover, in many cases subjects were able (spontaneously) to produce corroborating evidence such as the original battered book which had changed their lives. Finally, in a number of cases subjects appeared to be unaware that childhood events had led to the development of a life theme.

What does all this mean for our discussion of organization in autobiographical memory? The consensus view is that autobiographical memories are represented in hierarchical knowledge structures, the base of which are specific autobiographical memories. Intermediate levels in these hierarchies represent extended and generalized events and the highest levels represent extended-event time lines or lifetime periods. Clearly knowledge about goal attainment will be distributed throughout the hierarchical structure and, of course, goals will vary in their level of personal importance, and the nature of goal attainment will, accordingly, have more or less consequentiality for the individual. One possibility is that at more specific levels of representation in the hierarchy, goal-attainment knowledge will tend to be more proscribed and event specific. Goal-attainment knowledge represented at more abstract levels in the hierarchy will tend to be more wide ranging and general, although generality will, at least in part, be determined by how the individual conceptualizes the problem to which a goal or goals attach.

Life themes as described by Csikszentmihalkyi and Beattie should then be represented at the higher more abstract levels in the hierarchy, that is, they should act to structure lifetime periods. One further speculation I would like to introduce here is that it seems unlikely that a person should have only a single life theme. The discussion of self in Chapter 5 suggests that people may have many different types of selves and possibly these selves are structured around different sets of existential problems. For instance, the set of problems which confronts a person when they are at school (prior to any higher education) may generate a life theme which is specific to that lifetime period. Perhaps, each lifetime period or extended-event time line is associated with a life theme generated by existential problems specific to that period. Such lifetime-period-specific life themes might act as an important way in which autobiographical memories are organized within the hierarchy for that lifetime period. There is, as yet, no evidence bearing on these conjectures and the work of Csikszentmihalkyi and Beattie simply indicates that life themes may be critical in determining personality and the self. Certainly life themes are closely associated with autobiographical memories and in order to understand more fully the organization of autobiographical memories, thematic aspects of personal history will have to be investigated in further detail.

Theoretical aspects of structure: 'The past is another country'

The consensus view which is gradually developing within the study of autobiographical memory posits that autobiographical memory is hierarchically organized. But why should autobiographical memories be organized in this way? One answer to this question is being developed by Neisser (1986a, 1988) who, in recent papers, has attempted to draw researchers' attention to the actual nature of events. Consider, for example, a person's wedding day. Such an event has a complex structure composed of many sub-events and is embedded in a whole sequence of equally complex events which precede and postdate it. Neisser's point is that events are nested within events and it is this external structure which is at least partly preserved in memory, and which facilitates hierarchical organization of autobiographical memories.

More speculatively, Neisser (1988) takes these proposals one step further and argues that a specific brain structure might mediate the encoding of nested structure. The hippocampal system of the midbrain in mammals has been extensively investigated and heavily implicated in the processing of spatial information. Spatial information is, of course, also nested as Gibson (1979) pointed out. The hippocampus has been isolated as the main neural system which processes and represents nested spatial knowledge. Neisser proposes that this system has been adapted in the course of evolution to support the development of nested hierarchical structures in autobiographical memory. Indeed there are interesting neurological cases which lend some support to Neisser's proposals. For example, the patient H.M. suffered damage to the hippocampal regions of the midbrain and suffered from retrograde amnesia – an impairment of memory for past experiences and knowledge (impairments of autobiographical memory are reviewed in Chapter 9). Also worth noting is people's use of language to describe past events (and time in general) which is often dominated by the use of spatial metaphors, e.g. 'I'm glad all that's behind me now'; 'That event occurred between two very difficult periods'; or the subtitle of this section. Of course, this use of language could be based on some culturally specified beliefs rather than a dim awareness of the structure of autobiographical memory, but culturally specified beliefs have to come from somewhere, and it may be that characteristic ways of referring to the past do, in fact, reflect the structure of memory.

Neisser goes on to conjecture that knowledge at a low level in the hierarchy is forgotten at a faster rate than knowledge at high levels. Specific memories and the micro-events which are nested in them are susceptible to forgetting because similar events are likely to be experienced and similarity leads to interference with the original memory representation. Consider, for example, the micro-event of pinning a button-hole flower on a jacket on the morning of a wedding. When queried a person might be able to respond positively to the question 'Have you ever pinned a buttonhole on your jacket?' but might be unsure as to whether they had pinned a buttonhole on the day of their wedding: maybe someone else pinned the flower on, maybe the flowers were supplied with devices which did not require pinning. Although I am sure I wore a buttonhole on the day of my own wedding, I simply cannot remember whether I pinned it on, whether someone else pinned it on, or, indeed, whether we did in fact use pins! I simply cannot *remember* this event, although I'm absolutely sure it happened – indeed, I am also sure that I pinned buttonholes to my jacket at other weddings I attended, even though I cannot remember these actions. (A quick examination of family photograph albums confirms that I am correct.) But, note, that it would be very unusual if I had forgotten my wedding day, or could remember I was married but not recall events, some vividly, which took place that day.

Microevents nested at the bottom level of the hierarchy are rather like the general actions described by Reiser *et al.*, they occur in many contexts and must be nested in myriads of memories; further up the hierarchy the levels of nesting become distinctive and unique. I have attended comparatively few weddings and I know that I can *remember* something from each of these events. When I remember sub-events from a wedding, recall tends to be partly in the form of images. Images are a ubiquitous form of autobiographical memory recall (see Conway 1988a and Brewer 1986, discussed in Chapter 1) and the fact that a person does recall an image often lends credence to the belief that the remembered event actually happened (Johnson 1988). Neisser (1988) proposes that images in autobiographical memory may serve a specific purpose which is to 'illustrate' subjectively important aspects of a remembered event. However, as images may often be of generic memories (Conway 1989), imagery itself may be misleading if images are taken as evidence that the remembered event actually happened. Maybe I have now attended so many weddings that I have formed a generic memory – an E-MOP – of these events and the images I recall represent generic aspects of my personal experiences of weddings rather than micro-events which actually occurred. Possibly it is in this way that people have the subjective experience of 'remembering' an event which they later discover did not take place or did not take place in the way they remembered it.

Hierarchical nested structure is, then, supported both by the empirical findings and by theoretical considerations and it can now be argued, with some justification, that the model constitutes a promising starting point for future research. One area in which the model is clearly deficient, and which points to a potentially fruitful area of research, is that of the detailed nature of specific autobiographical memories. Virtually no empirical studies have attempted to examine just what the structure of specific auto-biographical memories might be. Consider again the wedding-day example. Certainly we would want to argue that a memory of this day would be nested within more abstract levels of representation, but what about the actual memory itself – what is the structure of the memory? On Neisser's view the memory should contain nested structure in which events are embedded in sub-events. When, however, protocols are collected from subjects exhaustively describing events, nested structure usually does not dominate the description of the event. Consider the following extract from a protocol reported by Conway (1988a).

> Well the first thing which comes to mind is the registry office. I can clearly see (closes her eyes) Paul who was wearing a green velvet suit, my parents and my in-laws, also Susan and Dee who were my bridesmaids and Paul's friend Ian – he was best man – standing in a semi-circle around a big mahogany desk upon which the registrar was organising some papers. This was just before the ceremony started.

This account was from 35-year-old woman recalling her wedding day. What is interesting about this excerpt, and the subsequent account, was that sub-events were recalled which did not appear to be nested within each other. Indeed some of the sub-events which were recalled led the subject to recall other events and facts which occurred outside the wedding-day event altogether. In protocols such as these, subjects occasionally employ chronological organization as though they were searching a memory trace which was organized temporally – from start to end (see Barsalou and Sewell 1985 for related findings) – but this type of protocol is by no means the dominant form of recall. One aspect of these recalls which is common to all protocols is that subjects always recall images. But images do not seem to represent continuous action sequences but, rather, appear to act like 'snapshots' of groups of participants or scenery associated with the recalled event. A good example of this is provided by Brewer (1986) in describing a response to the cue word *California*.

> I might experience a mental image that corresponds to a particular episode in my own life, such as the time in California, while visiting Mt Palomar, when I made a snowball and threw it down the trail at my sons, starting a snowball fight (p. 26).

Lifetime-period knowledge (the time in California) and E-MOP knowledge (visiting Mt Palomar) are both present in this protocol, but so is the specific detail preserved in the image of who some of the principal participants were and also perhaps what the general tone of the visit was (fun).

Conway (1988a) argues that the function of images in autobiographical memory is to provide cues which can be further used to search the memory trace. If specific autobiographical memories are comparatively unstructured, then accessing knowledge in a trace cannot effectively occur by employing structure. It may be, as Neisser suggests, that nested structure at the level of micro-events is quickly forgotten and, if this is the case, then we would expect a memory of an event to contain a number of disconnected representations of event details – fragments of the original memory. In order to access these fragments information in an image can be selected and employed by retrieval processes to cue recall. In the wedding protocol mentioned above the subject 'jumped' ahead and recalled an incident occurring much later in the day, involving the best man's speech at the reception. Perhaps Brewer could use information in his image to recall further details of his trip to Mt Palomar. In protocols of exhaustive recalls, subjects occasionally 'surprise' themselves by the recall of 'forgotten' details.

Moreover, recall often moves outside the target event as other memories are apparently directly accessed by knowledge retrieved from the target memory.

Little is known about the structure of specific autobiographical memories. It seems reasonable, on intuitive grounds alone, that some memories would be highly structured perhaps because of their personal importance to the individual or because the events they represent were distinctive in some other way. Most memories, however, are probably comparatively unstructured and rapidly degrade, preserving knowledge of one or two specific micro-events and maybe some incomplete knowledge of chronological order. Once a memory is accessed through the hierarchical organization of autobiographical memory, then the actual trace may be searched by some process of repeated retrieval in which initially retrieved knowledge is recycled in an attempt to access other fragments of the memory. This may explain why specific cues such as smells, a chance comment, or some aspect of the environment, might lead to the direct access of a memory – bypassing the hierarchical structure – and leading to the experience of spontaneous, surprising, and unexplained recall of a 'forgotten' event. In cases where a memory is directly accessed by a cue but not consciously retrieved, then an experience of *déjà vu* may result. These issues are considered further in Chapters 8 and 10.

Summary: the organization of autobiographical memory

The empirical findings indicate that autobiographical memories are represented at different levels of abstraction. The abstraction dimension ranges from specific representations of experienced events to representations of themes and goals which were associated with an extended period of time. Representations along this dimension are arranged hierarchically so that the most abstract representations (lifetime periods) index less abstract generic representations such as extended events or E-MOPs which, in turn, index specific autobiographical memories. Organization and the nature of representations within different levels of this hierarchical structure have not been extensively investigated. It seems possible that this organizational scheme might reflect, in part, the structure of events as they actually occur and Neisser (1988) has speculated that hippocampal regions of the brain may be centrally involved in the formation of organizational structures in autobiographical memory. Specific types of knowledge, activities, persons, locations, and time, seem to be equally effective in retrieving memories.

At the lowest level in the hierarchy specific autobiographical memories appear to be comparatively unstructured and this may be because information in the trace rapidly degrades, or becomes inaccessible for other reasons, leading to memories which represent fragments of knowledge. Once a memory is accessed by retrieval processes traversing the hierarchical organization, knowledge within the memory trace may then be retrieved by some process of cued recall. It may be that representations of specific memories are highly sensitive to cue information and, when a cue corresponds to information in a trace (cf. Tulving and Thomson 1973), access occurs automatically. Thus memories can be accessed indirectly through the structure of autobiographical memory or directly by an appropriate cue.

7 • REMEMBERING THE PAST: THE PROCESS OF RETRIEVAL

In the previous chapter we saw that researchers have converged on the view that autobiographical memories are organized in memory by a nested hierarchy of knowledge structures. At the top level of a hierarchy are abstract representations of lifetime periods containing knowledge about personally relevant goals and life themes. At the bottom level are autobiographical memories of specific events. Autobiographical memories themselves, however, may be relatively unstructured fragmentary records of experienced events. In this general model of autobiographical memory, retrieval proceeds by searches through the hierarchical structures and different levels of the hierarchy index one and other. But what if the hierarchy is bypassed? How can retrieval proceed then?

Supposing I knew that, when you were a schoolchild aged 9, you had taken a holiday in Italy with your school and I asked you to remember who else from your class went on this holiday. The hierarchical structure of autobiographical memory is bypassed by the query; the structure of the event is specified in my question, and let's assume that the same structure indexes in your memory a whole set of memories of events which occurred during your Italian holiday. What knowledge do you use to search these memories? Are there particular strategies you can use to access memories of specific events? Is there some general strategy which most people use to search through a complex set of memories?

At the end of the last chapter it was argued that searches of specific autobiographical memories might involve some type of repeated retrieval process in which already retrieved knowledge is recycled through the retrieval process in order to access other parts of the memory trace. In the present chapter this view is developed in much more detail. The research reviewed in Chapter 6 was chiefly concerned with how a subject locates a target memory, or set of memories (i.e. what structures are involved), and not with how a subject 'unpacks' the memory/memories once accessed. In contrast, research into autobiographical memory retrieval processes has mainly employed tasks – such as the one in the example above – which do not require the subject to utilize the hierarchical structure of autobiographical memory. Instead, a particular target event or set of events is specified by the experimenter and the behaviour of interest is how the subject goes about retrieving knowledge from their memory/ memories of the event(s).

The generate–search–verify model

Williams (1978) and his colleagues (Williams and Santos-Williams 1980; Williams and Hollan 1981) reported a protocol study of memory retrieval which indicated that memory retrieval was an effortful and elaborate process. Williams studied four subjects who were asked to think aloud while remembering the names of their high-school classmates. Subjects did this for sessions lasting about one hour, and after ten such sessions subjects were still recalling many names! In a stamina-sapping analysis Williams and Santos-Williams (1980) examined the full ten-hour protocol from one of their subjects, and Williams and Hollan (1981) overview characteristics of all four subjects' protocols. A number of particularly interesting aspects of the protocols were observed and these are reviewed below. It should be noted that one advantage of this task was that subjects' responses were verifiable as yearbooks kept by the schools contained the names and photographs of all students in a graduating year. Note also that for two of the subjects the number of potential classmates was in excess of three hundred and for the remaining two subjects the number of potential classmates was in excess of six hundred.

Here is an example of a typical first protocol collected by Williams (taken from Williams and Hollan 1981: 89–90):

> The first thing that comes to mind is . . . I mean it's almost like images of different snapshots of our high school. You know, I can think of our general science class, and waiting in the lunch line, and halls. Umm, Sort of, Jeff Thompson! He was a friend of mine. Sort of pops into mind and I think, umm, we used to stand in the lunch line together, and he was in our general science class. That's where I first met him, our freshman year. There was, umm, let's see I'm trying to think of people I interacted with a lot with. And some of them . . . are sort of people I've known after high school. Like Bill Newell. I . . . I lived with him for a while, in Portland. Umm, after school. So he sort of comes to mind immediately too. Umm, let's see. I mean I guess it's almost easier for me to think of our home town, and think of people . . . that I've still run into on occasion, when I go back there. And then sort of check to see if they meet the require- ments. Like were they in high school with me? And I can think of people like Buddy Collender, and John Tremble, who both live in our . . . Ah . . . home town. Umm . . . I guess it's. It also seems that I want to think of, sort of, it's clear that I have to think of some other situations. It's like I want to think of, sort of, prototypical situations and then sort of examine the people that were involved in those. And things like P.E. class, where there was . . . Ah . . . Gary Booth. Umm, and Karl Brist, were sort of, we always ended up in the same P.E. classes, for some reasons. Umm . . . I can think of things like dances. I guess then I usually

think of . . . of girls (chuckle). Like Cindy Shup, Judy Foss, and Sharon Ellis. I went to grade school with her. Umm . . . I mean it's sort of like I have a picture of the high school dance. You know, and these are the women I knew then. Umm . . . There's a girl I can think of, I have a very good picture of her but I can't remember her name. I can even remember she was, she was from Gales Creek. Ah . . . And . . . Ah . . . I mean I can see what she looks like. I just can't remember her name. She lived near John Randolf, who was another friend of mine.

Williams and Santos-Williams (1980) identified four very common aspects of the protocols which they called, *extended retrievals, partial recalls, contextual retrieval*, and *systematic hypothesizing*. Extended retrievals, which were to be the most ubiquitous aspects of the protocols, occurred when a subject recalled part of a target name or some features of a person and then retrieved a substantial amount of related knowledge as they focused in on the name. This is illustrated in the following protocol in which one of the subjects attempts to recall the name of a classmate who had also been a member of a high-school rock band.

Okay I was imagining the whole room and we were imagining the instruments set up and I'm trying to remember the name of this guy – who used to . . . Art! And he was also in our 10th grade art class . . . he would also bring a whole lot of people to – first on that – what's his name now? Let's see – (whistle) I'm trying to – remember his name. At his house was the first time I heard a Jefferson Airplane album. Umm . . . the bass guitar, really a strungout looking dude . . .

Extended recalls frequently resulted in the retrieval of a name. Partial recalls occurred when subjects recalled part of a name, such as first or second name or an initial letter. Contextual retrieval was evident when subjects used locations, activities, and other types of knowledge to generate a context with which to search memory. For instance, a subject might generate a context such as 'people I used to play tennis with' and use this to probe memory for classmate names. In a similar way a subject might generate a list of locations with which they had been familiar and use these to probe memory. Systematic hypothesizing involved subjects generating intelligent guesses. For instance, a subject might start with a letter, say 'P', and generate common names such as Paul, Peter, Pam, and so on. The names would be used as probes in subsequent memory searches.

Other characteristics of the protocols were overshoots, distractions, self-corrections, and the systematic application of search strategies. Overshoots occurred when subjects located a target name but continued to supply information associated with that person. Self-corrections were fairly frequent and occurred when subjects modified or rejected an already retrieved name. Both these characteristics of the protocols are fairly good evidence of a verification stage in retrieval. Overshoots convince the subject that they are right, and self-corrections can occur only if some type of verification is undertaken. Distractions, on the other hand, are interesting for a different reason. Distractions were also fairly frequent and occurred when the subject would, apparently, pursue a different, perhaps partly related, path in retrieval and later return to the main retrieval path. The digression into mentioning images of the high school in the first protocol above is an example of this. It is as though the cues employed in the memory search map on to a large number of memories, only some of which are directly relevant to the task in hand. Finally the systematic application of search strategies was also fairly common. A frequently used search strategy involved a subject creating some form of mental map and using this to guide the search process. For example, a subject might create an image of the local neighbourhood and mentally search through the streets 'looking' for houses in which high-school friends had lived.

Williams and Hollan propose a basic retrieval process and then show how this process responds to two general types of memory cue and how this is reflected in the characteristics of the protocols they collected. Their starting assumption is similar to that made by Schank (1982) discussed in Chapter 6 – events are processed by different knowledge structures and sub-event information is represented separately in 'packets' of knowledge. They also assume that not all event information is encoded. Thus memory representations are inherently impoverished and fragmentary. The general retrieval process they assume has three stages: *find-a-context*; *search*; *verify*. The find-a-context stage involves the generation of a context with which to search memory. Context is usually provided externally (or at least this is the case in experimental studies of autobiographical memory) and the starting context is used in a preliminary search. It is not clear how the search process actually operates in the Williams and Hollan model but let's assume that the start context maps on to the structure of memories. This does not seem an unreasonable assumption for a context such as 'high school' which Conway and Bekerian (1987) found to be a very common lifetime period listed by all their subjects. The search leads to the retrieval of fragmentary knowledge stored in a memory trace. A verification procedure then evaluates the output from memory and a decision is made as to whether to execute a response or not. If a positive verification cannot be made, then the new context (original context plus retrieved knowledge) is recycled through the search process. Note that this new context might also be recycled through the find-a-context procedure in order to shape or fine-tune the contextual-memory cue – perhaps context-cue information which was ineffective in the first search is omitted from subsequent searches. Thus memory retrieval operates in stages of context generation, memory search, and output verification, and the retrieval process is repeated on the basis of each verification stage through succeeding context–search–verify cycles.

Williams and Hollan consider two major problems faced by this type of retrieval process. The first occurs when the retrieval task contains insufficient information, that it to say that, if the retrieval cues are impoverished, then retrieval cannot immediately proceed. In this case elaboration takes place at the find-a-context stage and recall takes the form of extended retrievals, systematic hypotheses, and inferential recall. The second problem arises when the retrieval task contains too much information – the cues are over-elaborate or too rich. In this case, a context is focused by processes operating at the find-a-context stage. For example, in response to the cue '8th grade' a subject might search memory on the basis of the types of classes they took in that year at school (e.g. history, maths, English, classes, etc.). On a slightly different tack a person might select a particular aspect of the context and focus the search on that cue. For instance, a particular person might be employed or, as Williams and Hollan's subjects did, a memory of a class picture might be retrieved and mentally scanned in order to identify features which might lead to the retrieval of a name.

Clearly there are problems with this context–search–verify model. The central one seems to be that all the 'interesting' aspects of retrieval occur in context generation and verification – search is assumed to be an automatic process which simply takes an input and delivers an ouput. But the important questions, such as what aspects of context are selected for search, why, and how, are left unresolved. Similarly the immensely difficult problem of verification is not discussed: how can subjects know that they have retrieved the correct information if they did not know what the information was in the first place? Despite these problems the research of Williams and his colleagues is of particular interest for some of the issues considered at the close of Chapter 6. Importantly, retrieval from memories of specific events appears to be an essentially problem-solving process in which different stages in the retrieval process are cycled through as the search moves from general to specific. There are also further clues to memory structure evident in Williams and Hollan's data. For instance, in initial recall subjects frequently recalled names very quickly as though only the very briefest of memory searches was required to access this knowledge. Perhaps names of best friends, and significant others in general, are stored at the level of lifetime periods and can be directly accessed in processing the context of the retrieval cue provided by the memory probe. The use of categorical knowledge such as activities and locations in searching specific memories suggests that the events these memories represent may have been encoded in terms of categorical knowledge structures used to process the events. Perhaps specific autobiographical memories are structured, as Schank suggested, by the schemas and concepts used to process those events as they occurred (see also Barsalou 1988). Finally the use of imagery-based search strategies suggests that memories might be structured, at least in part, by the spatio-temporal context in which the events they represent were located, and this would seem to lend some support to Neisser's suggestions about nested structure, a point we will return to later in the chapter.

Recency, categories, and images

Whitten and Leonard (1981) also studied autobiographical-memory retrieval by requiring the retrieval of the names of teachers. Their study was, however, rather different from the Williams study. In their first experiment Whitten and Leonard required 161 first-year university undergraduates to recall the name of a teacher from each of their 12 pre-university school years. One group of students was instructed to start their recall at 1st grade and proceed through to the most recent year, 12th grade (forward recall). Other students retrieved teachers' names in the reverse order, starting with 12th grade and proceeding through to 1st grade (backward recall). Finally, a third group of students recalled teachers' names in random order.

Two main measures were taken, number of failures to retrieve a name and speed of retrieval. A trial was counted as a failure if a subject failed to retrieve all 12 teachers' names. The principal finding for failure rate was that 9.1 per cent of subjects failed to recall all twelve teachers' names in the backward-recall condition; forward recall led to 29.8 per cent retrieval failures, and random-order recall to 33.3 per cent retrieval failures. Statistically there were fewer errors for the backward-recall order than for either of the other two orders. Thus there was a marked recency effect in the recall of teachers' names with teachers from more recent grades being recalled far more frequently than teachers from more distant grades. This effect was also present in speed of retrieval, and backward recall gave rise to a mean retrieval time of 157 seconds, forward recall to a mean retrieval time of 179 seconds, and random-order recall to a mean retrieval time of 191 seconds, indicating that memory access was easier in backward recall.

These findings were replicated in a second experiment and the recency function in this case showed that 40 per cent of failures to retrieve occurred for 1st-grade teachers, whereas for 12th-grade teachers the failure rate was only 10 per cent. This finding is particularly interesting and clearly corresponds to the temporal gradients in autobiographical-memory retrieval observed by Rubin and his colleagues (see Chapter 3). It suggests that a general property of the human-memory system is to preserve, and keep available, memories of recent events compared to memories of more remote events. Such a function would serve the very useful purpose of keeping a person keenly aware of current developments in the environment, and help to keep track of a person's current location in space and time. Indeed, Baddeley (1986) suggests just such a function for recency in human memory. Baddeley and Hitch (1977) reported findings rather similar to those obtained by Whitten and Leonard, although in their case they assessed rugby players' memories for matches they had played in that season. They found that recent matches were well remembered and matches from earlier parts of the season more poorly remembered.

One interesting exception to the recency effect which was evident in Baddeley and Hitch's data was that one match, which occurred in the middle of the season, was remembered almost as well as the last match which had been played. It turned out this was the only match which the rugby club had won that season. Thus other aspects of an event may override recency effects. Conway and Montgomery (1990) report a similar finding in a study in which subjects attempted to date newsworthy events and pop songs occurring over a 10-year period. In this study strong recency effects were observed but, as in the Baddeley and Hitch study, some events, regardless of whether they occurred recently or not, were very accurately dated. In the Conway and Montgomery study subjects also 'thought aloud' while they dated events, and analysis of the protocols indicated that events which were not recent, but which were dated accurately, were highly associated with autobiographical memories. Conway and Montgomery propose that recency is only one general function which determines the availability of autobiographical memories. Another way in which memories may become highly available is by the attention and interest which is taken in original events. High levels of attention lead to encoding of the event in terms of the structure of autobiographical memory and so the availability of these memories remains high. The availability of memories of events which were not associated with high levels of attention at encoding is determined by recency of the event.

Recency then is clearly an important determinant of memory retrieval and may be independent of the structure of autobiographical memory (Chapter 6) and of the nature of the encoded events. Whitten and Leonard, however, also investigated the types of knowledge and strategies used by their subjects in retrieving memories. In their second experiment they required subjects to 'think aloud' as they recalled the names of their grade teachers and subsequently analysed the resulting protocols. One important factor in the Whitten and Leonard study is that US school children have the same grade teacher for grades 1 to 6 and a different grade teacher for each of the grades 7 to 12 (of course, even during grades 1 to 6 children have different teachers, but these are not grade teachers). Whitten and Leonard found that different types of knowledge and retrieval strategies were employed in the retrieval of teachers from grades 1 to 6 and 7 to 12.

The most common retrieval strategy was the *subject-enumeration strategy*. Using this strategy a subject would think of different topics they had been taught at school and then attempt to retrieve the name of the teacher for that subject. However, the subject-enumeration strategy was most common for retrieval of teachers' names in grades 7 to 12 and was barely evident at all for recall from grades 1 to 6. For grades 1 to 6 a whole range of other types of retrieval strategies and knowledge types were evident, and these were most common for these grades and less common for grades 7 to 12. These latter strategies were overall more frequent than the subject-enumeration strategy and this shows that more thought was required in the retrieval of older information – this is, of course, what would be expected when recency is a factor influencing recall.

The second most frequent strategy observed by Whitten and Leonard was that of locational search. In this strategy subjects would imagine a location from their school environment and then mentally explore this representation in the hope of coming across a teacher's name. For instance, Whitten and Leonard (1981: 573) quote the following statement by one of their subjects: 'I'm thinking about where my locker was and where I used to walk and which classrooms I went into – with the hopes that I'll see a teacher there.' Other strategies and knowledge used by the subjects were partial name cues (e.g. first letter), emotional responses, recall of specific physical attributes of teachers, and recall of personality attributes (see Whitten and Leonard 1981: Table 4, p. 573, for a complete list). Finally, a very common type of knowledge employed by Whitten and Leonard's subjects, but curiously not discussed by the authors, was retrieval of specific autobiographical memories of events involving grade teachers.

The studies reviewed in this and the preceding section quite clearly demonstrate that a whole range of different types of retrieval strategies and knowledge types are employed when a memory cue is sufficiently specific to bypass the structure of autobiographical memory. A general tactic involves cue elaboration by cyclic retrieval-verification passes through memory. Recent knowledge is more accessible than older knowledge and the retrieval process for older knowledge is, accordingly, more elaborate. Overall, subjects use a range of retrieval tactics and category enumeration, and imagined-location searches appear to be the most frequently employed techniques for constructing an effective retrieval context. Note that these two strategies would seem to capitalize upon original features of the encoding environment (different types of teachers, spatial layout of the environment) and, as such, might be taken as evidence of the use of nested structure in autobiographical memory. Finally, specific autobiographical memories are often directly retrieved and these provide the detailed knowledge which is the object of the memory search.

Single-case studies

Probably the best evidence that retrieval strategies vary with retention interval (age of memory) comes from Linton's (1975, 1978, 1982, 1986) pioneering study of her own memory. In Chapter 3 we saw that Linton set herself the task of recording events which occurred each day in her own life over a six-year period. Subsequently, Linton tested her ability to remember and accurately date the recorded events. However, at the end of each year of the study Linton also set herself the task of exhaustively recalling memories from the preceding year. Of particular interest here were the strategies Linton observed herself using during these lengthy recalls. Moreover, as these recalls were repeated over a 12-year period (1972 to 1983), Linton was able to compare changes in her recall strategies.

Linton (1986) reports five broad classes of retrieval strategies which she employed:

1 *Simple chronological order (62.3 per cent)*
In this strategy memory search started with the oldest memory retrieved and worked forwards towards the present.

2 *Categorical summaries (23.2 per cent)*
In this case the retrieval process employed some personally relevant theme and memories relating to the theme were retrieved.

3 *Reverse chronological order (5.8 per cent)*
This is the opposite of (1); retrieval starts with the most recent memory retrieved and works backwards towards the most remote memory.

4 *Graphical and time-line expressions (5.8 per cent)*
It is not exactly clear what Linton means by this retrieval strategy but her description suggests that she brought to mind some type of image which represented the 'shape' of her life in a particular period and employed this analogically represented graph in the retrieval process.

5 *Unclassified (2.9 per cent)*
Only two of the memory searches were unclassifiable.

The percentages show the frequency of use of particular types of strategies. Consider the chronological searches. Perhaps the first point here is that backward retrieval (reverse chronological order) is infrequently used and this finding stands in sharp contrast to the findings of the previous section. It seems clear that, in Linton's case at least, backward retrieval was not a preferred strategy, and it seems reasonable to conclude that this is because this strategy was not an effective means of recalling autobiographical memories. In contrast forward retrieval (simple chronological order) was a very frequently employed strategy and seemed overall to be the most effective retrieval strategy – again in marked contrast to the findings of Whitten and Leonard. It is unclear why these differences emerged in Linton's study but one possibility is that searching a comparatively short-time period (one year) might favour retrieval strategies which are ineffective when searching a long-time period (the 12 school years).

Linton's study does, however, lend strong support to other aspects of Whitten and Leonard's findings. The second most frequent retrieval strategy noted by Linton was that of categorical search of autobiographical memory. In this case the categories denoted themes relating to professional/work and social/self-interest domains. The important finding was that categorical searches of memory became much more frequent as the age of the target time-period increased. Conversely, chronological searches dominated searches of more recent time periods. In fact Linton (1986: 64) comments. 'Chronological search strategies that are speedy, accurate, and complete for memories less than a couple of years old . . . are difficult, if not impossible, to perform for older materials. Categorical searches, with the chronology of the events and episodes within the categories still remarkably well fixed, become the norm.' So, as in the Whitten and Leonard study, older memories appear to be organized categorically and not temporally. Linton argues that memory is rewritten in the passage of time so that specific events become unified in representations of thematic aspects of a person's life and it is this thematic structure which guides the retrieval of older memories. Memories of events which occurred only a year or two prior to retrieval appear to be organized in terms of chronology and are most effectively accessed by retrieval strategies which exploit temporal information. Thus Linton's findings closely agree with the findings reported in Chapter 6 and lend further support to the notion of a hierarchically structured autobiographical memory.

Linton's (1986) study did not, however, bypass the structure of autobiographical memory. By free-recalling events which took place over a period of a year the structure of autobiographical memory could be employed (at least for older memories) to access groups of theme-related memories. In an extension of Linton's work, Wagenaar (1986) examined more closely the effectiveness of different types of cues in directly accessing autobiographical memories. Like Linton, Wagenaar kept a diary for a period of six years and each day recorded events from his life. Wagenaar, however, recorded his events in terms of *who*, *what*, *where*, and *when* providing an entry for each of these categories for every event. He also recorded a distinctive detail for each event and rated each event on various scales, e.g. emotionality, salience, personal importance, etc. At test, Wagenaar systematically varied the specific cues available for recall, the aim being to determine which cues were most effective in remembering.

The principal findings were as follows. *What* cues were most effective, followed by *where* and *who* cues, and *when* cues were barely effective at all in promoting recall. However, when cues were combined, *when* proved to be a highly effective second cue, so that given some non-temporal information about an event, recall would improve markedly when a temporal cue was also provided. In general, multiple cues were more effective than single cues. These findings lend some support to the views of Reiser and Barsalou outlined in Chapter 6. Knowledge of locations, activities, and persons can be effective cues for autobiographical-memory retrieval. However, it is clear from Wagenaar's findings that combinations of cues are far more effective in promoting retrieval than single cues. We should not be surprised by this; after all, memories are complex representations of complex occurrences and presumably a combination of cues will always be more effective in discriminating between individual memories. Perhaps action, location, and person cues are effective in accessing *sets* of memories, and combination cues facilitate in the discrimination of specific memories within a set. One reason for this may be that cue combinations more exactly specify the structure of the encoding environment (and hence the structure of the resulting memory) than single cues alone.

Events and thoughts

The most extensive study of specific autobiographical memories has been reported by Brewer (1988). Brewer investigated memory for randomly sampled autobiographical events and for subject-selected autobiographical events. Events were randomly sampled by requiring subjects to carry an electronic 'beeper' which was programmed to beep at randomly selected times, with the constraint that events should be sampled at an approximate rate of one every two hours. When the beeper sounded subjects filled out a response card on which they provided a short description of the current event and various ratings of event characteristics. Subject-selected or memorable events were sampled by requiring subjects to record at the end of each day one event which they judged would be memorable.

In the first experiment reported by Brewer subjects recorded the following aspects of each event: time, thoughts and actions, thoughts, actions, and rated the co-ordination of actions and thoughts for that event. The various ratings of the event were: category frequency (i.e. frequency of that type of action/thought), instance frequency (i.e. frequency of that particular action/thought), pleasantness, significance, excitement (emotional arousal), and how goal directed that particular action/thought was. The same procedure was followed for memorable events. There were eight subjects in the experiment and subjects averaged 17 days recording memories. Subjects were tested immediately, after a delay of 69 days, and after a delay of 140 days. At test, subjects were shown an event description (in their own handwriting) and rated their memory for the event on a 7-point scale where a '1' meant *no memory* and a '7' *certain that I remember the event*.

Overall, recognition memory was good and the forgetting curves showed a gradual decline over time so that best memory performance was evident at immediate test and slightly lower memory performance at final test. Recognition accuracy proportions collapsed across sampling periods was 79 per cent for randomly sampled actions, 68 per cent for randomly sampled thoughts, 87 per cent for memorable actions, and 72 per cent for memorable thoughts. Thus memory for actions was superior to memory for thoughts and memory for memorable events superior to memory for randomly sampled events.

In terms of the rating scales, memorable events (actions and thoughts) were associated with higher ratings of pleasantness and emotionality than randomly sampled events. Overall, memory for actions were associated with low ratings of category frequency and high ratings of excitement and significance. Memory for thoughts were associated with high levels of pleasantness, significance, and excitement. Regression analyses found that memory for actions was reliably predicted by ratings of category-instance frequency so that low ratings were associated with highest levels of memory. Good memory performance for thoughts was best predicted by high levels of excitement. Finally, events to do with college work were high on ratings of significance, goal-directedness, and co-ordination of thought and action, and low on ratings of affect and pleasantness. Conversely, events to do with recreation were high on ratings of affect and pleasantness but low on significance, goal-directedness, and co-ordination.

The findings from Brewer's first experiment demonstrate that memory for randomly sampled and memorable events differ in various ways, thus questioning the generality of conclusions reached on the basis of studies of memorable events only (e.g. Linton, Wagenaar). Forgetting appears to be somewhat more rapid for random than for memorable events and shows a steady but shallow decline over time. Memory for actions is superior to memory for thoughts, and memory for actions is related to the uniqueness of an event, whereas memory for thoughts is related to emotional arousal.

In a second experiment Brewer essentially confirmed his early findings and extended the use of random sampling to cued recall. In this second experiment the data-collection procedure was basically the same as that used in the first experiment – subjects wrote descriptions and made ratings of events and thoughts in response to randomly timed beeps. At test subjects were presented with a single cue from an event and asked to recall other aspects of the event and make a global judgement of whether they remembered the event or not. Cues used to prompt recall were taken from subjects' event descriptions and were divided into five cue-types: *time, location, time and location, thought, action*. In addition to this, subjects also completed a questionnaire designed to assess the nature of their phenomenal experience of remembering. In this questionnaire subjects judged to what extent they (re)experienced the following characteristics of the remembered event: *visual, auditory, tactile, smell, taste, emotion,* and *thought*.

Once again there was a shallow incline in the forgetting curves so that events tested immediately were very well remembered and events tested last were less well remembered. There appeared to be no marked serial position effects, although there was some evidence of a 'weekend' effect where events occurring at weekends were rather better remembered than events occurring during weekdays. Marked differences in the cued recall of event knowledge were observed and the ordering was: times 75 per cent, emotions 78 per cent, thoughts 84 per cent, actions 89 per cent, and locations 92 per cent. These findings are, however, somewhat misleading because subjects could probably infer locations and actions on the basis of a presented cue more accurately than they could infer times and emotions. A better measure are the ratings on the 7-point scale of how well an event is remembered and in this case the ordering of cue types was: time 2.38, location 2.51, time and location 2.92, thought 3.85, and action 4.31. (It will be recalled that a '1' means no memory and a '7' means 'certainly I can remember the event'.) In general, these findings would seem to support the findings considered earlier. For example, the poor utility of time cues in Brewer's experiments supports Wagenaar's finding that 'when' cues were the least effective cues to recall. That time cues improve when linked with location cues in Brewer's experiments also supports Wagenaar's findings that cue combinations are more effective for recall than single cues, and that 'when' cues are particularly effective in the context of other cues. Brewer's finding that action cues are very effective for recall lends some support to the claims of Reiser that autobiographical memories might be organized in terms of activities (see Chapter 6).

A more complex picture emerged when Brewer examined the relations between the various ratings and cued recall for the different types of cues. For action cues, goal-directedness was a good predictor of recall, and highly goal-directed actions were associated with high levels of remembering. For locations, location frequency was a reliable predictor, and infrequent locations were associated with high levels of recall. As in the first experiment, thought cues were effective aids to remembering when the thought serving as a cue had been associated at encoding with high levels of excitement. Time was an effective cue when the to-be-recalled event was of a low-frequency action, and time plus location was effective when the event occurred in a low-frequency location.

Recall accuracy also varied with cue-type and, as can be seen from the recall percentages listed in Table 7.1, time cues were virtually ineffective in prompting recall.

Thus different types of cues appear to be associated with different aspects of events; actions are associated with goal-directedness whereas thoughts are associated with excitement or arousal. Overall, actions and thoughts are better cues to recall than other types of event knowledge.

Finally, Brewer reports a very interesting analysis of subjects' phenomenal experiences of remembering. Items which subjects were highly confident in recalling (and where the recall was correct) were associated with very high ratings of visual imagery, recall of thoughts, emotions, and some tactile phenomena. As recall confidence declined, so did ratings on these phenomenal-experience scales. Overall, the most dominant form of phenomenal experience at the time of recall was visual imagery. For incorrect items, however, ratings of visual imagery were essentially flat – that is, subjects were equally likely to have images, no matter how confident they were about the accuracy of their recall. This occurred partly because of the recall of the wrong event – although the event had actually happened – in response to a cue. Thus incorrect recalls were a mixture of retrieving a true memory to the wrong cue – which gave rise to high imagery ratings – and of guesses which did not give rise to imagery.

This very complex set of findings can be related fairly directly to Neisser's arguments concerning nested structure in autobiographical memory. Brewer proposes that one way to understand the pattern of remembering observed in his study is to consider the structure of the environment of college students and he comments (1988: 77):

> the experienced environment for these undergraduates takes the following form: They carry out a variety of actions in locations, often with other people around, and they have a variety of thoughts and feelings while carrying out the actions. They experience one location (their rooms) with enormous frequency, have moderate exposure to a number of other locations (e.g. classrooms), and infrequent exposure to a range of other locations (e.g. a particular restaurant). They carry out a wide range of very different actions, some fairly frequently (e.g. reading academic material, dressing), others relatively infrequently (e.g. using the

Table 7.1 Recall rates to different types of cues

Actions		Thoughts	
	%		%
Time	25	Time	7
Location	33	Location	9
Time + location	49	Time + location	14
Thought	58	Action	42

(Based on Brewer 1988)

library, going to the doctor). There are certain people they see frequently; however, they engage in a variety of actions with respect to these individuals. They experience a range of thoughts, but for some thoughts there is little or no relation to the concurrent actions and location (e.g. thinking about an upcoming fraternity party during a lecture). There appear to be a limited number of emotions that reoccur in association with particular events and thoughts.

Essentially Brewer's thesis is that some aspects of events are distinctive and these aspects determine memorability. Many different actions may take place in the same location, so that a frequently experienced location is unlikely to be an effective recall cue. Conversely, an infrequent location, because it is distinctive, will be an effective cue for both thoughts and actions. Clearly, the goal-relatedness of an action will also determine its memorability and one reason for this is that actions which are goal-directed probably map on to pre-existing memory structures and so can be effectively encoded. The memorability of thoughts was found to be associated with high levels of excitement and it is not clear from Brewer's experiments why this should be so. Perhaps, once again, high levels of emotion indicate that an event is being processed in terms of personally relevant goals, so is integrated in memory and made more retrievable (see Chapter 5). Also, when actions and thoughts are co-ordinated, then either thought or action will be a comparatively good cue to remembering. Finally, time appears to be a very poor cue to recall and Brewer concludes that absolute time (date) is typically not encoded in autobiographical memory.

Conclusions: retrieval of specific memories

The findings from the studies reviewed in this chapter suggest that three main factors may mediate the retrieval of specific memories. The first factor is the general retrieval process outlined by Williams, the find-a-context–search–verify model. This general retrieval strategy is sensitive to cue specificity and, when a cue is highly specific, an elaborate retrieval context must be developed. To see this, try retrieving a memory to the following cue: 'Recall a specific memory of an event which took place on 26 September 1979.' When a cue is less specific, the retrieval process can utilize the structure of autobiographical memory. For example, given a cue such as 'going to the cinema', a person might recall a period from their own life when they frequently attended cinemas (e.g. 'when at university') and search memories indexed by this period.

The second factor is recency. Memories of recent events appear to be generally more available than memories of more remote events and, when a cue or set of cues is in a form which permits a temporal search, then recency effects in retrieval will be evident. (Try recalling events which happened every 26 September from the present time back to 1979.) Recency effects will, however, be attenuated by the occurrence of events of high personal importance which will be well remembered independently of retention interval, and we will return to this point in a moment. Recency effects may also diminish or change as memories become integrated with the structure of auto-biographical memory – perhaps after a retention interval of one or two years, as Linton suggested.

The third factor mediating remembering is the structure of the encoding environments, what Neisser called *nested structure*. The findings clearly illustrate that aspects of the original encoding environment are utilized by the retrieval process in accessing memories. For instance, types of teachers, spatial layout of school, lecture hall vs. college room, all have been strongly implicated as effective retrieval contexts and as environmental determinants of qualitatively different types of memories.

One important question for present concerns is how do these aspects of structure and retrieval fit with the hierarchical organization of autobiographical memory outlined at the close of Chapter 6? Perhaps one useful way to think about these different aspects of autobiographical memory is as follows: the hierarchical structure of autobiographical memory might be viewed as representing the *thematic* structure of one's life. Lifetime periods and general events instantiate various aspects of personally relevant themes – such as goal-attainment – and index sets of memories which are associated with specific themes and attributes of themes. The thematic structure of autobiographical memory can be utilized to retrieve specific memories (as the experiments in Chapter 6 showed) but this structure may also serve other purposes (see Chapter 5 and Chapter 8). Within sets of memories, however, other forms of organization appear to be dominant. In particular, aspects of the encoding environment – the nested structure of events – which are encoded with specific memories provide ways of discriminating between memories and focusing memory retrieval on specific memories.

For example, when subjects retrieve a memory of an event which occurred during their Italian holiday, they might do this by traversing the thematic structure of autobiographical memory and simply access the first memory they come across. Such a memory is likely to be highly theme related and encoded distinctively. (Maybe these are the sorts of events which subjects in diary studies single out to record in their diaries – as Brewer's data suggest.) When, however, the task is to recall places one visited in Italy or people one met when travelling, then the nested structure of the encoding environment (which is preserved in memories) is drawn upon in order to discriminate between appropriate memories and inappropriate memories. Perhaps a person would recall a general outline of their schedule, categories of different types of people, or categories of different types of places (i.e. museums vs. restaurants). Or, if the holiday had occurred recently, then a backward search from the first retrieved event might be possible. Thus autobiographical memory appears to have two fairly distinct forms of organization, one which I have called the *thematic structure* is comprised of personally relevant themes which index sets of memories and the other reflects the (nested) structure of the encoding environment(s) as this is preserved in specific memories. It is this structure which is used to discriminate between memories within a set.

8 • THE DEVELOPMENT AND THE DECLINE OF AUTOBIOGRAPHICAL MEMORY

In the first part of this chapter we will consider the phenomenon of 'childhood amnesia' and the emergence of autobiographical memory in infancy. The second part deals with impairments of autobiographical memory in old age and with the meaning of autobiographical memory for the elderly. The aim of both this chapter and of Chapter 9 is to provide at least some insight into much more complex aspects of autobiographical memory than we have considered previously, and to extend theoretical positions outlined in previous chapters to these more complex areas.

The development of autobiographical memory: childhood amnesia

We saw in Chapters 2 and 3 that 'childhood amnesia' refers to the frequently made observation that most people can remember few events which occurred in their life prior to the age of six to eight years. One of the first people to make this observation was Freud (1905/1953) who commented 'What I have in mind is the peculiar amnesia which, in the case of most people, though by no means all, hides the earliest beginnings of their childhood up to their sixth or eighth year.' Waldfogel (1948, see Chapter 2) in his pioneering study of recall of events dating from the first seven years of life found that very few memories were retrieved from the earliest years, and increasingly more from later years. Recent studies have confirmed this basic finding. Crovitz and Harvey (1979) persuaded college undergraduates to recall episodes which occurred before their eighth birthday and to do this for one hour every week for twelve weeks. The resulting distributions of the proportions of memories recalled by year showed that very few memories were recalled from ages 1 to 3 years, and most memories from ages 6 to 7 years. In a follow-up study Crovitz, Harvey, and McKee (1980) required subjects to recall memories from their earliest years to cue words. The cue words were taken from the memory descriptions collected in the earlier study and selected on the basis of the frequency with which they were mentioned. One group of cue words named items which had been very frequently mentioned by most subjects (*animal, car, damage, fear, girl, house, mother, play, school, water*) and a second group named items which had only been infrequently mentioned (*amount, brick, bucket, ink, knee, moon, page, suggestion, tongue, worm*). Although the high-frequency cues led to the retrieval of more memories than the low-frequency cues, both types of cues produced the same distribution of memories by age as observed in the previous study: fewest memories from the earliest years and more memories from the later years.

The work of Crovitz and his colleagues has then clearly established that there is an amnesia for the earliest years of life. However, this amnesia is far from complete and, as we shall see in Chapter 9, is rather different from the pattern of amnesia typically found in retrograde amnesia following brain injury. In this latter case a person usually cannot recall events immediately preceding the onset of their illness but can recall more remote events. One further problem is that research into childhood amnesia has typically not compared retention curves for the earliest years of life with later years. It will be recalled that Rubin and his colleagues (Chapter 3) argued that retention across the life-span can be modelled by a retention function in which progressively fewer memories are recalled as the retention interval increases (but see Chapter 3 for important qualifications of this view). Thus childhood amnesia may be nothing more than the asymptote of the retention curve and may be fully accounted for by the Rubin retention function. In order to explore this possibility Wetzler and Sweeney (1986) reanalysed part of the data reported by Rubin (1982, Experiment 1). Taking only the distribution of memories from the time of testing back to the subject's eighth year, they calculated a retention function. They then used this retention function to predict the proportions of memories which would be expected to be present for the period from eight years to birth. As Rubin's data actually sampled this period it was possible to compare expected, with observed, distributions of memories. Wetzler and Sweeney found that the Rubin retention function did not account for the observed distribution of memories from the earliest years and that the distribution of memories from about the age of five years to birth was characterized by an accelerated forgetting function.

Childhood amnesia is then a robust phenomenon observed under different cueing conditions, with different testing procedures, and appears to differ from retention for other time periods in a person's life. But how can we explain it? There are essentially two general classes of explanation for childhood amnesia. The first type of explanation comes from the work of Freud (1916–17, see Chapter 2) and provides a psychodynamic account of childhood amnesia. The second type of explanation represents a whole constellation of models which have in common their emphasis on cognitive changes in development (e.g. Waldfogel 1948; Schachtel 1947; Neisser 1962; White and Pillemer 1979).

Freud and the repression of the past

In Freud's model of psychosexual development the infant passes through various stages in which needs and desires are localized to different erogenous zones: the oral, anal, phallic, latency, and genital stages. From the age of three to five years the child passes through an Oedipal stage which is characterized by desires to possess the opposite-sex parent and eliminate the same-sex parent. It is proposed that the child resolves this complex by making a successful identification with the same-sex parent. The desires, thoughts, and fantasies which preoccupy the child during these stages are highly emotionally charged and represent threats to the ego which eventually emerges from the resolution of the various stages. Accordingly, memories of events, thoughts, and feelings, from the active phase of psychosexual development are repressed and cannot be recalled in later life – hence childhood amnesia. Indeed, Freud's treatment of neurotic patients essentially entailed locating and resolving memories from the childhood phase which were 'screened' by apparently nonvalent memories.

Screen memories are a type of repression of more disturbing memories. It is not clear, however, from Freud's writings whether he considered screen memories to be complete fabrications or whether he thought of them as fragments of memories of real episodes which defence mechanisms of the psyche have, as it were, sanitized for remembering (see White and Pillemer 1979 for further discussion of this point). Certainly, many of the case histories reported by Freud seem to indicate that memories from the earliest years are indeed memories for real events but are used in such a way as to screen or hide memories of more emotionally charged events. For example, Freud (1917) analysed an event described by Goethe in his biography in which the poet recalled throwing his parents' crockery out of a bedroom window and feeling much exhilaration as the valuable china smashed in the street below. At the time this happened, Goethe was 4 years old. In fact, Freud had treated a neurotic patient with a virtually identical childhood memory. For both cases, Freud argued that the china-smashing episode screened a memory (or memories) of the child's desire to throw a sibling out into the street; the adult only remembers the excitement and, perhaps, hostility of breaking valuable objects. These feelings are, however, ones originally directed at a younger sibling. Note that, in this particular analysis, Freud apparently agrees that the actual (remembered) events did take place, but this does not detract from their power to screen the earlier more emotionally charged and disturbing memories. In the case of Freud's patient the neurosis was apparently healed as the patient resolved and understood the significance of the china-smashing episode. A very clear example of a neurosis arising from a repressed memory, for which there was no screen memory, is provided by Nemiah (1969: 111):

> Another patient came to our ward because of acute anxiety over a recurrent, obsessional image of herself and her father in a naked sexual embrace. In the course of treatment she recollected, with near panic, and in a direct train of associations to the symptom, having seen her parents having sexual intercourse when she was 5 years old – a memory that had been totally beyond conscious recall for 15–20 years. (Incidentally, it is of interest to note that following the return of this memory, her obsessional symptom vanished.)

According to Freud's interpretation, childhood amnesia arises in response to memories of emotional episodes which the adult would find threatening and disturbing. These memories are screened by memories of less disturbing events or, perhaps, directly repressed by other defence mechanisms. (More detailed accounts of the Freudian view on childhood amnesia are provided by Neisser 1962 and White and Pillemer 1979.) What evidence is there to support Freud's views on childhood amnesia? Obviously there is the clinical evidence supplied by Freud and his colleagues, some of which was described above, but this amounts to only a very small number of cases and an even smaller number of memories. Moreover, one implication of the screen memory view is that most memories of childhood experiences before the age of 6 to 8 years should be comprised of memories of banal, largely trivial events. This, however, was not the finding of Waldfogel or of Crovitz and his colleagues who observed that childhood memories were very often of emotionally significant events such as the births of siblings, deaths in the family, accidents, and so on. More recently Kihlstrom and Harackiewicz (1982) have attempted directly to relate screen memories with personality factors. In their study, high-school and college students recalled and described their earliest memories and then completed a personality questionnaire. One factor which was measured by the personality questionnaire was harmavoidance which can be taken as an index of how neurotic a person is. Kihlstrom and Harackiewicz found the usual distribution of proportions of memories across the early years, with more memories being recalled to more recent time periods and very few memories to the earliest years. These authors also developed a scoring system which allowed them to categorize different childhood memories as screen memories or not. Their principal finding was that students who had screen memories scored reliably more highly on the harmavoidance scale than students who did not have such memories, indicating that people with screen memories are more fearful and anxious than those who do not have screen memories. Thus it seems likely that screen memories may play some role in childhood amnesia (and influence subsequent personality) but not such a central role as Freud originally thought – only a minority of Kihlstrom and Harackiewicz subjects did in fact show screen memories.

Knowledge structures and the emergence of autobiographical memories

Cognitive theories, in contrast to the Freudian approach, have not focused on the content and significance of childhood memories but rather have emphasized more general aspects of developing cognition. Waldfogel suggested that childhood amnesia might reflect the emergence of intelligence and linguistic skills and noted that the childhood-amnesia curve paralleled the curve for gradually increasing intelligence and linguistic abilities. Piaget and Inhelder (1973) proposed that infants have not developed the appropriate schema for sequencing events and so cannot encode event knowledge effectively. Other theories, such as those of Schachtel (1947), Neisser (1962), and White and Pillemer (1979), have variously argued that developmental changes in stored knowledge, short-term processing capacities, and retrieval strategies, directly affect the ability to encode, integrate, and retrieve knowledge.

Recent research, however, now indicates that at least some of these cognitive accounts can be ruled out. Work by Nelson and her colleagues (Nelson, Fivush, Hudson, and Lucariello 1983; Nelson 1986, 1988; Fivush 1984) has clearly demonstrated that children below the age of 3 years have both knowledge of events in general and memories of specific events. For instance, O'Connell and Gerard (1985) found that children as young as 20 months could mime sequences of actions involved in common routines when prompted with a verbal cue. Interestingly, the same children were poor at miming when the cues named unconnected action sequences, showing that they were sensitive to the coherent nature of event knowledge. In other studies Nelson and her co-workers have found that most children between the ages of 3 and 8 years can provide detailed accounts of events such as visits to McDonalds and birthday parties – indeed these children even design their account of an event to suit their audience, leaving out 'obvious' information if their listener has also taken part in the remembered event (Fivush 1984). These findings would seem to rule out explanations of childhood amnesia in terms of failures to process, encode and/or organize knowledge.

A rather different view of childhood amnesia has been suggested by Nelson (1988). In this study Nelson tape-recorded the spontaneous pre-sleep monologues of a child, Emily, over a period of approximately 15 months (Emily was aged 21 months when the study began and three years when it ended). Here is an extract from one of the early monologues:

> We bought a baby ... cause ... the, well, because, ... when she, well, we *thought* it was for Christmas, but when we went to the s-s-store we didn't have our jacket on, but I saw some dolly and *yelled* at my mother and said 'I want one of those dolly.' So *after* we were finished with the store, we went over to the dolly and she *bought* me one ... So I have one.
>
> (Nelson 1988: 269)

Although Emily's monologues contained many such examples of memories of past experiences, they were, in fact, dominated by monologues concerning the correct ordering of events. For instance, action sequences which had occurred in the past and future routines were extensively discussed by Emily in her monologues. Essentially Emily seemed to be running through likely action sequences (of fairly common routines) in her own mind, while thinking aloud. Nelson's argument is that this reflects the emergence of event knowledge in memory and that memories of specific episodes are rehearsed as the child actively attempts to develop scripts or schemas for routine activities. As the study of Emily's monologues progressed, it became clear that episodes which were prominent early in the study were soon dropped and replaced by other episodes. It seemed as though the earlier episodes had been incorporated into knowledge structures representing routine activities (getting dressed, shopping for toys, etc.). Thus memories of specific events are used to build knowledge structures representing routine activities, and in the process the initial memories of specific events are lost – hence, childhood amnesia.

Later in development the child is taught, implicitly, by parents, older siblings, etc., to generate narrative accounts of experienced events. Nelson claims that these narratives form the basis of autobiographical memory and, as the child matures, they can be used to structure autobiographical memory. In Nelson's view earlier autobiographical memories do not constitute narratives but rather represent lists of actions, actors, and props, which are rehearsed as part of the process of building the basic knowledge structures which will eventually support the representation of a narrative-based autobiographical memory.

Nelson's view on the functional role of early autobiographical memories is interesting and her emphasis on the role of socialization and cultural factors in determining the narrative form of autobiographical memories an important factor for future research to consider. There are, however, some reasons for supposing that her particular account of childhood amnesia may be open to debate. For instance, Fivush, Gray, and Fromhoff (1987) found that 2.5-year-olds were able to recall 'special' one-off events. Moreover the events recalled by these children all occurred over six months prior to the time of recall. In other words very young children appear to have autobiographical memories which cannot be script based (one-off events) dating from their very earliest years (see also Fivush 1984). Similarly, Forbes (1988) in a particularly interesting review of the memory abilities of a 2-year-old concludes that very young children have surprisingly detailed and accurate memories for experienced events. The script-based account of childhood amnesia proposed by Nelson offers no explanation of accurate and detailed recall by children.

It seems most likely that childhood amnesia is a product of many factors. We have already seen that repression in the form of screen memories may play some role in obscuring memories of infancy and that the emergence of basic knowledge structures may also contribute to inabilities to remember very early experiences. Other factors which may act to promote childhood amnesia may relate more specifically to the developing structure of autobiographical memories. For example, it is unlikely that an infant would be able to construct a lifetime period structure for the years from birth to 8 years. Perhaps socialization factors within a culture (e.g. nursery school, primary school, etc.) provide the 'natural' breaks in life experience which can be used to segment one's autobiography – at least initially. Indeed, it may be difficult for infants to construct the event structures (e.g. E-MOPs, see Chapter 6) with which to index memories of specific experiences. Infants, it might intuitively be argued, do not have representations such as 'when we were in Italy', 'when I played with X', 'when I was fascinated by insects', etc. Thus memory from infancy may be relatively unstructured. If it were the case that the thematic structure of autobiographical memory could not be used to access memories of events from the earliest years of life (because no thematic structure existed for those periods), then access to autobiographical memory would have to involve some more direct route. We have already seen that direct access to autobiographical memory, bypassing the thematic structure of memories, is possible and typically involves the use of cues (often self-generated) which map on to specific memories. However, it might be expected that the types of event knowledge which an infant attends to, and perhaps encodes in such a way as to facilitate retrieval, are rather different from the types of event knowledge which an older child or adult employs. Thus, it may be that even this more direct form of access for childhood memories is largely ineffective because memories encoded in childhood employ cues which an adult cannot use. As Proust pointed out, childhood memories may be spontaneously retrieved in response to a cue which directly coresponds to a memory of a childhood experience (in his case a particular taste), but this type of retrieval is rare and unexpected. Finally, it should be noted that another factor which may contribute to childhood amnesia is that of the changing nature of self-system (see also Fivush 1988). The self of the older child and adult is undoubtedly very different from the emerging self of the infant and it may be that the nature of the current self (and memories of past selves) limits access to autobiographical memories in some general way (see Chapter 5). Clearly much more research is required to clarify these issues.

Autobiographical memory in old age

The study of autobiographical memory in the elderly (people over the age of about 70) is currently at a very early stage and few experimental reports have directly addressed this issue. Nevertheless the rapidly expanding population of elderly citizens is giving rise to wide-ranging research projects with a focus on cognition in later life. Thus the research to be considered in this section represents the initial attempts by psychologists to explore a vastly understudied area. As such, the research described below should be seen as preliminary – the aim has been to raise important questions and not to provide definitive answers. Research into autobiographical memory in the elderly can be divided into two more or less discrete areas. The first area has used experimental and sampling techniques in order to examine theoretical conjectures concerning changed memory functioning in the elderly. The second area has been more concerned with the meaning of autobiographical knowledge and has focused on data from interviews, self-report studies, and biographical accounts of memory in works of literature.

The decline of autobiographical memory

As an example of the experimental/sampling approach consider a study reported by Burke, Worthley, and Martin (1988). In this study young adults (mean age 19.7 years) and old adults (mean age 70.5 years) recorded in a diary, over a 4-week period, occasions when they had failed to recall a word in the course of their everyday life. Such word-finding failures are usually referred to as tip-of-the-tongue experiences or TOTs (Brown and McNeill 1966; Reason and Lucas 1983; Cohen and Faulkner 1986). The TOT state has certain characteristic features and, in particular, people experiencing TOTs usually recall some knowledge to do with the orthography and phonology of the sought-for word (e.g. initial letter, number of syllables, what the word rhymes with or sounds like). Often a TOT is resolved when the word 'pops' into mind and this usually occurs after active attempts to access the word have ceased and attention is focused on other tasks. Burke *et al.* and Cohen and Faulkner report that elderly subjects often complain of such word-finding difficulties. For example, Burke *et al.* claim that the impetus for their study arose when an elderly subject said to them 'If you want to study something really important, find out why I can't remember the name of my friend of 20 years when I go to introduce her.' Burke *et al.* found that older adults did indeed have more TOTs than younger adults and that they used different strategies in resolving their TOT experiences. Older subjects apparently were prepared to wait until the sought-for word popped into mind and used strategies such as extended memory search, consulting books, and asking people less frequently than younger adults. Interestingly, there were marked age differences in the types of words which featured in the TOTs. For younger adults the TOT words were either person/place/movie names or the names of abstract words. For older adults the words in TOTs were either person/place/movie names or the names of objects – younger adults rarely had TOTs which featured object names. Also younger adults had fewer TOTs for person/place/movie names than did older adults. These findings largely confirm the earlier findings of Cohen and Faulkner (1986) who also studied age effects in TOT states.

These age differences in TOTs demonstrate that elderly people do suffer from an increase in word-finding problems as they age and that failures to locate people and place names are more common in older than younger people. The connection between this and autobiographical memory is not, however, so obvious. Well-learnt knowledge such as the names of people and places might not be stored in memories of specific experiences but rather might be indexed by knowledge structures representing the thematic organization of autobiographical memory. Perhaps, names of people and places are directly represented in lifetime periods, including the current period. Why names should be difficult to access in the elderly is not clear (see Cohen 1988 for a brief overview of potential accounts of this and other age effects) but it may, however, reflect a general impairment in processing capacities. One possibility is that, as people age, the efficiency of processes centrally involved in most forms of cognition (e.g. working memory – see Baddeley 1986) decreases.

This possibility was explored by Winthorpe and Rabbit (1988) and Holland and Rabbit (1989), using an autobiographical-memory retrieval task. In their studies subjects recalled and described specific autobiographical memories for a period lasting 40 minutes. Subjects who 'dried up' were prompted with lifetime period cues such as 'Tell me about an event from your school days' and subjects were explicitly instructed to recall specific and detailed events. Various other measures of intellectual function and memory for text were also collected from the same subjects. The autobiographical memories were scored in terms of specificity, and four categories were used: highly specific; general event; very little detail; and little autobiographical information. Two groups of subjects took part, a 'young' elderly group with a mean age of 65.7 years and an 'old' elderly group with a mean age of 73.5 years, and within these groups subjects were subdivided by IQ score into high- and low-ability groups. The principal findings were that the high-ability groups (regardless of age) were more likely to recall specific and detailed autobiographical memories than the low-ability group. There was, however, an age effect in the low-ability old group such that memories for this group contained fewer details. Overall, the lower-ability old group showed poor integration of details with central thematic knowledge and Holland and Rabbit interpret this as an impairment of central processing capacities.

The elderly then appear to experience an increased frequency of lapses-of-everyday-memory errors and, for lower-ability elderly, there is some evidence that autobiographical memory may be impaired. It seems likely that this impairment arises from a reduced ability to integrate details and themes. This latter finding corresponds quite closely with the overall view of autobiographical memory developed in Chapters 6 and 7, that memories can be accessed more or less directly by a sufficiently detailed cue or less directly by traversing the thematic structure of autobiographical memory. The findings of Rabbit and his colleagues suggest that elderly subjects in general have few problems in accessing thematic knowledge but do experience difficulties in integrating thematic knowledge and detailed event knowledge and that this is most marked for low-ability elderly subjects. We will return to this type of impairment of autobiographical memory when we consider amnesia in Chapter 9.

The meaning of life

Autobiographical memory in the elderly is also interesting for other reasons. Salaman (1970; 1982) in her important book *A Collection of Moments: A Study of Involuntary Memories* describes with great insight her own experience of her memory and provides valuable reviews of various great writers on autobiographical memory. Salaman's thesis is that the recall of autobiographical memories is often involuntary or spontaneous, that some memories take the form of detailed episodes, whereas other memories may represent mere fragments of an experienced event, and that the ability to recall, particularly childhood memories, increases and changes as a person grows older. Finally Salaman stresses the point that memories may serve a purpose in the present, such as providing a sense of self and/or important psychological support in a time of stress. Let us consider some of Salaman's examples and arguments for these views.

Salaman argues that there are many types of fragmentary autobiographical memory: a poorly remembered telephone number, a face, an object, and so on. These fragments contrast with other memory fragments such as a memory of reading a specific book (Salaman describes her own childhood memory of reading *Uncle Tom's Cabin*), or of interacting with a particular object. She claims that the former types of fragmentary knowledge are not spontaneously or involuntarily recalled, whereas the latter are. This is probably the most questionable of Salaman's suggestions and it seems highly unlikely that, for example, an image of a long 'forgotten' face would not be involuntarily recalled. Perhaps the critical difference Salaman is after here is that fragmentary 'factual' knowledge (autobiographical or otherwise) is not accompanied by the feeling of remembering – this knowledge is just suddenly in mind and, although one might *recognize* it as being from the past, even from a specific time period, no phenomenal experience of remembering occurs. In contrast, other types of fragmentary knowledge are accompanied by a powerful feeling of remembering, even of being transported into the past.

Salaman provides numerous accounts, both from her own memory and from the writings of other authors, of these involuntary rememberings. Here are some examples:

The first is from Chateaubriand's *Mémoires d'Outre-Tombe.*

> Walking alone in the evening, I was drawn from my reflections by the warbling of a thrush perched upon the highest branch of a birch tree. At that instant the magical sound brought my paternal estate before my eyes; I forgot the catastrophes of which I had been a witness and, transported suddenly into the past, I saw again that country where I had so often heard the thrush sing.

Another example is De Quincey's memory of Altrincham market-place. It comes in the revised version of the *Confessions of an English Opium Eater*. When De Quincey was 17 he ran away from school. He set out that morning on foot for Altrincham in a disturbed state of mind and full of misgivings. It was a heavenly early morning in July and, when he reached the town, a memory of just such a dazzling morning when he stayed at Altrincham with his nurse when he was 3 years old came back to him. He had waked early and woken up the nurse and, when she lifted him in her arms and threw open the window, he saw the gayest scene he had ever seen: the market-place at Altrincham at eight o'clock in the morning. It was market day:

> fruit, such as can be had in July, and flowers were scattered about in profusion: even the stalls of the butchers, from their brilliant cleanliness, appeared attractive: and the bonny young women of Altrincham were tripping about in caps and aprons coquettishly disposed . . .

He was refreshed by the walk and the memory, and after a rest and breakfast 'all my gloom and despondency were already retiring to the rear.'

Note that the examples cited by Salaman do not always lead to feelings of joy; on the contrary, involuntary recollections may cause anxiety, fear, even depression. Salaman cites an involuntary memory of her own in which she vividly and poignantly recalled the premature death of a younger sister. One characteristic of these 'involuntary' remindings, particularly in the examples described by Salaman, is that there is also a cue in the environment which the rememberer singles out as the focus for their recall (the song of a thrush or the beauty of a July morning). It is, of course, very probable that at (random?) times in a person's life a cue will be encountered in the environment which corresponds directly to knowledge stored in a single specific memory and so lead to the 'spontaneous' recall of that memory. Of course, it could be argued that virtually any cue in any environment would correspond to knowledge in at least some memories. It does not, however, follow that cues generally correspond uniquely to specific memories. Perhaps the cues which initiate involuntary recall are processed prior to recall in a way which parallels very exactly the processing of that same cue when the original experience was encoded. The probability of the same cue being processed in an analogous way, say 50 years after an experience, is undoubtedly very low. Nevertheless when this does occur, the effect of the cue is so powerful as to lead to the involuntary retrieval of the memory. In a sense this could be regarded as a *failure* of memory, for, if we involuntarily recalled all the memories to which any given cue was associated, we would be seriously incapacitated. Perhaps the evolution of human memory has capitalized upon the fact that no two events are ever processed in the same way. For, if similar events are encoded in different ways, then cues can be used to access memories – the only consequence being that a cue will access more than one memory and no single memory uniquely. Such a memory-access system would not lead to a particularly efficient memory system but, if that same memory system could develop cyclic retrieval processes in which cue information is progressively refined, then specific memories could be accessed. Moreover, if the memory system contained more abstract knowledge which indexed sets of memories, then further refinements of cue-base retrieval would be possible. This is the general model of autobiographical memory suggested by the work reviewed in Chapters 6 and 7.

A further complication of Salaman's view is that it is not until maturity or late middle-age that involuntary remembering becomes particularly marked: 'For many years my experience of involuntary remembering was, unpredictable, sporadic, and elusive.

Only in maturity, when a large number came back within a comparatively short period of time, did a pattern of their general nature begin to appear' (1982: 50). Why should involuntary recall of autobiographical memories increase in later life? By the above arguments one possible explanation is that as time passes and more and more cues are processed, the probability of (re)processing a previously processed cue in the same way, or nearly the same way, increases. This speculative line of argument does have some plausibility and certainly it seems that involuntary recall of autobiographical memories is associated with specific cues. Nevertheless other factors may play an even more significant role in the spontaneous retrieval of autobiographical memories, especially in later life.

The major point made by Salaman is that autobiographical memories carry personally relevant meanings and it is the meaning of memories which is critical in her analysis. In particular, Salaman argues that in maturity (she was in her 50s when writing *A Collection of Moments*) the meaning of childhood memories becomes clearer and the pain of past events may be psychologically resolved – the parallels with Freud's views on neuroticism are evident here. As an example, Salaman (1982: 57–8) provides the following account from her own experience:

> One more example from the age of nine. While trying to write about a teacher who had a great influence upon me, I dwelt on a painful memory of her calling me a chatterbox. I rationalised it thus: the memory makes me miserable because I annoyed my teacher, and also, being sensitive to words, I was upset by the harsh, ugly Russian word for chatterbox – *treschotka*. I carried that painful word in my conscious mind for years. Once, still in Russia, an involuntary memory brought me back to the exact place where I was sitting in the classroom when it happened, and with it my bewilderment. Since we changed classrooms each year, I could tell that I was in my first year, and that I was nine. Now this is what happened some forty-five years later. Another involuntary memory brought me back the moment immediately after I had heard the word 'chatterbox': I am looking round, wondering whom it is meant for, I hear the teacher say: 'I mean you, Polianovskaya,' and I see a grey-haired woman with clever penetrating green eyes turned sternly on me. But I was not aware that I had been talking! Now another panel was revealed: As soon as the bell had rung for break, I had turned with a feeling of relief to the girl on my right. The teacher must have told us to be quiet for another moment; the noise must have subsided, while I continued to talk. But how did it all happen without my knowing? I had neither heard her command, nor known that I had been talking. Now I knew why I looked so bewildered in the original involuntary memory. I recaptured with complete certainty, myself not at ease, afraid inside, the room too long, the ceiling far away. These panels fitted perfectly into the picture of the conscious memory, and they account for the fact that I never had a feeling of shame or guilt about this incident, a feeling familiar enough to me, nor had ever felt resentment against the teacher.

Salaman clearly feels that she herself, and the writers she discusses, went through periods of life-review (Butler 1963) in which many memories from childhood, which previously had not been recallable, suddenly became available for recollection. The personal meaning of these memories was slowly revealed as the rememberer meditated upon them. We saw in Chapter 3 that the process of life review might underlie the distribution of memories across the life-span for older subjects. For younger subjects most memories were recalled from recent time periods and decreasingly less as the sampled time period increased in remoteness from the present. For older subjects, however, a large reminiscence 'bump' was present in the distribution of memories and these subjects apparently recalled many memories from the ages of 10 to 30 years.

Recently Fitzgerald (1988) has reported very interesting data bearing on this issue. In his study a group of elderly subjects (mean age 68.7 years) recalled three highly vivid memories from their own lives and provided the usual ratings of these memories (see Chapter 4). Fitzgerald plotted the distribution of these vivid memories across the life-span and found, in contradiction to the retention curve usually observed, that most of these memories were drawn from ages 3 to about 25 years of age. Content analysis of the memories found them to cover a very wide range of topics and, more importantly, to be written in a first-person narrative form, and to present a coherent story. Clearly these findings are similar to those of Cohen and Faulkner (1987, reviewed in Chapter 3) who found that vivid memories of the elderly were drawn from childhood and early adulthood (see also McCormack 1979, in Chapter 3). Taken together these separate data sets indicate that many of a person's most vivid memories are of events which occurred in childhood and early adulthood – but see Fitzgerald (Figure 1, p. 265) for evidence that older subjects also sample other time periods for vivid memories. Fitzgerald's interpretation of these findings is that they represent the narrative structure of the self-system. The collection of vivid memories might be thought of as personal stories which define and integrate various aspects of the self into a unified whole. Perhaps such a unification only becomes possible as a person matures.

Life review, reworking and revelation of memories, and generally resolving past experiences, appear to be a feature of autobiographical memory in the elderly. But how common are these processes? Do all older people meditate upon the past? Do many people experience the resolution of memories of difficult events in later life? Csikszentmihalkyi and Beattie (1979, see Chapter 5) provided some evidence to suggest that existential problems posed by early life experiences in conjunction with specific socialization processes may act to influence subsequent personality development. Not all of Csikszentmihalkyi and Beattie's subjects were confronted with such problems, nor were many exposed to socialization practices which might predispose them to resolve an existential problem and, perhaps, to engage in reminiscence practices such as those describe by Salaman.

Recently important research on these issues has been reported in an excellent longitudinal study by Coleman (1986). Over a 15-year period Coleman studied elderly people living in sheltered housing in and around London. Coleman's account of his interviews with his elderly subjects is complex and detailed and here we will focus only on the different roles reminiscence appeared to play in the lives of these elderly people. It should, however, be noted that Coleman goes to some lengths to emphasize that a person's current environment may be more significant in determining the use of autobiographical memory than is their age. For instance, as Salaman found, a person living under conditions of stress may reminisce about more pleasant times, indeed memories of other times may spontaneously come to mind under these conditions. It is a well-documented failing of our society that many old people do, in fact, live under stressful and emotionally damaging conditions. Thus it is likely that many aspects of the behaviour of the elderly arise from their current circumstance rather than from their age.

The elderly people visited and studied by Coleman were, with some exceptions, generally well cared for and did not suffer from extreme economic hardship (but see Coleman 1986, Chapter 9). Many, however, were depressed to at least some extent and suffered from the inevitable physical declines of old age. In an initial sample of 50 elderly people Coleman assessed attitudes to, and extent of, reminiscences and the relationship of these to current morale as assessed by various standard tests. His principal finding was that 21 (42 per cent) of these subjects valued their memories of the past and had high morale. A further 15 people (30 per cent) saw no point in reminiscing and also had high morale. Of the low-morale elderly, eight (16 per cent) were troubled by memories of the past and six (12 per cent) avoided recall of the past because of the contrast between past and current events. In order to illustrate characteristics of these sub-groups Coleman describes a number of case studies from each.

The group who apparently valued their past generally showed high morale. Their pasts did not, however, comprise idyllic childhoods and successful adulthoods. Rather, many of these people had lived through the most difficult times in this century and lost family and friends in various wars, suffered personal injuries, had careers thwarted by army service, and experienced childhoods of extreme poverty. None the less, they were all generally at peace with their past finding much to rejoice in and claiming to have come to terms with their most difficult experiences:

> They referred a lot to coping with and learning from difficulties. Mrs Parson for example described experiencing her life now as 'a pattern rolled out behind her'. She had learned from the difficulties in her life and now felt a 'wiser' person. Many were proud they had overcome difficulties and not been overwhelmed by them. Mr Turner had been through difficulties in the First World War, in service together with his wife and then bringing up his daughter on his own when his wife died young in the 1920s. He had high self-esteem, both based on his achievements in the past where he had been 'a bit of a rebel' – he had once been sacked from his job as a gardener for giving away apples that were lying on the ground to an orphanage – and in the present where he 'kept going' doing gardening and other jobs for people despite his advanced age of 88 years.
>
> (Coleman, 1986: 40)

For some of these subjects their memories represented times which were judged to be superior in some respects to the present time, i.e. more fun when children, better education, better nutrition, more personally fulfilling, etc. Miss Smith, who was over 88 years old and had spent most of her life on the low wages of a nanny, commented 'Now wasn't I happy with that little bit of money that I was earning? Aren't I happier now to sit in my nice little room and think to myself and look back on those happy memories? . . . No one could look back like I do could they?' (Coleman 1986: 48). In contrast, Mr Austin also valued the past but in his reminiscences, focused on his memories of the First World War and the remarkable, painful and surreal events he had experienced. He conveyed the impression that he still felt (50 years later) a great relief and sense of luck at being alive. In somewhat similar vein Mr Cook concentrated on his memories of when he had worked as a tugboat engineer. The impression gained is of a time in his life which was fully rewarding and captivating and in which he made his major achievements. For this group then the past, although comprised of memories of difficult and painful events, is also a source of joy and pride. For these elderly subjects their pasts are an important part of their current self and there is an integrity to the whole of their autobiography (cf. Erikson 1978).

The second sub-group of elderly subjects apparently thought little about their past lives. Three of these subjects, who were in their late 80s and early 90s, showed signs of having successfully completed life reviews and, when interviewed initially, provided detailed reviews of their life, but did not mention their pasts in any detail in subsequent interviews. Even when pressed, these elderly people simply commented that the past was not of much relevance. One of this group of three, Mrs Stanton, aged 87 years, initially described some preoccupation with her mother's cruelty to her as a child. But apparently Mrs Stanton was able to resolve the set of memories associated with her difficult childhood and expressed no further interest in extensively discussing the past. Coleman comments that 'she expressed an appreciative attitude towards young people and the present world'. A further group of three people expressed some dissatisfaction with their past lives and recalled events which disturbed or threatened them. However, this group was able to live with the past and simply did not think about it over much. Of the remaining elderly most expressed positive attitudes towards their pasts, although none seemed particularly to value reminiscence. Many of these subjects expressed a view that old people needed to 'keep going' and they actively maintained hobbies, friends, and social commitments. For this group reminiscence did not appear to impinge on their psychological well-being. The present was more interesting and psychologically significant for these elderly people.

Of the elderly with low morale the past and reminiscence were something of a problem. For some of these people errors made in the past haunted them into old age; a bad marriage, inability to love one's children, a term spent in prison, a life wasted in casinos, and the regrets of a petty crook, all affected later adjustment to the past. Many of these people felt that their lives had been subject to forces beyond their control, and this apparently compounded their difficulties in coming to terms with the past. But not all of this group felt particularly guilty or regretful about the past. Miss Martin had been born into a wealthy Belgian family and her father had been a celebrated pianist. Prior to the First World War she had been brought up in the creative and Bohemian social world of an international pianist. The First World War saw the destruction of her home life by the Germans, the death of her mother, and was followed by the life of a refugee in London. For Miss Martin in old age, both the past and the present were equally appalling. She saw prejudice and humankind's animal nature as factors which contributed to the inhumanity of the present and the past. She did not reminisce a great deal and regarded her past as a tragedy which, if given the choice, she would disown. In fact, as time progressed, Coleman reports that Miss Martin gradually came to terms with both the past and the present and appeared in better spirits shortly before her death. It is probably noteworthy that this group of elderly people were the youngest in Coleman's study and it seems quite likely that for many of them the process of life review was not yet complete. The case of Miss Martin suggests that, for at least some of this group, a resolution of the past would be possible.

The final group studied by Coleman were elderly subjects who did not reminisce despite the fact that their past lives were happy and contained memories of pleasant events. For all six of these elderly subjects a spouse had recently died and it seemed likely that the past, although represented by pleasant memories, was too painful to contact in the context of the present. There was some evidence that, as the bereavement process progressed, the past became approachable and reminiscence could recommence. We will return to the effects of emotion, especially depression, on memory in Chapter 9.

The research reviewed in this chapter suggests that memory in the elderly may be impaired compared to younger groups of subjects; everyday failure of memory may increase and it may be difficult to integrate details of remembered events with thematic aspects of one's life. Yet the most important aspect of autobiographical memory in old age is represented by the processes of life review. The function of autobiographical memory in maintaining the self and in leading to further developments of self – the emergence of integrity – is of critical importance for at least some people. It seems likely that the purpose of life review and the role of autobiographical memory in this process are determined more by the existential problems set by the past and nature of current circumstances than by any predetermined cognitive process. Indeed some elderly people may not indulge in life review at all and, nevertheless, have a positive attitude to their past. For these elderly, the meaning of life lies in the present and not in the past and, consequently the life-review process appears to hold few attractions.

9 • THE IMPAIRMENT OF AUTOBIOGRAPHICAL MEMORY

In this Chapter we will review some of the research into the functioning of auto-biographical memory after brain injury. The main part of the chapter reviews research into amnesia and, following this, the nature of autobiographical memory in clinical depression is briefly considered. The research on amnesia is complex and the findings are often contradictory; nevertheless a general theoretical position is outlined, based on Shallice (1988). We will see that a model of autobiographical memory which emphasizes thematic structure and specific memories (see Chapter 7) receives support from at least some of the studies reported in this area.

Amnesia

Amnesia is often characterized as taking two forms, *anterograde* amnesia and *retrograde* amnesia. Anterograde amnesia refers to the inability of a patient following brain damage to encode information into long-term memory. Such patients show striking deficits, often repeating the same story many times, failing to recognize a person they were introduced to only minutes before, and generally showing no signs of being able to learn new information. Note, however, that such patients apparently can learn new information 'implicitly'. For instance, prior exposure to a word list may influence how the patient subsequently responds to the same words when re-presented, even though the patient has no explicit memory of the words nor, in most cases, any memory of the experimenter who presented the words only a few minutes previously (see Schacter 1987 for a review). Perhaps because of its striking effects and experimental tractability, anterograde amnesia has been extensively studied, whereas retrograde amnesia has received comparatively little attention from researchers (Butters and Cermak 1986). Retrograde amnesia, as the name implies, refers to an inability to remember past events and knowledge following brain injury. Retrograde amnesias typically are densest for a period immediately preceding the brain injury and much milder, if present at all, for remoter events in a person's life. Even within a period of retrograde amnesia 'islands' of memories may be preserved.

Our main concern in the remainder of this chapter will be with retrograde amnesia. It is important to note that retrograde amnesia is often accompanied by an anterograde amnesia. So, for example in Korsakoff's syndrome – one of the most extensively studied amnesias – patients often have anterograde amnesia and dense retrograde amnesia. Korsakoff's syndrome can arise from a number of causes, the most common being chronic alcoholism leading to the atrophy of certain brain areas. Other causes can be strokes, tumours, encephalitis, and progressive brain disorders such as Alzheimer's disease. In some cases, e.g. close-head injury, patients regain access to their memories.

In reviewing research into amnesia we will chiefly focus on chronic alcoholics with severe Korsakoff's syndrome, although we will also consider patients with amnesias associated with other types of brain injury. Korsakoff patients typically have very dense retrograde amnesias stretching back a number of decades and showing preservation of memories from early adulthood and childhood only (see the discussion of Ribot in Chapter 2). The retrograde amnesias of these patients have been studied in two slightly different ways. One approach has confined itself to examining impairments of knowledge for public events, whereas the other has investigated impairments of auto-biographical memory. This immediately brings us to a conceptual problem which was raised in Chapter 1 – namely, what type of knowledge is *not* 'autobiographical'? In Chapter 1 it was suggested that one way in which this problem might be thought about is in terms of a continuum. Memories of specific episodes one has directly experienced characterize the autobiographical end of the continuum and depersonalized knowledge (e.g. $3 \times 3 = 6$) characterize the semantic end of the continuum (see Tulving 1983 and Table 1.1 in Chapter 1). According to this scheme, factual knowledge specific to one's autobiography would be placed towards the autobiographi-cal end of the continuum. For example, knowledge about the public figures and events which occurred in one's life might be thought of as autobiographical knowledge. Indeed Conway and Montgomery (1990) found that public events were frequently dated by relating a target event to lifetime periods and specific memories, suggesting that this 'public' knowledge might intersect in memory with representations of the 'private' knowledge of one's own life. Conway (1987), however, found evidence suggesting that autobiographical factual knowledge (e.g. which bank one is with, whether one drives or not, etc.) might be directly associated in memory with semantic knowledge. We will return to these points below; for the moment let us first consider the impairment of autobiographical knowledge relating to public figures and public events.

Impairments of 'public' knowledge

Sanders and Warrington (1971) were the first to attempt to quantify long-term impair-ments of public knowledge. In their study they used descriptions of famous events and the faces of famous people. They selected their stimuli so that within a decade the events and famous people were indeed famous, but their fame was limited to a comparatively short time span. Of course, they tried to hold constant the level of fame for the events and the famous faces, but it is difficult to see how this could be done in any but the crudest of ways. For example, was Richard M. Nixon more or less famous than John F. Kennedy during their respective presidencies? To decide this we would need some independent objective measure of 'fame' and this we clearly do not have. Moreover, as was argued in Chapter 4, what a person remembers of public events is likely to be determined by their emotional reaction to specific events, and the type of knowledge and interest they have in those events. Many surveys in the popular press have demonstrated that people may be quite unaware of who are the leading political figures of their day; the names of famous athletes, artists, musicians, and so on, may also not be known. Thus we should be aware at the outset that in attempting to assess knowledge of public events researchers have had to employ rather crude measures and, as we shall see, this may account for some of the contradictory findings in this area.

In the Sanders and Warrington study a group of five amnesics were tested using these items (only three of the amnesics were Korsakoff's) along with matched control subjects. The principal finding was that the amnesics showed severe impairments for all decades – in other words memories for more remote time periods were not 'spared'. Thus these amnesics remembered very little of the famous people and events of their lives. But these findings contrast markedly with the outcome of a study reported by Albert, Butters, and Levin (1979). These authors also created their own test battery for memory for public events, but in doing so adopted a different procedure from that of Sanders and Warrington. Albert *et al.* created three tests featuring public figures and events from the 1920s to the mid-1970s. The first test was a face-recognition test, the second test was a recall questionnaire about famous people and events, and the third test was a multiple-choice questionnaire also dealing with public events and famous people. Items were selected for the tests on the basis that normal (non-brain-damaged) controls could get about 85 per cent of the items correct. Moreover the famous-faces test was subdivided into 'hard' and 'easy' faces on the basis of control subjects' responses. The 'easy' faces tended to be of celebrities whose period of fame spanned more than a decade, whereas the 'hard' faces tended to be of celebrities whose fame was limited to a few years or less. These tests were administered to a group of 11 alcoholic Korsakoff patients and a group of non-alcoholic matched controls. The principal findings were that the Korsakoff patients were severely impaired in responding to public events and famous people from recent years and much better at remembering the famous events and people from earlier years (1920s and 30s) – although still not as good as the controls. Strikingly, the Korsakoff patients were better at remembering 'hard' famous faces from the 1930s than 'easy' famous faces from the 1970s (Butters and Albert 1982).

Thus the findings of Albert *et al.* are in marked contrast to those of Warrington and Sanders, and the findings from other groups of amnesic patients are rather different again. For example, patients with Huntington's Disease, suffer from progressive motor and intellectual impairments, and also often show signs of amnesia. Albert, Butters, and Brandt (1981), employing the Albert *et al.* remote-memory battery, found that these patients, unlike Korsakoff patients, showed an essentially flat distribution of retention in which they were equally impaired for all time periods sampled – rather like Sanders and Warrington's amnesic patients. Other patients with more focal brain injuries tend to have retrograde amnesias for only short time periods (a few years) immediately preceding the onset of their illness. Thus retrograde amnesia is associated with a complex set of findings indicating different types of amnesias for different types of brain injury.

A number of different types of theory have been put forward as explanations of these diverse findings. Warrington and Weiskrantz (1982) propose that amnesia is primarily a disconnection syndrome, that is, due to brain injury parts of the memory system have become disconnected from retrieval processes or from other systems which are critical in the processing of memories. How could this theory explain the findings of Butters and his colleagues? The argument goes something like this: amnesia represents a disconnection of *episodic* memory from the rest of the cognitive system. The increased retention shown by some Korsakoff patients for very remote memories occurs because these memories have been transferred to *semantic* memory – which, it is proposed, is not disconnected from the rest of the cognitive system. There is in fact some plausibility in this argument and Squire and Cohen (1982) argue that two events or two pictures of celebrities, one from the 1930s and one from the 1970s, are not equated simply because control subjects remember both equally well – rather the reverse seems more probable, that an event from the 1930s which is remembered as well as a recent event is probably *more* memorable than a recent event. After all, it is highly unlikely that the recent events which feature in the various tests will in fact be remembered by anyone 40 years hence! It is argued that events from the remote past are memorable because they are represented in semantic and not episodic memory. Thus Korsakoff patients' retention of remote memories is an artefact of testing procedures and, it is claimed, these patients are, in fact, completely amnesic for episodic memories. Other types of patients have less severe disconnections in which islands of recent memories are disconnected, or even totally removed, from the cognitive system.

An alternative theory has been proposed by Cermak (1984) and an application of this theory to Korsakoff patients has also been developed by Butters and his colleagues. The Cermak theory proposes that amnesics suffer from an impairment of episodic memory such that they cannot transfer episodic knowledge to semantic memory. Amnesics, then, typically have anterograde amnesia because they cannot encode episodes. Moreover, if we assume that in many cases the episodic impairment is a progressive one which has developed over years as the severity of the alcoholism increased, then it is reasonable to assume that recent events will have been less well encoded than more remote events. Thus it is proposed that recent events are not remembered, because they were never encoded, but remote events which were encoded, preceding the onset of the progressive disease, can be recalled. Butters and his colleagues argue that this is just the case for alcoholic Korsakoff patients. Their alcoholism has led to a progressive impairment in their ability to encode episodic information and hence their temporally graded retrograde amnesia and dense anterograde amnesia. As Korsakoff patients are also typically poorer than normals even in knowledge which they can remember, it is also proposed that overlaid on this progressive impairment is a disconnection type of amnesia in which access to various sets of memories is physically no longer possible.

Both these theories are equally plausible and both can account for much of the data (which in any case is ambiguous). Recent evidence reported by Butters and his colleagues (e.g. Butters and Cermak 1986) has provided only marginal support for the 'dual-process' account of amnesia. For instance, if the dual process account is correct, then chronic alcoholics who have yet to develop Korsakoff's syndrome should also show something like a mild retrograde amnesia with a temporal gradient. This would be predicted if these patients are suffering from a progressive impairment in their ability to encode episodic knowledge. In fact, Butters and Albert (1982) found some support for this view when they administered the Albert *et al.* battery to chronic alcoholic non-Korsakoff patients, but the amnesia was very mild and was not present for all tests. More recently Butters and Cermak (1986) studied a case of a scientist (P.Z.) who, after a period of chronic alcoholism, developed Korsakoff's syndrome. This case presented a unique opportunity to examine the retention of knowledge which, it could be established beyond doubt, the patient had known prior to the onset of his illness. P.Z. was administered test batteries similar to those employed by Albert *et al.* but in this case the tests were comprised of events and colleagues taken from P.Z.'s own published autobiography and published academic work. The principal finding was that P.Z. showed a retrograde amnesia with a temporal gradient such that information from his early academic life was well preserved compared to information from the more recent past. Of course, the problem remains that this knowledge may have been stored in semantic, rather than episodic, memory. Indeed, it seems quite likely that the frequently rehearsed information used by Butters and Cermak would have been part of P.Z.'s semantic knowledge. Intriguingly Butters and Cermak also examined P.Z.'s semantic knowledge for definitions of scientific terms and found this knowledge to be mildly impaired.

The findings then do not allow us to choose clearly between the disconnection and dual-process accounts of amnesia. For the moment we will leave this debate and later return to a more recent theory advanced by Shallice (1988). Perhaps the most important point of the findings reviewed in this section is simply that autobiographical memory for the public events of one's life can be selectively impaired.

Impairments of autobiographical memory

There have, in fact, been even fewer studies of impairments of autobiographical memory in amnesia but, like studies of public knowledge, the findings are equally contradictory. Wood and his colleagues (Kinsbourne and Wood 1975; Wood, Ebert, and Kinsbourne 1982) report a cue-word study (see Chapters 1 and 6) of auto-biographical-memory retrieval in which alcoholic Korsakoff amnesics and various types of matched controls took part. In this study the amnesics were presented with single words such as *ship, bird, tree, flag*, and required to recall a memory which featured the named object. When a subject responded, 'the experimenter led the subject, encouraging him in whatever way possible, to produce a discrete personal memory of the word in question' (Wood *et al.* 1982: 170). The amnesic patients were, however, severely impaired in producing autobiographical memories, managing on average only 9 successful retrievals out of 20 trials. In contrast, the various controls averaged about 17 successful recalls. Wood *et al.* comment that it is extremely difficult to encourage Korsakoff patients to retrieve memories and that once some knowledge is recalled, e.g. 'flags are for waving', the patient typically becomes disturbed when pressed further to recall a specific episode. A similar finding emerged with a highly intelligent post-encephalitic patient (SS) extensively studied by Cermak and O'Connor (1983; Cermak 1976). SS had been found to have a temporal gradient for recall of public events and to perform reasonably normally when asked factual questions about his past life. When, however, he was tested with the cue-word technique it became apparent that he was quite unable to recall any memories whatsoever. Rather his 'memories' were of lifetime periods and general events; he was unable to recall specific events.

Striking as the above findings are, they are directly contradicted by the findings of a cue-word study conducted by Zola-Morgan, Cohen, and Squire (1983). They employed the cue-word technique with alcoholic Korsakoff patients and various types of controls. Like Wood they prompted and encouraged their patients to recall memories and included this in their scoring measure. Their principal finding was that Korsakoff patients were impaired compared to alcoholic control subjects, but only when compared on their first responses to the cue words. When the responses were compared taking prompting into account, then no overall differences were evident between the two groups. The list of example memories reported by Zola-Morgan *et al.* (1983: 492) show memory descriptions very similar to those obtained with normal subjects. One difference which was apparent, however, was that the Korsakoff patients drew most of their memories from their late childhood and early adulthood, whereas the controls drew most of their memories from recent time periods, clearly suggesting a retrograde amnesia for recent time periods only.

A disconnection-type of model could be used to account for patients' inabilities to retrieve specific autobiographical memories, but such a model could not be simply applied to the findings of Zola-Morgan *et al.*, demonstrating a temporal gradient in memory access. Interestingly a recent study by Dall Ora, della Sala, and Spinnler (1989) also questions the notion of a simple disconnection model. In their study, patients with Alzheimer's disease, focal brain damage, or widespread brain damage, were administered an autobiographical-memory questionnaire. The questionnaire required subjects to recall memories from all periods of their life (childhood, adulthood, and later life) and scored responses in terms of the detail and contextual information provided by the subjects (Borrini, Dall Ora, della Sala, Marinelli, and Spinnler 1989). Patients with Alzheimer's disease and widespread brain damage were severely impaired in auto-biographical-memory retrieval and basically could provide only a few details in response to the autobiographical-memory questionnaire. In contrast, patients with focal brain injuries were comparatively good at memory retrieval and provided fairly detailed and appropriate memory descriptions to the questionnaire. These findings demonstrate that widespread brain injuries are more likely to lead to amnesias for the events of one's life than are focal brain injuries, suggesting that a simple disconnection model is unlikely to account for autobiographical-memory amnesia.

The findings of Dall Ora *et al.* have, however, to be considered in the light of a study reported by De Renzi, Liotti, and Nichelli (1987). They studied a patient L.Z. who had apparently suffered a severe impairment of semantic memory with full preservation of autobiographical memory. This patient could not generate the meaning of simple noun concepts but could still perform routine actions and, remarkably, had an intact (and exact) memory for personally experienced events from the past and was normal in her encoding of events after her illness. Interestingly this patient had little knowledge of public events and showed a severe impairment for public events, except where an event had impinged on her own life:

> even public events could sometimes be recalled, limited, however, to the aspects that happened to establish a link with her personal experience or had a profound impact on her feelings. Of the Chernobyl episode she remembered that something had exploded and polluted the atmosphere, 'because the vegetables and house plants I kept on the deck had suffered' (vegetable sales were prohibited in Italy for two weeks), but ignored where the accident had occurred and that it had concerned nuclear energy. Questioned about the wedding of a member of the English Royal Family a few months after it had been televised, she immediately commented that the poor boy had been ensnared by a girl, whose past history was not immaculate and expressed fear that the same could happen to her own child, but she was unable to add other information on the episode.
>
> (De Renzi *et al.* 1987: 587)

This intriguing case shows that semantic knowledge can become disconnected from the cognitive system, while autobiographical knowledge, procedural knowledge, and some semantic knowledge relating to personal experiences remains intact (assuming, that is, that knowledge of public events can be classified as 'semantic' – see below). If this is the case, then it does not seem unreasonable to suppose the reverse, that episodic knowledge may become disconnected from the cognitive system, while semantic memory remains unaffected, and we will return to this point shortly.

Finally, in this section we must consider amnesias arising from damage to the frontal lobes, an area of the brain implicated in problem-solving, planning, and, perhaps, in supervising complex cognitive processes such as memory retrieval (see Shallice 1988). Baddeley and Wilson (1986) compared autobiographical-memory retrieval to cue-words by a range of brain-damaged subjects, including frontal-lobe patients. Their principal findings were that some patients, including some of their frontal-lobe patients, showed what the authors called a 'clouding' of autobiographical memory. In essence this was an inability by the patients to produce detailed specific episodes to the cue words, although they were able to recall lifetime periods, general events, and, on occasion, some few specific details of a remembered event. There appear to be strong parallels here between clouding of autobiographical memory following brain damage and the clouding of autobiographical memory noted by Holland and Rabbit in their elderly subjects (see Chapter 8). We will return to this point later.

Other of Baddeley and Wilson's frontal-lobe patients showed a strikingly different pattern of responding in which they would quite often provide lengthy and elaborate accounts of past events; unfortunately most of these events, it turned out, had never occurred. For example, one patient described the death of his younger brother Martin in a car crash at the age of 10/12 years. In fact, his younger brother was in contact with the patient while he was hospitalized and had not died prematurely in a car crash. Indeed, the patient himself subsequently denied this story. These confabulations in autobiographical-memory recall were apparent in some of Baddeley and Wilson's frontal-lobe patients and often could be easily detected because of their implausibility. Moreover Shallice (1988) reports a similar case in which a frontal-lobe patient accurately recalled the details of an event (at which Shallice had been present) but misattributed the location of the event. Baddeley and Wilson point out that striking confabulations such as these are in fact rare in brain-damaged patients and in their sample, at least, were confined to a small group of their frontal-lobe patients.

Taken together, these findings would seem to indicate that amnesics have severe problems in retrieving specific autobiographical memories. For some patients the impairments are so severe that no memories can be retrieved, while for other patients careful prompting and encouragement can assist recall. Furthermore some patients may be unable to judge whether an event they have in mind is or is not a memory of a past experience. In contrast to these impairments of memories for specific events, the thematic structure of a person's life appears to be comparatively spared in amnesia and subjects are able apparently to retrieve information concerning lifetime periods and general events. How then can we explain this pattern of autobiographical-memory impairment in amnesics?

Shallice (1988) proposes that these aspects of amnesia can be understood within a general model of the cognitive system in which information retrieved from long-term knowledge structures is further processed in a supervisory system which co-ordinates and interprets retrieval processes. Shallice argues that this supervisory system is located in the frontal lobes. Focusing on the structure of long-term knowledge Shallice also argues that well-learnt autobiographical knowledge is stored in semantic memory. Indeed, this was one of the points arising from the findings of Conway and Bekerian (1987) and Conway (1987), that lifetime periods and even some general event knowledge may be part of a person's semantic knowledge. It also seems likely that some specific autobiographical memories might be represented along with semantic knowledge (see Chapter 10). Memories which have been recounted many times and memories upon which a person has frequently reflected might be stored in this way. If we then suppose, as Shallice does, that in amnesia episodic memory has become disconnected from the supervisory system and only autobiographical knowledge in semantic memory can be accessed, then the pattern of amnesic memory retrieval begins to make some sense. Amnesics cannot retrieve autobiographical memories from episodic memory but they can retrieve the comparatively few autobiographical memories stored in semantic memory and access the thematic structure of autobiographical memory.

If the frontal lobes co-ordinate and interpret something like the autobiographical-memory retrieval process described in Chapter 7 (a cyclic process of generate–search–verify), then this system will be highly dependent on input from other parts of the cognitive system. In the case of a disconnection from episodic memory, then, of course, no memories can be retrieved; the search stage of the retrieval process fails and the supervisory system can respond only with information retrieved from other areas of memory. If the episodic system is not disconnected and the supervisory system is undamaged, then brain injury should not greatly affect memory retrieval – as in the case of Dall Ora *et al.*'s focal brain-damaged patients. When, however, the episodic system is not disconnected but the supervisory system is impaired, then memory may be 'clouded' – the retrieval process works fully, but inefficiently – or confabulations may result, indicating a failure of the verification stage of retrieval. Perhaps an inefficient retrieval process and/or similarly impaired verification process can also account for the failure of very elderly subjects to retrieve detailed and specific memories. One type of theory of cognition in the elderly does, in fact, propose that the very elderly suffer from the malfunctioning of a central executive processor or supervisory system (see Cohen 1988; Holland and Rabbit 1989).

Findings from the study of amnesia would then seem to support both the general model of autobiographical memory we considered at the close of Chapter 7, and specific aspects of the retrieval process also considered in Chapter 7. Other problems, however, remain. The findings of Zola-Morgan *et al.* cannot be accommodated without additional assumptions. And it seems likely that amnesia might also arise by a progressive inability to encode the experiences of one's life. Similarly the temporal gradients for knowledge of public events do not fit the disconnection/impaired supervisory model of amnesia. Once again, a progressive impairment of encoding could account for these findings. What does, however, seem likely is that knowledge of public events is typically not stored in autobiographical memory, unless those events intersect with one's own experiences in some fairly direct way (De Renzi *et al.* 1987; see also Conway and Montgomery 1990).

Methodological note

One problem with the research into amnesia is that different researchers tend to use different items with which to probe memory. For example, Sanders and Warrington and Albert *et al.* each developed their own remote-memory tests and each test contained different items, although items in both tests were similar in that they referred to public events and celebrities. Similarly different researchers employing the cue word 'technique' appear to employ slightly different sets of cue words (it is difficult to determine the extent of this as researchers usually do not list, in their papers, the items they have employed). One problem which arises with the use of different items is that different effects may be specific to the item set used in a particular study. This is an especially pressing problem when only small numbers of subjects and items are sampled. The usual way to treat this problem is to adopt a more conservative form of analysis which takes into account variance arising from subjects *and* from items (Clark 1973). Indeed this method of analysis is routinely employed in studies of autobiographical memory such as those reported in Chapters 6 and 7. Had this method of analysis been used in the remote-memory studies of amnesia and in the studies of impaired autobiographical memory (when the experiments featured more than one subject), it seems likely that the many contradictory findings described above would not have emerged. In other words it seems possible that many of the apparent differences, e.g. between flat and temporally graded memory distributions for amnesics' recall of public events, are most probably due to the specific items employed by a researcher in a particular study. Thus, if reanalyses were performed in which items were treated as random effects, then it might be found that amnesics are, in fact, globally impaired for knowledge of public and private events. The interesting question would then be why certain amnesics are occasionally able to retrieve such information.

One answer, suggested above, is that some of this knowledge is stored in a memory system which patients can still access (i.e. semantic memory).

Living with amnesia

Whatever the ultimate explanation for amnesia, the critical point for the sufferer is that recall of specific memories is impaired. In Chapter 5 and Chapter 6 we saw that auto-biographical memories are centrally involved with the self-system; indeed a self with no personal history would be a very strange self indeed. In 1986 Jonathan Miller presented a television programme on the tragic life of the Cambridge musician Clive Wearing. Wearing had contracted a rare virus which caused widespread brain damage and as a consequence of his illness had no recollections of any specific experiences from his past, and also suffered a dense anterograde amnesia. Remarkably Wearing could still hold a conversation, play music, and recognize his wife, knew he was married, and could use a telephone. Thus much of his semantic knowledge was spared, as was some well-learnt autobiographical knowledge. He was, however, a man who was greatly distressed. His semantic knowledge afforded him some awareness of his disorder and he would often say that each moment was like waking from the dead – as he had no memory of saying this, he would often repeat it. When he saw his wife he would hug her as though they were being reunited after a long separation, even though she had been in the room only minutes previously. When in hospital he would make repeated telephone calls home, unaware that each call was not the first. He was utterly perplexed about the past, retaining only the most general knowledge of his pre-illness life. Each morning when he awoke he believed that he awoke from being dead.

Cases similar to that of Clive Wearing are described with much sympathy and insight by Sachs (1985) in his book *The Man Who Mistook His Wife for a Hat*. One case, that of Jimmie G., was a Korsakoff patient with a severe retrograde amnesia and dense antero-grade amnesia. Unlike Clive Wearing, however, Jimmie G. had a good memory for his childhood and adolescence. When treated by Sachs, Jimmie G. was 49 years old but thought of himself as a 19-year-old. He had access to very few memories of events which had occurred after the age of 19 and his illness, which apparently commenced in the late 1960s when he would have been in his early 40s, had induced a dense retro-grade amnesia for the preceding 20 years or so. Jimmie G.'s anterograde amnesia meant that every meeting with a person was a first meeting and he seemed to be totally unable to encode into memory any current event knowledge. In contrast his fluid intelligence was clearly intact, and he was very good at puzzles, enjoyed mathematical games, and like many Korsakoff patients was able to acquire procedural knowledge. Jimmie G. generally seemed unaware of his problems, yet when pressed – for example when shown a photograph of the earth taken from space, which implied a technology not in existence as far he knew – he became distressed and keenly aware that something was wrong. Sachs describes how Jimmie G. became more restless, how he seemed to be existentially distraught and took to restlessly roaming the corridors of the hospice, perhaps seeking some type of fulfilment the nature of which he had no conception. Sachs reports the following conversation with Jimmie G.:

'How do you feel?'

'How do I feel,' he repeated, and scratched his head, 'I cannot say I feel ill. But I cannot say I feel well. I cannot say I feel anything at all.'

'Are you miserable?' I continued.

'Can't say I am.'

'Do you enjoy life?'

'I can't say I do . . .'

I hesitated, fearing that I was going too far, that I might be stripping a man down to some hidden, unacknowledgeable, unbearable, despair.

'You don't enjoy life,' I repeated, hesitating somewhat.

'How then *do* you feel about life?'

'I can't say I feel anything at all.'

'You feel alive though?'

'Feel alive? Not really. I haven't felt alive for a very long time.'

His face wore a look of infinite sadness and resignation.

(Sachs 1985: 34)

Many different tactics were tried in order to attempt to place Jimmie G. into a meaningful relationship with his environment, one in which he felt alive. And Sachs reports that in attending church and, eventually, in his role as a gardener, Jimmie G. found some ways in which he could meaningfully relate to the world. In particular it seemed that in activities which set up a mood or feeling, then Jimmie G. could persist in the emotion for some length of time, 'and there would be in him a pensiveness and peace we rarely, if ever, saw during the rest of his life at the Home'. Perhaps Jimmie G. was a rare or lucky case – certainly he was very different from Clive Wearing – nevertheless it seems that people with even the most devastating of neurological impairments can still find some meaning in life and maintain a self, of sorts.

Three other cases described by Sachs are rather different. Mrs O'C. at the age of 88 had a vivid dream of her childhood in which she re-experienced, or so it seemed to her, the songs of her childhood. When she awoke the music continued as if a radio was playing in her head, so vividly did she continue to rehear the forgotten songs of childhood. Neurological examination indicated that she was suffering from temporal lobe seizures (the brain area involved in many of the amnesias considered above). In fact, the re-experience of these songs was so acute that, when Sachs interviewed Mrs O'C., she could barely hear him over the noise inside her head. As she recovered from the symptoms of her stroke (the cause of the right temporal lobe seizures), the music gradually faded until she no longer heard the Irish music of her childhood. Mrs O'C., when asked by Sachs how she felt about her recovery, commented: 'Mostly I would say, it is a great relief. But, yes, I *do* miss the old songs a little. Now, with lots of them, I can't even recall them. It was like being given back a forgotten bit of my childhood again. And some of the songs were really lovely.' For Mrs O'C. then, her recovery was tinged with regret and she was pleased to have been so vividly reminded of her past; the experience for her had been like a door opening on to a lost past. In a similar case Mrs O'M., who was also in her 80s, also heard music in her head:

One day, Mrs O'M. recounted, while she was grating parsnips in the kitchen, a song started playing. It was 'Easter Parade', and was followed, in swift succession, by 'Glory, Glory, Hallelujah' and 'Good Night, Sweet Jesus'. Like Mrs O'C., she assumed that a radio had been left on, but quickly discovered that all the radios were off. This was in 1979, four years earlier. Mrs O'C. recovered in a few weeks, but Mrs O'M.'s music continued, and got worse and worse.

(Sachs 1985: 127)

For Mrs O'M. this was not a pleasant experience, especially as she claimed to have never particularly liked the songs which had no meaning for her whatsoever. As they kept replaying in her head, she grew to hate them. Fortunately, she responded to medication and the singing ceased. When asked if she missed the songs, she replied 'Not on your life, I'm much better off without them.'

Not everyone then finds meaning in what Sachs calls *incontinent nostalgia*, when brain malfunction leads to the involuntary and irrepressible recall of aspects of the past. Sachs describes another case of this type of nostalgia which occurred when a post-encephalitic patient was administered the drug L-dopa for the first time. Occasionally with this type of patient L-dopa leads to resumption of past behaviours, memories, and feelings, present in the very earliest stages of the disease and subsequently 'lost'. The drug was administered to a 63-year-old woman who had been in a virtual trance for 24 years of her life, being unable to speak normally and showing few signs of self-motivated behaviour. After receiving the drug her speech returned and motor activity resumed at an excitable level. She also showed signs of increased libido. Sachs comments (1985: 144):

This period was marked by nostalgia, joyful identification with a youthful self, and uncontrolled upsurge of remote sexual memories and allusions. The patient requested a tape recorder, and in the course of a few days recorded innumerable salacious songs, 'dirty' jokes and limericks, all derived from party-gossip, 'smutty' comics, night-clubs, and music-halls of the middle and late 1920s. These recitals were enlivened by repeated allusions to then-contemporary events, and the use of obsolete colloquialisms, intonations and social mannerisms irresistibly evocative of that bygone flappers' era. Nobody was more astonished than the patient herself: 'It's amazing,' she said. 'I can't understand it. I haven't heard or thought of those things for more than 40 years. I never knew I still knew them. But now they keep running through my mind.' Increasing excitement necessitated a reduction of the dosage of L-dopa, and with this the patient, although remaining quite articulate, instantly 'forgot' all these early memories and was never again able to recall a single line of the songs she had recorded.

These remarkable and tragic cases show us that the meaning carried by autobiographical memories can profoundly affect a person, either by their absence or by their irrepressible presence. The case of the L-dopa patient is particularly interesting because it suggested that a whole forgotten or 'submerged' self-system was reactivated, including memories and many other types of autobiographical knowledge. In contrast, the case of Mrs O'M. shows that the past is not always redolent with meaning and feeling, and whose past does not contain passages of tedium which, if automatically and irrepressibly retrieved as a consequence of brain injury, would only act as an irritant? The point of this section has been to try to provide some insight into the experience and meaning of brain injury for the patient. It seems that in our efforts to build models of how the brain might work, we have de-emphasized the experience and personal meaning of brain injury for the patient. In studies of autobiographical memory, however, personal meaning cannot be ignored.

Autobiographical memory in depression

In the review of research into amnesia we saw how brain injury can lead to the inability to recall specific memories or to the irrepressible retrieval of memories. In clinical depression there appears to be a bias towards retrieving memories of events with negative personal connotations. In a seminal study Lloyd and Lishman (1975) had clinically depressed patients recall memories to cue words which were selected to be emotionally neutral. Patients were asked to recall a memory of either a pleasant or unpleasant event and to indicate when they had a memory in mind. Retrieval time was recorded. The principal finding was that the more severely depressed the patient, the faster the retrieval of a negative memory. Striking though this mood-memory effect is, there are alternative explanations of these findings. For instance, it may be that severely depressed patients actually have more negative experiences and so have a larger pool of negative memories which they may quickly access and retrieve. Alternatively, very depressed patients may simply interpret rather neutral memories as being negative and so give the impression of retrieving more unpleasant memories more quickly than less depressed patients.

Research by Teasdale and his colleagues has effectively ruled out these alternative explanations. Teasdale and Fogarty (1979) employed non-clinical subjects and induced depressed or happy moods. Subjects then recalled memories to different types of cue words. The principal findings were that mood state determined speed of memory retrieval, elated groups recalled unpleasant memories more slowly than depressed groups. As subjects were randomly assigned to groups it can be assumed that depressing experiences were random across groups and so the mood-memory effects can only have arisen as a product of the mood and not as a product of biases in the subject's memories. Further studies demonstrated that depressed mood was unlikely to influence the (negative) judgement of neutral memories and so artefactually induce mood-memory effects. In a study which directly demonstrates the effects of depressed mood on memory; Clark and Teasdale (1982) used clinically depressed patients whose pattern of depression was cyclic. Subjects recalled memories in a cue-word experiment when they were clinically depressed and when they were on the part of their cycle where they were not depressed. Happy memories were very likely to be recalled when subjects were less depressed and negative memories less likely to be recalled. This pattern was reversed when subjects were more severely depressed.

Depression then seems to lead to a bias in memory retrieval in which memories of negative events are more frequently recalled as the depression increases – a sort of 'vicious circle' as Teasdale describes it. Maybe we have all experienced something like this but are able to 'snap' out of it and/or are fortunate enough to be in the company of people who can 'lift' our mood. More recently, Williams and Broadbent (1986) in a study of memory retrieval by suicide attempters, who are more emotionally disturbed and confused than depressives, also found mood-memory effects, and these patients retrieved memories of negative events more rapidly than memories of positive events. A further intriguing finding was that these patients tended to recall 'general' memories rather than specific detailed memories. Like Baddeley and Wilson's amnesics, the suicide attempters showed a 'clouding' of autobiographical memory. Perhaps this clouding serves an adaptive function, shielding the patient from memories of more pleasant events which might further exacerbate their mood and protecting the patient from the details of negative events which might deepen their mood.

Little is known about the effects of clinical disorders upon autobiographical memory. The findings, such as they are, suggest that mood may bias retrieval processes towards mood-congruent memories, but this typically only occurs in depression (see Williams, Watts, Mcleod, and Mathews 1988 for an overview). Intriguingly there is some suggestion that emotionally disturbed patients might also suffer from a 'clouding' of autobiographical memory and be unable to retrieve memories of specific events.

10 • AUTOBIOGRAPHICAL MEMORY AND COGNITION

In this final chapter we will first consider some of the general properties of auto-biographical memory suggested by the research reviewed in the preceding chapters. Research which suggests relationships between autobiographical memory, concepts, and learning will then be reviewed. The purpose here is to develop some initial and speculative perspectives upon the wider role of autobiographical memories in cognition. The final section considers possible theoretical (re)formulations of the notion of an 'autobiographical memory'.

Aspects of autobiographical memory

In Chapter 3 we saw that temporal properties of events are not encoded in memory according to calendar date. Instead, memories contain knowledge about the time of day or part of a week, month, or year, and this knowledge can be used to infer a date. The work of Robinson (1986b) demonstrated that the temporal structure of events can determine memory availability and, presumably, this structure might also be reflected in specific memories. The temporal structure of events is encompassed by Neisser's concept of nested structure and an event will have different types of temporal structure at different levels of nesting. As I write these sentences, there is a temporal structure which is determined by my speed of typing (slow), by the length of the period I have this morning to spend writing, by the various commitments of the day, by the deadline for submission of the manuscript, by the intervening event of Christmas, and so on. The influence of different layers of temporal structure upon the representation of auto-biographical memories in memory is currently unknown. However, the work of Robinson, Brown *et al.*, and others (reviewed in the latter part of Chapter 3) quite clearly demonstrates that temporal structure is a central component in autobiographical memories.

Although temporal structure has been found to be important, other factors appear to be equally important in autobiographical memory. For instance, in Chapters 4 and 5 emotions and the self were found to be critical in determining memory content and subsequent availability. Events which involve emotional experiences and/or which are of high personal importance are remembered more clearly and persistently than memories of events low in these qualities. Thus the interaction between an experiencer and an event also determines the nature of autobiographical memories. As in the case of temporal structure, however, exact details of how emotions and the self influence memory representation have yet to established.

One further way in which to conceptualize these aspects of autobiographical memory is in terms of the organization of memories. In Chapter 6 it was proposed that autobiographical memories are hierarchically organized. The highest level in the hierarchy represents knowledge concerning chronological periods from one's life. These lifetime periods or extended timelines represent thematic knowledge relating to a period, such as knowledge about goals, other people, and event features, which characterize that period. Extended timelines index representations of general or summarized events which denote shorter time periods within a lifetime period. At the lowest level of the hierarchy are specific autobiographical memories which are indexed directly by representations of general events. This then is the *thematic structure* of auto-biographical memory.

How might the temporal structure of events influence the nature of the thematic structure of autobiographical memory? There seem a number of possibilities. Lifetime periods are inherently chronological in that they represent periods with temporally marked beginnings and endings. This is not to say that specific dates which mark these points are stored in memory but rather that such endpoints may be 'fuzzy' in the sense that they span a period of time rather than an exact date. Moreover, different lifetime periods, although loosely denoting chronological time periods, are not exclusive in the sense that only one period relates to one unique passage of time. Chronologically different lifetime periods may overlap partly or fully. It is the general events and specific memories uniquely indexed by the thematic knowledge of a time period which distinguish one lifetime period from another. Nevertheless it seems possible that the external structure of a lifetime period might determine memory availability. Perhaps specific memories from the beginning and ending of a period are directly indexed by the period and so are highly available for retrieval. Similarly events associated with the period and which were highly relevant to that period – perhaps because of their emotional content and/or self-relevance – are also highly available for retrieval. Thus, at the level of lifetime periods, specific memories, because of their temporal or emotional/self-properties, may play a privileged role.

At the level of general events the same may be true and, as Robinson found, temporal structure can influence memory availability here. For instance, the temporal structure of the school term might be represented at the general-event level, and so influence the retrieval of specific memories. The work of Pillemer and his colleagues (see Chapters 4 and 5) suggests that emotional episodes tend to occur at the beginning of a novel period in a person's life. If so, there may simply be more memories of emotional events associated with the start of a general event than with other points in that event. These issues have yet to be investigated in detail and other possibilities seem equally likely. For example, memories of events which are highly associated with a lifetime-period theme – regardless of temporal and emotional properties – might also be represented in some distinctive fashion. Thus the suggestion of a hierarchically ordered thematic structure for autobiographical memory is useful for conceptualizing the findings from the sorts of studies considered in Chapter 6, and it might be possible to develop this view in further research to encompass findings related to temporal structure, emotions, and the self. Currently, however, proposals concerning the thematic structure of autobiographical memory are merely suggestive rather than definitive, and much research remains to be conducted if these proposals are to form a basis for a more comprehensive model of autobiographical memory.

In contrast, the research reviewed in Chapter 7 indicated that, when a memory probe is sufficiently specific, then the thematic structure of autobiographical memory may be rather peripheral to the process of memory access. In this situation a general cyclic or iterative retrieval process may be employed as a person gradually 'homes' in on a target memory. Presumably the thematic structure of memory is used at points in the cyclic retrieval process – perhaps for cue elaboration and retrieval verification – but the role of emotions and the self in this process remain obscure. On the other hand, the findings demonstrating recency effects in memory retrieval suggest a general function of temporal information in memory. Recent events are comparatively well remembered and this level of retention may be independent of thematic structure, temporal structure (as this was discussed above), emotion, and the self. As Baddeley suggested, memory may generally function to retain recent events in some detail and so provide us with a sense of 'now'. As an event becomes more remote in time, other types of retention – rehearsal and organization – determine the fate of a memory.

One final general aspect of autobiographical remembering is that of direct cued recall. In Chapter 8 this type of recall was briefly discussed with reference to Salaman's work on recollection. It seems that many people occasionally experience the 'spontaneous' recall of a 'forgotten' memory. In the cases discussed by Salaman this nearly always occurred in response to a cue of which the rememberer was aware. Specific cues, then, might directly correspond to the representation of an event in memory and so provide direct access to that memory, bypassing both the thematic structure of autobiographical memory and the cyclic retrieval process. Such direct access has not been experimentally studied and reports of this, although frequent, are anecdotal.

In summary, then, current research has established a number of general aspects of autobiographical memory. The temporal structure of events and the quality of the interaction between participant and event, both strongly influence the nature and accessibility of autobiographical memories. Autobiographical memories appear to be organized hierarchically in memory and this hierarchical structure represents thematic aspects of a person's life. Within this structure, knowledge about activities, people, and places, are focal points for memory access (see Chapter 6). A characteristic cyclic retrieval process is employed in autobiographical-memory retrieval and this is most evident when a memory cue specifies particular time periods and sets of target memories. Finally, some evidence suggests that memory cues may, occasionally, be specific enough to access single memories directly.

Facts, concepts, and memories

The research outlined in previous chapters focused almost exclusively upon the properties of and interrelations between different types of autobiographical memories. In contrast, the research to be discussed in this section is more concerned with the relations between autobiographical knowledge and other types of knowledge. Keenan and Baillet (1980) reported two studies which attempted to examine how people process and encode self-relevant information. They based their study on the well-established finding of Rogers and his colleagues (Rogers, Kuiper, and Kirker 1977) that people remember highly self-relevant information far better than information low in self-relevance. In Keenan and Baillet's first experiment subjects responded 'yes' or 'no' to a series of questions. One set of questions asked whether a personality characteristic was appropriate for a particular person. The people named in the experiment ranged from 'yourself' to Jimmy Carter (who was president at the time of the study). A second set of questions asked subjects to judge whether two words were the same in meaning – a semantic task. Reaction times to respond to the questions were recorded and after a filled delay subjects were then given a surprise recognition test in which they had to discriminate between the words in the study phase of the experiment and new words. The principal findings were that subjects were far quicker at responding to questions when they were self-referring than in any other condition. Similarly subjects recognized many more of the words when they had been judged to refer to them. In addition to this, reaction times systematically increased as the target person became less well known and, similarly, recognition rates declined for less well-known persons. Thus subjects recognized few of the personality traits they had attributed to Carter and many which they had attributed to their best friend.

In their second experiment, Keenan and Baillet presented subjects with true and false facts about people and places, and subjects made either a *factual* or an *evaluative* judgement of each fact. Facts for people and places differed in their self-relevance for the subjects and, as in the first experiment, subjects first made timed judgements, followed by a surprise recognition test. The main finding was that recognition memory was influenced by how well the subjects knew the target people and places but only for evaluative judgements. When subjects made factual judgements, no effect of self-relevance was present.

The findings of Keenan and Baillet demonstrate that factual knowledge which is highly self-relevant and evaluative is processed more rapidly, and retained more accurately than factual knowledge which is low in these qualities. This suggests that factual knowledge which has direct autobiographical reference may be represented somewhat differently from factual knowledge which is not directly self-referring. This finding is difficult for theories of memory which make a sharp distinction between autobiographical knowledge and other types of knowledge. For instance, in Chapter 1 a distinction between semantic memory and autobiographical memory was introduced in which semantic memory was viewed as memory for the meanings of words or concepts (i.e. factual knowledge), whereas autobiographical memory was characterized as memory for experienced events. It is often assumed.in such models that semantic knowledge is comprised of decontextualized abstract knowledge, whereas autobiographical knowledge is comprised of context-specific knowledge. But, in

Keenan and Baillet's study, facts, which we can assume were roughly equivalent in terms of the semantic processing they were likely to engender, were none the less processed differently according to their self-reference.

In order to explore this further Conway (1987) conducted a study in which subjects made judgements about 'semantic facts' and 'autobiographical facts'. Semantic facts took the form of true and false statements which referred to the category membership of various items, e.g. a true semantic fact would be 'Is an apple a fruit?'; and a false semantic fact would be 'Is an express train a fruit?' Autobiographical facts were collected individually from subjects who completed a questionnaire in which they listed, among other things, their favourite fruits. An example of a true autobiographical fact would be 'Are apples your favourite fruit?'; and a false autobiographical fact would be 'Are pears your favourite fruit?' Subjects responded 'yes' or 'no' as accurately and as quickly as they could to these questions and speed of responding was recorded. The interesting manipulation in this study, however, was that the questions were preceded by a prime word which either named the category of the questions (e.g. *fruits*) or named a neutral word. The reasoning behind the prime manipulation was that the category names should speed the processing of true semantic facts and hence produce faster responding, than speed of responding following the processing of true semantic questions which had been preceded by a neutral prime. This should occur because the category prime is automatically processed and, in the course of this processing, related semantic knowledge about category members is activated and so can be processed more rapidly when encountered in the true semantic fact question. If, however, semantic knowledge is depersonalized and decontextualized, it would not be expected that a category prime would facilitate responding to a true autobiographical fact. This is because specific personal preferences would not be stored in memory with semantic knowledge and so the prior processing of the category prime would not activate this knowledge. In fact, Conway found that semantic-category primes facilitated responding to both true semantic facts and true autobiographical facts and that the magnitude of the priming was the same in both cases. This finding is also surprising when contrasted with the findings of Conway and Bekerian (1987), discussed in Chapter 6. These authors found that semantic-category names did *not* prime the retrieval of specific memories. Conway (1987) argues that frequent and current autobiographical knowledge might be stored in memory with semantic knowledge and so help 'customize' the semantic system.

The interconnectedness of autobiographical and semantic knowledge may, however, be even more extensive than these studies suggest. Conway (1990) carried out a series of experiments designed to explore the relations between autobiographical memories and different types of concepts. In these experiments subjects retrieved memories to cue words and phrases naming different types of concepts. Two types of concepts were employed: taxonomic categories and goal-derived categories. Examples of taxonomic categories are *clothing, furniture, fruits*, etc., and these are similar to the categories used by Conway and Bekerian (1987) in their autobiographical-memory retrieval experiments. Examples of goal-derived categories are *birthday presents, things to take on a picnic, foods to eat on a diet*, etc. (see Barsalou 1985, 1986, for further details of these types of categories). In Conway's first experiment subjects retrieved memories to members of these categories and were primed with the category name or a neutral word. For example, a subject might be primed with *furniture* and then retrieve a memory to the word *chair* and might be primed with *foods to eat on a diet* and retrieve a memory to the word *carrot*. The main finding was that goal-derived-category primes speeded memory retrieval, whereas taxonomic-category primes gave rise to slow memory-retrieval times and no prime effects were present for these categories. In subsequent experiments Conway found that a cue word such as *jumper*, when preceded by a taxonomic prime such as *clothing*, gave rise to slow memory-retrieval times, whereas the same cue word when preceded by a goal-derived category prime such as *birthday present* gave rise to reliably faster retrieval times. These findings demonstrate that goal-derived concepts are closely associated in memory with records of experienced events, whereas taxonomic categories appear to be less directly associated with autobiographical memories.

Thus factual knowledge which is highly self-referring may be processed differently from factual knowledge which makes no direct self-reference. Frequently repeated and current facts about oneself may be stored along with semantic facts, and certain types of concepts, such as goal-derived categories, may be directly associated with autobiographical memories. These findings indicate that autobiographical memories and, more generally, autobiographical facts may play some role in the representation of semantic or conceptual knowledge. Perhaps autobiographical knowledge helps us to link the processing of abstract decontextualized knowledge to practical and self-relevant issues. Another function of autobiographical memories in conceptual processing is that they may provide knowledge which goes well beyond current processing and so facilitates problem-solving and creativity. We will return to these points in the next section. The studies outlined above strongly suggest that autobiographical memories and facts are closely associated with conceptual knowledge which, previously, was thought to be depersonalized and abstract. The exact role of memories in conceptual processing has yet to be established.

Although memories and recurrent autobiographical facts from one's life may be closely associated in memory with conceptual knowledge, it seems that these types of associations must change, or be updated, fairly frequently. Thus the set of items that comprise likely *birthday presents* for adolescents are rather different from the same set of items for the adult. Indeed, Conway (1990) found that items named by older adults as members of goal-derived categories were not named by younger adults. Moreover, younger adults had difficulties in retrieving memories to cue words from goal-derived categories when those words were based on responses by adults. For example, young adults who found it difficult to view a *jumper* as a *birthday present* were not primed when *jumper* was the target cue. When questioned, young adults claimed that they had not received or been given jumpers as birthday presents. Older adults, however, were primed by *birthday present* when retrieving memories to *jumper*. More generally, it might be the case that as the current facts of one's life change, so the autobiographical knowledge stored with concepts also changes.

Bugelski (1977) reports a particularly interesting finding relating to these suggestions. Bugelski's experiment was similar to Galton's original cue-word study (see Chapter 1) and subjects noted the first few thoughts to come to mind when they read a cue word. The difference was that the subjects were all bilingual, having spoken Spanish as children and American English as adults. At the time of testing none of the subjects had spoken Spanish for at least ten years and many had not spoken Spanish since their childhood. Two lists of cue words were employed, one in English and the other in Spanish. After recording their 'thoughts', subjects then identified the time period in their life from which the 'thoughts' were taken. For English words most thoughts (70 per cent) were from recent time periods and fewest thoughts were from childhood (13 per cent). As the subjects' thoughts were mainly comprised of images of experienced events, we can take these findings as corroboration of the retention function for auto-biographical memories described by Rubin and his colleagues (Chapter 3). For Spanish words, however, a quite different picture emerged and 43 per cent of thoughts were from recent periods compared to 45 per cent of thoughts from childhood. Indeed, Bugelski reports that many of his subjects were surprised by the apparently unexpected and spontaneous recall of 'forgotten' events. One intriguing interpretation of these findings is that, when it is possible to access the meanings of words which a person had at some earlier point in their life, then associated autobiographical memories from that period also become available.

In some respects it might be thought remarkable that Bugelski's subjects could remember any Spanish words learnt in childhood. After all, for most of his subjects these words had not been used for many years and we have already seen that memory recall from the earliest period of childhood is severely impoverished. Bugelski's subjects would have learnt Spanish during the period 0 to 8 years, which corresponds to the period of childhood amnesia discussed in Chapter 8. The very long-term retention of knowledge has, however, been extensively documented by Bahrick and his colleagues (Bahrick, Bahrick, and Wittlinger 1975; Bahrick 1983; 1984). The main findings of these studies is that memory for a language learnt in adulthood shows a rapid fall in retention for the first six years or so after acquisition. Retention then stabilizes and up to 40 per cent of the originally learnt information is retained for periods in excess of 40 years. Similar findings were obtained in studies of the retention of the names and faces of classmates over 57-year retention intervals. Recognition memory for names and faces was at about the 90 per cent level over a 15-year retention interval and recall of names and faces declined to about 40 per cent over a 48-year period. In a study in which graduates recalled the relative position of streets, names of streets, names of buildings, and names of landmarks, from their university town, it was found that memory for street positions and names rapidly declined, whereas knowl-edge concerning the names of buildings and landmarks declined less rapidly. Note that this latter study examined memory over 1- to 46-year retention intervals. Thus knowl-edge about the facts of one's life appears to be surprisingly well retained and it may be that such knowledge is associated in memory with 'forgotten' autobiographical memories, as in Bugelski's study.

How can these findings be conceptualized in terms of the general aspects of auto-biographical memory outlined earlier? Consider the notion of thematic structure in autobiographical memory. One way in which to think about a set of lifetime periods relating to a specific period of time is in terms of the self. The lifetime periods and life themes which they represent might be viewed as a sort of 'fossilized' account of an earlier self. Presumably, when the particular period in question was experienced, the themes relevant to that time permeated most aspects of cognition and consciousness and, of course, influenced cognitive activities such as conceptual processing. The 'relics' of this time are preserved in the structure of autobiographical memory – in lifetime periods, general events, and memories of specific events. Thematic structure, however, probably provides only limited access to a small number of memories from a time period. This is because not all goals and themes are preserved in such structures. Perhaps only summary goals and themes are preserved. If, however, conceptual processing relating to the time period can be reinstated, then this might cue the retrieval of versions of knowledge specific to that time. In other words, just as a particular cue might correspond directly to a specific memory, so a particular type of processing might correspond to a previous type of knowledge: processing in the way we once did might give rise to (partial) retrieval of a past self – including memories, knowledge base, and characteristic types of processing. Maybe something like this occurred with Bugelski's subjects. Whatever the case these ideas are largely speculative, although some of the neuropsychological findings reviewed in Chapter 9 indicate that they may have some applicability.

Learning, problem-solving, and explanation

One feature of learning is that a learner often remembers, or is reminded of, previous learning episodes. Indeed, the view that reminding plays a central role in learning has strongly influenced the recent theories of Schank (see Chapter 6 and below) and other researchers more directly concerned with learning (see, for example, Anzai and Simon 1979). Despite the interest in reminding and learning and the commonly held belief that remindings do occur during learning, there is very little evidence that this is, in fact, the case. There is, however, one excellent study by Ross (1984) which carefully documents the interrelations of reminding and learning.

The starting point for Ross's experiments was based upon the idea that knowledge is retrieved from memory by an elaborated retrieval cue or memory description (see Chapter 7). Ross proposes that, during a learning episode, the learner's representation of the task environment constitutes a memory cue and that this representation is used to retrieve related knowledge from memory. It is assumed that in most cases the learner is unaware of this because s/he is preoccupied with an attempt to solve the current problem. Thus, during the course of learning some task a memory of a related previous learning episode may 'pop' into mind and assist current processing. Ross assumes that remindings most often occur when the learner is a novice at some task and remindings bring to mind knowledge about how to apply procedures and rules. This is because the recalled episodes contain examples of procedure and rule application. Of course, as a learner becomes proficient with a task and/or as the number of learning episodes increase, then the learner may draw upon knowledge abstracted from multiple episodes, and remindings correspondingly decrease.

In order to investigate these assumptions Ross conducted a series of experiments. In his first experiment Ross taught a group of subjects to use a word-processor. For each editing operation subjects learnt two editing methods. For example, if the editing operation was to put a word into the text, then subjects learnt that this could be done by either 'inserting' a word before the selected text or by 'appending' a word after the selected text. Initially subjects learnt these editing operations on different types of text. At test either similar or different texts were supplied and subjects 'thought aloud' while they performed the editing operations. Analysis of subjects' protocols indicated that remindings occurred on 30 per cent of the trials. Many of these remindings were highly specific and subjects would recall, when performing the test trials, how they had failed or succeeded in editing a similar word in the initial learning trials. For example, one subject commented 'Do it way we did "molasses" ', referring to a previous operation on that word (see Ross 1984, Table 2, for other examples). Moreover, when subjects were reminded of a previous text-editing episode, they were also much more likely to employ the editing method they had previously employed in that episode rather than an equally plausible alternative method. Ross's other experiments essentially replicate and extend these findings using a range of different tasks, and show that remindings do not decrease with short periods of practice. Thus it seems likely that specific episodic/autobiographical memories do come to mind in a learning sequence and provide useful knowledge for the learner.

More recently Kolodner and Riesbeck (1986) have collected together a set of readings on what they call 'case-based reasoning'. Case-based reasoning can be contrasted with 'rule-based reasoning'. In rule-based reasoning abstract, decontextualized rules such as 'if-then' rules are acquired and applied by a learner. In contrast, in case-based reasoning knowledge is viewed as being stored in memory representations of previous problem-solving episodes and the learner develops effective ways of indexing memories during the course of learning. One of the major problems facing models of case-based reasoning is how effective indices are constructed and utilized during problem-solving. It is not, however, the intention here to provide a detailed account of the many interesting models which have been developed in this area and the interested reader should refer to the papers in Kolodner and Riesbeck (1986) for more detailed accounts. Rather the purpose of this section is simply to provide something of the flavour of case-based reasoning and indicate how autobiographical memories *might* be used in problem-solving and understanding.

Consider the following example provided by Kolodner and Simpson (1986). A woman is reading a newspaper report on the dispute between Egypt and Israel over possession of the Sinai. As she reads, she is reminded of similar disputes such as that resulting from the Korean War and the dispute between the USA and Panama. These remindings occur because the woman classifies the Egypt–Israel dispute as being one of 'political conflict', involving 'dispute over land ownership', between 'two countries who have histories of military conflicts'. These classifications provide the indices with which to search and access prior knowledge which can be used in understanding the current issue. The woman obviously concludes that the Sinai will be divided, with half going to Egypt and half to Israel. Consequently she is surprised when, later in the newspaper article, she reads that *both* sides have rejected this solution. As she considers this failure of the 'divide-equally' strategy she recalls the following autobiographical memory concerning her daughters:

> Two sisters are quarrelling over an orange. Their mother surveys the situation, and proposes that each sister should take half the orange. One of the sisters complains, since she wants to use the whole peel for baking. Realizing the real nature of the conflict, the mother suggests that the sisters divide the orange agreeably: one will take the fruit and eat it, while the other will take the peel and use it for baking.

(Kolodner and Simpson 1986: 100)

At this point the woman realizes that a similar solution was reached in the Panama Canal dispute, when the real goals of the participants were recognized and the US relinquished economic and political control of the region to Panama but retained military control. Accordingly she predicts that Egypt will regain political and economic control of the Sinai and Israel will retain military control.

In case-based reasoning, then, classification of the current problem is used to index related episodes in memory and the retrieved memories employed in understanding the current problem. The impetus behind case-based reasoning was Schank's original work on dynamic memory, discussed in Chapter 6. More recently Schank (1986 a and b) has extended this work to encompass models of explanation generation and understanding. In this work Schank has attempted to classify different uses of memories in explanation generation and different patterns of explanations. One feature of the model is that understanding and explanation are essentially the same process. That is they both involve indexing appropriate knowledge structures, perhaps by generating appropriate classifications of an event. Explanation, however, differs from understanding in that retrieved knowledge is explicitly and consciously applied to the current task. For instance, in order to understand how to behave in a restaurant one does not need consciously and explicitly to retrieve previous memories of eating in restaurants – although this may occur anyway. Rather, very well learnt knowledge structures such as scripts can be directly applied in understanding these sorts of stereo-typed events. As Schank points out, it is only when an expectation fails that explicit remindings occur and this, of course, is where explanation begins.

Let us briefly consider one of the examples of explanation generation collected by Schank.

> During the ice storm last night, Suzie and I were in my apartment. Neither of us realized that the snow had turned to freezing rain. We heard a long series of crackles and whooshing sounds. I said that it sounded like trees falling. During the ice storm of '79 (my first real winter) I was nearly killed by a falling limb, and I suppose I am now sensitized to that noise. Suzie was sure that it wasn't trees because there were so many similar noises. When we awoke, it turned out to be dozens of fallen trees.
>
> (Schank 1986a: 147)

This is a very clear example of how a memory might provide an explanation for some current feature in the environment. Perhaps, as the rememberer claims, the sound of the falling trees directly accessed the memory, in which case no classification of the event was required and the memory came 'spontaneously' to mind. Schank (1986a) provides many other such examples across a range of different domains, e.g. social contexts, behaviour patterns, etc.

The research reviewed in this section can best be seen as providing preliminary evidence that autobiographical memories may play some role in problem-solving, reasoning, and explanation. However, many more investigations will be required if we are to understand this wider role of autobiographical memory. For instance, do remindings occur for all types of explanations? Maybe in areas where expertise has developed remindings play no role at all. More importantly it might be argued that remindings are epiphenomena. That is, although memories do come to mind when problem-solving, reasoning, and explaining, these recalls occur *after* the critical knowledge has been accessed and applied to the current task. In this case the conscious recollection of past events would play no determining role in problem-solving, reasoning, and explaining. Indeed, the Korsakoff patients discussed in Chapter 9 might be a paradigm case in which remembering cannot occur but, none the less, tasks can still be learnt. Thus the present findings are suggestive rather than conclusive.

What is an autobiographical memory?

In Chapter 1 we saw that researchers have identified a number of distinguishing features of autobiographical memory – such as imagery and self-reference. Indeed, it was suggested in Chapter 1 that autobiographical memories might differ from other types of long-term knowledge on the basis of a characteristic pattern of features: the pattern of these features is specific to autobiographical memories but any single feature might be shared with other types of knowledge (see Table 1.1, p. 14). In later chapters we saw that many of these features have been extensively investigated in subsequent research. However, this 'featural' approach does not help us greatly in understanding how specific autobiographical memories might be employed in conceptual processing and reasoning. The problem is that, currently, there is no model of the representation of specific memories. One of the few suggestions about the form of specific memories was made by Schank (1982) when he suggested that memories are encoded in a fragmentary way with different fragments stored with the specific knowledge structures used to process particular event features. It is not clear, however, just what an autobiographical memory might be according to this proposal. This final section considers, first, one way in which Schank's proposal might be developed and, second, speculates on some purely theoretical aspects of autobiographical memories.

Kahneman and Miller (1986) outlined a model of knowledge representation which contained many features pertinent to understanding the representation of specific experiences. The central component of their model is the idea of a 'norm'. A norm is a temporary pattern of activation in memory arising in response to some type of probe, e.g. event, object, concept. A norm might contain activation patterns of probe-related memories, semantic knowledge, and other types of knowledge. Within the norm, different elements are activated to different degrees and the activation is aggregated over elements to define the norm. Kahneman and Miller (1986: 136) comment:

> The central idea of the present treatment is that norms are computed after the event rather than in advance. We sketch a supplement to the generally accepted idea that events in the stream of experience are interpreted and evaluated by consulting precomputed schemas and frames of reference. The view developed here is that each stimulus selectively recruits its own alternatives . . . and is interpreted in a rich context of remembered and constructed representations of what it could have been, might have been, or should have been. Thus, each event brings its own frame of reference into being.

Thus a norm not only consists of a diffuse set of activated knowledge but also specifies alternatives to the current interpretation. Three further important aspects of this model are that norms, their elements, and constructions, do not have to be conscious;

norms can be constructed and reconstructed during a processing episode; norms which are frequently evoked/constructed will eventually be stored in memory. On this later point Kahneman and Miller argue that only 'summary statistics' are stored rather than raw data – in other words, some abstract rather than detailed record of processing is retained in memory.

Before applying this model to the representation of specific autobiographical memories we will introduce two modifications. First, assume that *all* normative models are stored in long-term memory but that accessibility is determined by the amount of subsequent retrievals and/or integration of a model with complex and elaborate pre-existing knowledge structures. If a stored model is not accessed frequently or is not integrated in some way with other knowledge, then accessibility rapidly diminishes. Second, assume that, when a normative model is stored in memory, the resulting representation contains both summary information and some detailed norm-specific knowledge. Perhaps summary knowledge represents a record of how the norm was constructed and used, whereas detailed knowledge represents fairly literal accounts of, say, major processing changes made on-line to the norm.

Consider now the encoding of a fairly commonplace experience: eating out at a restaurant with some friends. The first point to note is that this is a complex event which is extended in time, contains multiple actors, actions, and locations. Moreover, this type of event would inevitably be associated with a variety of emotions and meanings for the different actors involved. At the outset a norm is constructed which is comprised of various types of knowledge activated to different degrees and specifying alternative outcomes and interpretations. As the event unfolds over time the norm is constantly updated and modified and new alternatives and interpretations constructed. At the close of the event a summary record of the norm is stored in long-term memory and it is this norm which is the specific autobiographical memory of the event.

Much of what occurred at the restaurant will not be memorable in the sense that this can be directly retrieved from memory. Rather the norm will contain only detailed records of event features which correspond to changes in the structure and content of the norm. These might be expectation failures such as those discussed by Schank – maybe the restaurant had sold out of wine and so customers had to drink beer or non-alcoholic soft drinks with their meal. Norm changes might also relate to distinctive breaks in activity, for instance, first entering the restaurant, having a drink in the bar, being shown to the table, eating, paying, and then leaving the restaurant. Maybe detailed records of specific event features which marked these activity changes are preserved in the norm.

A norm for the event of eating out with friends will also, however, contain much non-event information. For instance, knowledge about why one chose to be there, how interpersonal relations proceeded, what the event meant for the self, and how one felt during and after the event. Particularly rich sets of norm alternatives may have been computed for these aspects of the event. Perhaps the changes in these alternatives are also stored in some detail. Indeed, alternatives here should, presumably, relate to a person's current self, past self, and possible selves (see Chapter 5).

Already then we have a highly complex (summary!) representation of a comparatively simple and familiar event. Clearly the representation of this norm can be accessed by many different routes in memory. For instance, the norm might be accessed through the subsequent activation of a knowledge structure which represented stable rather changeable knowledge in the norm. Perhaps the norm simply contained a record to the effect that a restaurant script had been followed when ordering the meal. Thus a restaurant script can be used to access the norm even though no event-specific knowledge connects the two structures. On the other hand, the norm might be accessed through a single concept such as 'beer', maybe the expectation failure has become strongly connected to the conceptual representation of this concept. The norm could be further processed once in memory so that it becomes more closely integrated with other knowledge structures. For example, perhaps an event which occurred during the dinner led to a re-evaluation of the self and so the norm becomes integrated with the self-system and the structure of autobiographical memory.

The main point of this norm account of the representation of autobiographical memories is that memories become entangled in many knowledge structures during the process of encoding – much as Schank originally suggested (see also Barsalou, 1986). It is, therefore, hardly surprising that memories 'pop' into mind during activities such as conceptual processing, problem-solving, reasoning, and explaining. It would be remarkable if this were not the case. Moreover, memories serve an important function in that they provide examples of norms created in the past; they provide illustrations of how knowledge can be, or has been, used. Unlike Schank's suggestions, however, the norm account of memories assumes that the features which make up complex events are linked together by virtue of the summary record of their processing. Thus, although there may be bidirectional connections between memories and (many) other knowledge structures, the knowledge within a memory is held together by the norm constructed in the processing of a specific event. A single autobiographical memory is then a complex representation with elaborate intersections with many other parts of the knowledge system and is held together by a summary normative account of on-line, and subsequent, processing.

There are a number of advantages to this norm model of the form of specific auto-biographical memories. If autobiographical memories are summary records of dynamic online processing then they will inherently tend to preserve the external structure of an event – changes in the composition of a norm will, at least in part, correspond to changes in the structure of an event. Thus the nested structure of events, as described by Neisser (see Chapter 6), will be at least partly reflected in the normative model of on-line processing. A norm will also represent implicit and explicit interpretations of an event – the personal meanings of experience. Norms, however, are also vulnerable to overwriting and/or interference. When a person next has dinner at a restaurant with friends, the norm which is constructed will, presumably, recruit the previous norm. The two representations which result will be highly confusable. Unless the original norm has been integrated in memory in some distinctive way, then it may become impossible to differentiate that norm from others. It seems possible that norms are representations which cannot be directly accessed in the sense that they are simply retrieved and inspected. Rather, norms have to be reconstructed in the context of some current norm. This may explain why 'clouding' of autobiographical memories occurs in certain types of brain damage, emotional disorders, and old age (see Chapters 8 and 9). The cognitive resources required to reconstruct a norm are impaired in some way and memories then lack details and the role and status of knowledge indexed by the norm cannot be evaluated.

Specific autobiographical memories are complex representations and one way in which to think about these representations is in terms of summary records of on-line dynamic processing. But autobiographical memories also have other unique characteristics, one of which is that they represent *personal meanings*. Indeed, this appears to be a defining feature of autobiographical memories. Other types of knowledge also represent meaning, but not necessarily personal meaning. For instance, the propositions that '2 + 2 = 4' and 'A canary is a bird' are meaningful, and these types of knowledge have been extensively investigated, but they do not carry personal meaning in the sense that my memory of 'two canaries given to me as a birthday present when a child' does. The dominant philosophy in cognitive psychology is that of *functionalism* or, less formally, the computational view of the mind. One of the main beliefs of functionalism is that an abstract description can be constructed which will adequately describe all cognition. Just as a mathematical theorem can be constructed which exactly describes, say, computation, so a similar abstract theory can be constructed which exactly describes human cognition. Indeed, the computational approach to cognition takes the theory of computation as, at least, the starting point for a functional model of mind. The representation in human memory of propositions such as '2 + 2 = 4' and 'A canary is a bird' have long been modelled in this way, and we saw in Chapters 6 and 7 that similar computational models of autobiographical memory are currently popular in cognitive psychology. Recently, however, some reservations about this approach have begun to emerge (see, for example, Putnam 1988). Certainly one major problem for an abstract description or theory is how to encompass the personal meaning for individuals of representations such as autobiographical memories.

Kolers and Smythe (1984) have raised some of these issues within cognitive psychology by conducting a reappraisal of the concept of a *symbol*. They point out that there are different classes of symbols and that different symbol classes give rise to different types of symbol systems. Consider the distinction between *dense* and *articulated* symbols. One key difference between these symbols is that dense symbols cannot be copied exactly (and are said to be 'uncopiable'), whereas articulated symbols can be copied exactly:

> The distinction is illustrated by an appeal to the arts, where copiable arts are called allographic and uncopiable arts are called autographic. A novel or musical score is normally allographic inasmuch as true copies exist when the letters or notes and the spaces between each are put down in proper order; the nature of the surface on which the copy is printed, the color of its ink, the device doing the printing are all irrelevant to the production of a true copy of the score or script. A painting, in contrast, is autographic in that changing any of its features changes the work, the symbol, itself; here the symbol is a particular rather than copiable template.
>
> (Kolers and Smythe 1984: 293)

The symbols employed in the computational approach to mind are allographic copiable symbols and they exist within an articulated symbol system in which (computational) rules specify unambiguously and exactly how symbols may be combined. Kolers and Smythe's general point is that symbols in human cognition are dense, non-copiable, and exist in a system in which rules and reference are not exactly defined. One more important point made by Kolers and Smythe is that symbols in human cognition are necessarily historic. That is to say that particular representations of knowledge in human cognition entail a specific history. Autobiographical memories, then, correspond very closely to Kolers and Smythe's characterization of dense symbols. More generally, it might be argued that personal meanings must be represented in dense symbol systems which preserve their unique history and unique status for the individual.

This does not mean, however, that an abstract description of cognition is not possible. Rather, the aim in recognizing that different types of symbols have different properties is simply to point to the drawbacks of assuming that human cognition can be described by one particular type of symbol system. Presumably some aspects of human cognition can, and should, be modelled within articulated-symbol systems. Other aspects will require different types of symbol systems and it may be that autobiographical memories and personal meanings are best modelled within a dense-symbol system. The problem facing cognitive psychology is how to integrate these two different modes of symbolization. More particularly, the problem facing students of autobiographical memory is how to build models which account for personal meaning and, within the bounds of the present discussion, this would be the problem of how to operate upon dense symbols.

Conclusions

The research reviewed in this chapter has demonstrated that autobiographical memories play a role in certain types of conceptual processing and in problem-solving. In order to accommodate these findings the nature of the representation of specific autobiographical memories was considered. The view was developed that specific autobiographical memories are summary records of dynamic models built on-line in the processing of an event. One implication of this view is that memories are entangled with many other types of knowledge in long-term memory and so have multiple access routes which inevitably means that memories will be involved in a wide range of different types of cognitions. Perhaps the thematic structure of autobiographical memory outlined at the start of the chapter is chiefly employed in representing aspects of the self and only directly utilized when explicit memory retrieval must be undertaken. Finally, we touched upon the problem of personal meaning and it was proposed that a defining feature of autobiographical memories was that they inherently represent personal meanings for a specific individual. This led to a reappraisal of the class of theory that can be used to model autobiographical memory. It was argued that computational models do not appear to offer any way in which to capture the personal meaning and idiosyncratic history of autobiographical memories. Memories are like paintings in that they cannot be exactly copied and a model of autobiographical memory must encompass this. The study of autobiographical memory, then, represents a challenge to the cognitive psychologist and the challenge is how to understand personal meanings.

• REFERENCES

Albert, M.S., Butters, N. and Brandt, J. (1981). 'Patterns of remote memory in amnesic and demented patients.' *Archives of Neurology*, 38, 495–500.

Albert, M.S., Butters, N. and Levin, J. (1979). 'Temporal gradients in retrograde amnesia of patients with alcoholic Korsakoff's disease.' *Archives of Neurology*, 36, 211–16.

Anzai, Y. and Simon, H.A. (1979). 'The theory of learning by doing.' *Psychological Review*, 86, 124–40.

Baddeley, A.D. (1986). *Working Memory*. Oxford, Clarendon Press.

Baddeley, A.D. and Hitch, G. (1977). 'Recency re-examined.' In Dornic, S. (ed.). *Attention and Performance, VI*. Hillsdale, NJ, Erlbaum.

Baddeley, A.D., Lewis, V. and Nimmo-Smith, I. (1978). 'When did you last . . .?' In Gruneberg, M.M., Morris, P.E. and Sykes, R.N. (eds.). *Practical Aspects of Memory*. London, Academic Press, 77–83.

Baddeley, A.D. and Wilson, B. (1986). 'Amnesia, autobiographical memory, confabulation.' In Rubin, D.C. (ed.). *Autobiographical Memory*. Cambridge, Cambridge University Press, 225–52.

Bahrick, H.P. (1983). 'The cognitive map of a city: 50 years of learning and memory.' In Bower, G. (ed.). *The Psychology of Learning and Motivation: Advances in Research and Theory*, vol. 17. New York, Academic Press, 125–63.

Bahrick, H.P. (1984). 'Semantic memory content in permastore: 50 years of memory for Spanish learned in school.' *Journal of Experimental Psychology: General*, 113, 1–29.

Bahrick, H.P., Bahrick, P.O. and Wittlinger, R.P. (1975). 'Fifty years of memory for names and faces: a cross-sectional approach.' *Journal of Experimental Psychology: General*, 104, 54–75.

Barclay, C.R. (1986). 'Schematization of autobiographical memory.' In O.C. Rubin (ed.). *Autobiographical Memory*. Cambridge, Cambridge University Press, 82–99.

Barclay, C.R. and DeCooke, P.A. (1988). 'Ordinary everyday memories: some of the things of which selves are made.' In Neisser, U. and Winograd, E. (eds.). *Remembering Reconsidered: Ecological and Traditional Approaches to the Study of Memory*. New York, Cambridge University Press: 91–125.

Barclay, C.R. and Subramaniam, G. (1987). 'Autobiographical memories and self-schemata.' *Applied Cognitive Psychology*, 1, 169–82.

Barclay, C.R. and Wellman, H.M. (1986). 'Accuracies and inaccuracies in autobiographical memories.' *Journal of Memory and Language*, 25, 93–103.

Barsalou, L.W. (1985). 'Ideals, control tendency and frequency of instantiation.' *Journal of Experimental Psychology: Learning Memory and Cognition*, 11, 629–54.

Barsalou, L.W. (1986). 'The instability of graded structure: implications for the nature of concepts.' In Neisser, U. (ed.). *Concepts and Conceptual Development*. Cambridge, Cambridge University Press, 101–40.

Barsalou, L.W. (1988). 'The content and organization of autobiographical memories.' In Neisser, U. and Winograd, E. (eds.). *Remembering Reconsidered: Ecological and Traditional Approaches to the Study of Memory*. New York, Cambridge University Press, 193–243.

Barsalou, L.W. and Sewell, D.R. (1985). 'Contrasting the representation of scripts and categories.' *Journal of Memory and Language*, 24, 646–65.

Bartlett, F.C. (1932). *Remembering: A Study in Experimental and Social Psychology*. Cambridge, Cambridge University Press.

Bohannon, J.N. (1988). 'Flashbulb memories for the Space Shuttle disaster: A tale of two theories.' *Cognition*, 29, 179–96.

Borrini, G., Dall Ora, P., della Sala, S., Marinelli, L. and Spinnler, H. (1989). 'Autobiographical memory. Sensitivity to age and education of a standardized inquiry.' *Psychological Medicine*, 19, 215–24.

Brewer, W.F. (1986). 'What is autobiographical memory?' In Rubin, D.C. (ed.). *Autobiographical Memory*. Cambridge, Cambridge University Press.

Brewer, W.F. (1988). 'Memory for randomly sampled autobiographical events. In Neisser, U. and Winograd, E. (eds.). *Remembering Reconsidered: Ecological and Traditional Approaches to the Study of Memory*. New York, Cambridge University Press, 21–90.

Brown, N.R., Rips, L.J. and Shevell, S.K. (1985). 'The subjective dates of natural events in very-long-term memory.' *Cognitive Psychology*, 17, 139–77.

Brown, N.R., Shevell, S.K. and Rips L.J. (1986). 'Public memories and their personal context.' In Rubin D.C. (ed.). *Autobiographical Memory*. Cambridge, Cambridge University Press, 137–58.

Brown, R. and Kulik, J. (1977). 'Flashbulb memories.' *Cognition*, 5, 73–99.

Brown, R. and McNeill, D. (1966). 'The "tip-of-the-tongue" phenomenon.' *Journal of Verbal Learning and Verbal Behaviour*, 5, 325–37.

Bugelski, B.R. (1977). 'Imagery and verbal behaviour.' *Journal of Mental Imagery*, 1, 39–52.

Bunuel, L. (1985). *My Last Breath*. London, Fontana.

Burke, D., Worthley, J. and Martin, J. (1988). 'I'll never forget what's-her-name: ageing and tip of the tongue experiences in everyday life.' In Gruneberg, M.M., Morris, P.E. and Sykes, R.N. (eds.), *Practical Aspects of Memory: Current Research and Issues*, vol. 2. Chichester, John Wiley, 113–18.

Butler, R.N. (1963). 'The life review: an interpretation of reminiscence in the aged.' *Psychiatry*, 26, 65–76.

Butters, N. and Albert, M.S. (1982). 'Processes underlying failures to recall remote events.' In Cermak, L.S. (ed.), *Human Memory and Amnesia*. Hillsdale, NJ, Erlbaum.

Butters, N. and Cermak, L.S. (1986). 'A case study of the forgetting of autobiographical knowledge: implications for the study of retrograde amnesia. In Rubin, D.C. (ed.), *Autobiographical Memory*. Cambridge, Cambridge University Press, 253–72.

Cermak, L.S. (1976). 'The encoding capacity of a patient with amnesia due to encephalitis.' *Neuropsychologia*, 14, 311–26.

Cermak, L.S. (1984). 'The episodic/semantic distinction in amnesia.' In Butters, N. and Squire, L.R. (eds.), *The Neuropsychology of Memory*. New York, Guilford Press, 55–62.

Cermak, L.S. and O'Connor, M. (1983). 'The anterograde and retrograde retrieval ability of a patient with amnesia due to encephalitis.' *Neuropsychologia*, 21, 213–34.

Christianson, S. (1989). 'Flashbulb memories: special, but not so special.' *Memory and Cognition*, 17, 435–43.

Clark, D.M. and Teasdale, J.D. (1982). 'Diural variations in clinical depression and accessibility of memories of positive and negative experiences.' *Journal of Abnormal Psychology*, 91, 87–95.

Clark, H.H. (1973). 'The language-as-fixed-effect fallacy: a critique of language statistics in psychological research.' *Journal of Verbal Learning and Verbal Behaviour*, 12, 335–59.

Cohen, G. (1986). 'Everyday memory.' In Cohen, G., Eysenck, M.W. and LeVoi, M.E. (eds.). *Memory: a cognitive approach*. Milton Keynes, Open University Press.

Cohen, G. (1988). 'Memory and ageing: toward an explanation.' In Gruneberg, M.M., Morris, P.E. and Sykes, R.N. (eds.). *Practical Aspects of Memory: Current Research and Issues*, vol. 2. Chichester, John Wiley, 78–83.

Cohen, G. and Faulkner, D. (1986). 'Memory for proper names: age differences in retrieval.' *British Journal of Developmental Psychology*, 4, 187–97.

Cohen, G. and Faulkner, D. (1987). 'Life span changes in autobiographical memory.' *Human Cognition Research Laboratory, Tech. Report No. 24*.

Cohen, N.J., McCloskey, M. and Wible, C.G. (1988). 'There is still no case for a flashbulb-memory mechanism: reply to Schmidt and Bohannon.' *Journal of Experimental Psychology: General*, 117, 336–8.

Colegrove, F.W. (1899). 'Individual memories.' *American Journal of Psychology*, 10, 228–55.

Coleman, P.G. (1986). *Ageing and Reminiscence Processes: Social and Clinical Implications*. Chichester, John Wiley.

Conway, M.A. (1987). 'Verifying autobiographical facts.' *Cognition*, 25, 39–58.

Conway, M.A. (1988a). 'Images in autobiographical memory.' In Denis, M., Engelkamp, J. and Richardson, J.T.E. (eds.). *Cognitive and Neuropsychological Approaches to Mental Imagery*. The Hague, Martinus Nijhoff, 337–46.

Conway, M.A. (1988b). 'Vivid memories of novel, important, and mundane events.' Unpublished manuscript.

Conway, M.A. (1989). 'Conceptual representation of emotions: the role of autobiographical memories.' In Gilhooly, K.J., Keane, M.T.G., Logie, R.H. and Erdos, G. (eds.). *Lines of Thinking*, vol. 2, 133–43. Chichester, John Wiley and Sons Ltd.

Conway, M.A. (1990). 'Associations between autobiographical memories and conceptual knowledge.' *Journal of Experimental Psychology: Learning, Memory and Cognition*, in press.

Conway, M.A. and Bekerian, D.A. (1987). 'Organization in autobiographical memory.' *Memory and Cognition*, 15(2), 119–132.

Conway, M.A. and Bekerian, D.A. (1988). 'Characteristics of vivid memories.' In Gruneberg, M.M., Morris, P.E. and Sykes, R.N. (eds.). *Practical Aspects of Memory: Current Research and Issues*. Chichester, John Wiley, 519–24.

Conway, M.A. and Montgomery, S. (1990). 'On the intersection of public and private history: recency and autobiographical memory.' Manuscript submitted for publication.

Crovitz, H.F. and Harvey, M.T. (1979). 'Early childhood amnesia: a quantitive study with implications for the study of retrograde amnesia after brain injury.' *Cortex*, 15, 331–5.

Crovitz, H.F., Harvey, M.T. and McKee, D.C. (1980). 'Selecting retrieval cues for early-childhood amnesia: implications for the study of shrinking retrograde amnesia.' *Cortex*, 16, 305–10.

Crovitz, H.F. and Quina-Holland, K. (1976). 'Proportion of episodic memories from early childhood by age.' *Bulletin of the Psychonomic Society*, 7, 61–2.

Crovitz, H.F. and Schiffman, H. (1974). 'Frequency of episodic memories as a function of their age.' *Bulletin of the Psychonomic Society*, 4, 517–18.

Csikszentmihalkyi, M. and Beattie, O.V. (1979). 'Life themes: a theoretical and empirical exploration of their origins and effects.' *Journal of Humanistic Psychology*, 19, 45–63.

Dall Ora, P., della Sala, S. and Spinnler, H. (1989). 'Autobiographical memory. Its impairment in amnesic syndromes.' *Cortex*, 25, 197–217.

De Renzi, E., Liotti, M. and Nichelli, P. (1987). 'Semantic amnesia with preservation of autobiographical memory. A case report.' *Cortex*, 23, 575–97.

Dudycha, G.J. and Dudycha, M.M. (1941). 'Childhood memories: a review of the literature.' *Psychological Bulletin*, 38, 668–82.

Edwards, D. and Middleton, D. (1988). 'Conversational remembering and family relationships: how children learn to remember.' *Journal of Social and Personal Relationships*, 5, 3–26.

Erikson, E. (1978). *Adulthood*. New York, W.W. Norton.

Fitzgerald, J.M. (1988). 'Vivid memories and the reminiscence phenomenon: the role of a self narrative.' *Human Development*, 31, 261–73.

Fitzgerald, J.M. and Lawerence, R. (1984). 'Autobiographical memory across the life-span.' *Journal of Gerontology*, 39, 692–8.

Fivush, R. (1984). 'Learning about school: the development of kindergartener's school scripts.' *Child Development*, 55, 1697–1709.

Fivush, R. (1987). 'Scripts and categories: interrelationships in development.' In Neisser, U. (ed.). *Concepts and Conceptual Development: Ecological and Intellectual Factors in Categorization*. New York, Cambridge University Press, 234–54.

Fivush, R. (1988). 'The functions of event memory: some comments on Nelson and Barsalou. In Neisser, U. and Winograd, E. (eds.). *Remembering Reconsidered: Ecological and Traditional Approaches to the Study of Memory*. New York, Cambridge University Press, 227–82.

Fivush, R., Gray, J.T. and Fromhoff, F.A. (1987). 'Two year olds talk about the past.' *Cognitive Development*, 2, 393–410.

Forbes, D.D.S. (1988). 'A two-year-old's memory observed.' *The Psychologist: Bulletin of the British Psychological Society*, 1, 27–31.

Franklin, H.C. and Holding, D.H. (1977). 'Personal memories at different ages.' *Quarterly Journal of Experimental Psychology*, 29, 527–32.

Freud, S. (1905/1953). 'Fragment of an analysis of a case of hysteria.' In Strachey, J. (ed.). *The Standard Edition of the Complete Psychological Works of Sigmund Freud*, vol. 7. London, Hogarth Press.

Freud, S. (1909/1962). 'Two short accounts of psycho-analysis.' In Strachey, J. (ed.). *The Standard Edition of the Complete Psychological Works of Sigmund Freud*, vol. 10. London, Hogarth Press.

Freud, S. (1916–17/1963). 'Introductory lectures on psychoanalysis.' In Strachey, J. (ed.). *The Standard Edition of the Complete Psychological Works of Sigmund Freud*, vols. 15 and 16. London, Hogarth Press.

Freud, S. and Breuer, J. (1893/1974). 'Studies on hysteria.' In Strachey, J. (ed.). *The Standard Edition of the Complete Psychological Works of Sigmund Freud*, vol. 2. London, Pelican Books.

Friedman, W.J. and Wilkins, A.J. (1985). 'Scale effects in memory for the time of events.' *Memory and Cognition*, 13, 168–75.

Galton, F. (1883). *Inquiries into Human Faculty and its Development*. London, Macmillan, 1st edition.

Garofalo, J. and Hindelang, M.J. (1977). *An Introduction to the National Crime Survey*. Washington D.C., US Department of Justice.

Gathercole, S.E. and Conway, M.A. (1988). 'Exploring long-term modality effects: vocalization leads to best retention.' *Memory and Cognition*, 16(2), 110–19.

Gibson, J.J. (1979). *The Senses Considered as Perceptual Systems*. Boston, Houghton Mifflin.

Gilligan, S.G. and Bower, G.H. (1984). 'Cognitive consequences of emotional arousal.' In Izard, C., Kagan, J. and Zajonc, R. (eds.). *Emotions, Cognitions, and Behaviour*. New York, Cambridge University Press.

Harvey, J.H., Flannary, R. and Morgan, M. (1986). 'Vivid memories of vivid loves gone by.' *Journal of Social and Personal Relationships*, 3, 359–73.

Holding, D.H., Noonan, T.K., Pfau, H.D. and Holding, C.S. (1986). 'Date attribution, age, and the distribution of lifetime memories.' *Journal of Gerontology*, 41, 481–5.

Holland, C.A. and Rabbitt, T.M.A. (1990). 'Autobiographical and text recall in the elderly: an investigation of a processing resource deficit.' *Quarterly Journal of Experimental Psychology.* (42A) 3, 441–70.

Huttenlocher, J., Hedges, L. and Prohaska, V. (1988). 'Hierarchical organization in ordered domains: estimating the dates of events.' *Psychological Review*, 95, 471–84.

James, W. (1890/1950). *The Principles of Psychology*, vol. 1. New York, Dover Publications.

Johnson, M.K. (1983). 'A multiple entry, modular memory system.' In Bower, G.H. (ed.). *The Psychology of Learning and Motivation: Advances in Research Theory*, 17, 81–123. New York, Academic Press.

Johnson, M.K. (1985). 'The origin of memories.' In Kendall, P.C. (ed.). *Advances in Cognitive-Behavioural Research and Therapy*, 4, 1–27. New York, Academic Press.

Johnson, M.K. (1988). 'Reality monitoring: an experimental phenomenological approach.' *Journal of Experimental Psychology: General*, 117, 390–4.

Johnson, M.K., Foley, M.A., Suengas, A.G. and Raye, C.L. (1988). 'Phenomenal characteristics of memories for perceived and imagined autobiographical events.' *Journal of Experimental Psychology: General*, 117, 371–6.

Johnson, M.K. and Raye, C.L. (1981). 'Reality monitoring.' *Psychological Review*, 88, 67–85.

Kahneman, D. and Miller, D.T. (1986). 'Norm theory: comparing reality to its alternatives.' *Psychological Review*, 93, 136–53.

Keenan, J.M. and Baillet, S.D. (1980). 'Memory for personally and socially significant events.' In Nickerson, R.S. (ed.). *Attention and Performance, VIII*. Hillsdale, NJ, Erlbaum, 651–70.

Kihlstrom, J.F. and Harackiewicz, J.M. (1982). 'The earliest recollection: a new survey.' *Journal of Personality*, 50, 134–48.

Kinsbourne, M. and Wood, F. (1975). 'Short-term memory processes and the amnesic syndrome.' In Deutsch, D. and Deutsch, J.A. (eds.). *Short-term Memory*. New York, Academic Press.

Kolers, P.A. and Smythe, W.E. (1984). 'Symbol manipulation: alternatives to the computational view of mind.' *Journal of Verbal Learning and Verbal Memory*, 23, 289–314.

Kolodner, J.L. (1978). 'Memory organization for natural language data-base inquiry.' *Yale University Department of Computer Science, Research Report*, 142.

Kolodner, J.L. (1983). 'Maintaining memory organization in a dynamic long-term memory.' *Cognitive Science*, 7, 243–80.

Kolodner, J.L. and Riesbeck, C.K. (1986). *Experience, Memory, and Reasoning*. Hillsdale, NJ, Erlbaum.

Kolodner, J.L. and Simpson, R.L. (1986). 'Problem solving and dynamic memory.' In Kolodner, J.L. and Riesbeck, C.K. (eds.). *Experience, Memory, and Reasoning*. Hillsdale, NJ, Erlbaum, 99–114.

Linton, M. (1975). 'Memory for real-world events.' In Norman, D.A. and Rumelhart, D.E. (eds.). *Explorations in Cognition*. San Francisco, Freeman, 376–404.

Linton, M. (1978). 'Real-world memory after six years: an in vivo study of very long-term memory.' In Gruneberg, M.M., Morris, P.E. and Sykes, R.N. (eds.). *Practical Aspects of Memory*. London, Academic Press, 69–76.

Linton, M. (1982). 'Transformations of memory in everyday life.' In Neisser, U. (ed.). *Memory Observed: Remembering in Natural Contexts*. San Francisco: Freeman, 77–81.

Linton, M. (1986). 'Ways of searching and the contents of memory.' In Rubin, D.C. (ed.). *Autobiographical Memory*. Cambridge, Cambridge University Press, 50–67.

Livingston, R.B. (1967). 'Brain circuitry relating to complex behaviour.' In Quarton, G.C., Melnechuck, T. and Schmitt, F.O. (eds.). *The Neurosciences: A Study Program*. New York, Rockefeller University Press, 499–514.

Lloyd, G.G. and Lishman, W.A. (1975). 'Effect of depression on the speed of recall of pleasant and unpleasant experiences.' *Psychological Medicine*, 5, 173–80.

Loftus, E.F. and Marburger, W. (1983). 'Since the eruption of Mt. St. Helens, has anyone beaten you up? Improving the accuracy of retrospective reports with landmark events.' *Memory and Cognition*, 11, 114–20.

McClelland, J.L., Rumelhart, D.E. and the PDP research group (1986). *Parallel Distributed Processing: Explorations in the Microstructure of Cognition*, vol. 2. Cambridge, MA, Bradford Books.

McCloskey, M., Wible, C.G. and Cohen, N.J. (1988). 'Is there a special flashbulb-memory mechanism?' *Journal of Experimental Psychology: General*, 117, 171–81.

McCormack, P.D. (1979). 'Autobiographical memory in the aged.' *Canadian Journal of Psychology*, 33, 118–24.

Markus, H. (1977). 'Self-schemata and processing information about the self.' *Journal of Personality and Social Psychology*, 35, 63–78.

Markus, H. and Nurius, P. (1986). 'Possible selves.' *American Psychologist*, 41, 954–69.

Meltzer, H. (1937). 'The present status of experimental studies on the relationship of feeling to memory.' *Psychological Review*, 37, 124–39.

Neisser, U. (1962). 'Cultural and cognitive discontinuity.' In Gladwin, T.E. and Sturtevant, W. (eds.). *Anthropology and Human Behaviour*. Washington DC, Anthropological Society of Washington.

Neisser, U. (1976). *Cognition and Reality*. New York, W.H. Freeman.

Neisser, U. (1981). 'John Dean's memory: a case study.' *Cognition*, 9, 1–22.

Neisser, U. (1982). 'Snapshots or benchmarks?' In Neisser, U. (ed.). *Memory Observed: Remembering in Natural Contexts*. San Francisco, Freeman, 43–8.

Neisser, U. (1986a). 'Remembering Pearl Harbor: Reply to Thompson and Cowan.' *Cognition*, 23, 285–6.

Neisser, U. (1986b). 'Nested structure in autobiographical memory.' In Rubin, D.C. (ed.), *Autobiographical Memory*. Cambridge, Cambridge University Press, 71–81.

Neisser, U. (1988). 'What is ordinary memory the memory of?' In Neisser, U. and Winograd, E. (eds.). *Remembering Reconsidered: Ecological and Traditional Approaches to the Study of Memory*. New York, Cambridge University Press, 356–73.

Neisser, U. (1989). 'Five kinds of self-knowledge.' *Philosophical Psychology*, 1.

Nelson, K. (1986). *Event Knowledge: Structure and Function in Development*. Hillsdale, NJ, Erlbaum.

Nelson, K. (1988). 'The ontogeny of memory for real events.' In Neisser, U. and Winograd, E. (eds.). *Remembering Reconsidered: Ecological and Traditional Approaches to the Study of Memory*. New York, Cambridge University Press, 244–76.

Nelson, K., Fivush, R., Hudson, J. and Lucariello, J. (1983). 'Scripts and the development of memory.' In Chi, M.T.H. (ed.). *Contributions to Human Development (Vol. 9): Trends in Memory Development Research*. New York, Kargar.

Nemiah, J.C. (1969). 'Hysterical amnesia.' In Talland, G.A. and Waugh, N.C. (eds.), *The Pathology of Memory*. London, Academic Press, 107–16.

Nigro, G. and Neisser, U. (1983). 'Point of view in personal memories.' *Cognitive Psychology*, 15, 467–82.

O'Connell, B. and Gerard, A.B. (1985). 'Scripts and scraps: the development of sequential understanding.' *Child Development*, 56, 671–81.

Piaget, J. and Inhelder, B. (1973). *Memory and Intelligence*. London, Routledge & Kegan Paul.

Pillemer, D.B. (1984). 'Flashbulb memories of the assassination attempt on President Reagan.' *Cognition*, 16, 63–80.

Pillemer, D.B., Goldsmith, L.R., Panter, A.T. and White, S.H. (1988). 'Very long-term memories of the first year in college.' *Journal of Experimental Psychology: Learning, Memory, and Cognition*, 14, 709–15.

Pillemer, D.B., Rinehart, E.D. and White, S.H. (1986). 'Memories of life transitions: the first year in college.' *Human Learning*, 5, 109–23.

Putnam, H. (1988). *Representation and Reality*. Cambridge, MA, Bradford Books, MIT Press.

Reason, J.T. and Lucas, D. (1983). 'Using cognitive diaries to investigate naturally occurring memory blocks.' In Harris, J.E. and Morris, P.E. (eds.). *Everyday Memory, Actions and Absent-mindedness*. London, Academic Press, 53–70.

Reiser, B.J., Black, J.B. and Abelson, R.P. (1985). 'Knowledge structures in the organization and retrieval of autobiographical memories.' *Cognitive Psychology*, 17, 89–137.

Reiser, B.J., Black, J.B. and Kalamarides, P. (1986). 'Strategic memory search processes.' In Rubin, D.C. *Autobiographical Memory*. Cambridge, Cambridge University Press, 100–21.

Ribot, T. (1882). *Diseases of Memory: An Essay in the Positive Psychology* (W.H. Smith, trans.). New York, Appleton.

Robinson, J.A. (1976). 'Sampling autobiographical memory.' *Cognitive Psychology*, 8, 578–95.

Robinson, J.A. (1980). 'Affect and retrieval of personal memories.' *Motivation and Emotion*, 4, 149–74.

Robinson, J.A. (1986a). 'Autobiographical memory: a historical prologue.' In Rubin, D.C. (ed.). *Autobiographical Memory*. Cambridge, Cambridge University Press, 19–24.

Robinson, J.A. (1986b). 'Temporal reference systems and autobiographical memory.' In Rubin, D.C. (ed.). *Autobiographical Memory*. Cambridge, Cambridge University Press, 159–90.

Rogers, T.B., Kuiper, N.A. and Kirker, W.S. (1977). 'Self-reference and the encoding of personal information.' *Journal of Personality and Social Psychology*, 35, 667–88.

Rosch, E. (1975). 'Cognitive representations of semantic categories.' *Journal of Experimental Psychology: General*, 104, 192–233.

Ross, B.H. (1984). 'Remindings and their effects in learning a cognitive skill.' *Cognitive Psychology*, 16, 371–416.

Ross, M. (1989). 'Relation of implicit theories to the construction of personal histories.' *Psychological Review*, 96, 341–57.

Ross, M. and Conway, Michael (1986). 'Remembering one's own past: the construction of personal histories.' In Sorrentino, R.M. and Higgins, E.T. (eds.). *The Handbook of Motivation and Cognition: Foundations of Social Behaviour*. New York, Guilford Press, 122–44.

Rubin, D.C. (1982). 'On the retention function for autobiographical memory.' *Journal of Verbal Learning and Verbal Behaviour*, 21, 21–38.

Rubin, D.C. and Baddeley, A.D. (1989). 'Telescoping is not time compression: a model of the dating of autobiographical events.' *Memory and Cognition*, 17, 653–61.

Rubin, D.C. and Kozin, M. (1984). 'Vivid memories.' *Cognition*, 16, 81–95.

Rubin, D.C., Wetzler, S.E. and Nebes, R.D. (1986). 'Autobiographical across the lifespan.' In Rubin, D.C. (ed.). *Autobiographical Memory*. Cambridge, Cambridge University Press, 202–21.

Sachs, O. (1985). *The Man who Mistook his Wife for a Hat*. London, Duckworth.

Salaman, E. (1970). *A Collection of Moments: A Study of Involuntary Memories.* London, Longman.

Salaman, E. (1982). 'A collection of moments.' In Neisser, U. (ed.). *Memory Observed: Remembering in Natural Contexts.* San Francisco, W.H. Freeman, 49–63.

Sanders, H.I. and Warrington, E.K. (1971). 'Memory for remote events in amnesic patients.' *Brain,* 94, 661–8.

Schachtel, E. (1947). 'On memory and childhood amnesia.' *Psychiatry,* 10, 1–26.

Schacter, D.L. (1987). 'Implicit memory: history and current status.' *Journal of Experimental Psychology: Learning, Memory, and Cognition,* 13, 501–18.

Schank, R.C. (1982). *Dynamic Memory.* New York, Cambridge University Press.

Schank, R.C. (1986a). *Explanation Patterns: Understanding Mechanically and Creatively.* Hillsdale, NJ, Erlbaum.

Schank, R.C. (1986b). 'Explanation: A first pass.' In Kolodner, J.L. and Riesbeck, C.K. (eds.). *Experience, Memory, and Reasoning.* Hillsdale, NJ, Erlbaum, 139–66.

Schank, R.C. and Abelson, R.P. (1977). *Scripts, Plans, Goals, and Understanding.* Hillsdale, NJ, Erlbaum.

Schmidt, S.R. and Bohannon, J.N. (1988). 'In defense of the flashbulb-memory hypothesis: A comment on McCloskey, Wible, and Cohen.' *Journal of Experimental Psychology: General,* 117, 332–5.

Shallice, T. (1988). *From Neuropsychology to Mental Structure.* New York, Cambridge University Press.

Smith, M.E. (1952). 'Childhood memories compared with those of adult life.' *The Journal of Genetic Psychology,* 80, 151–82.

Snyder, M. and White, P. (1982). 'Moods and memories: elation, depression, and the remembering of the events of one's life.' *Journal of Personality,* 50, 149–67.

Squire, L.R. and Cohen, N.J. (1982). 'Remote memory, retrograde amnesia, and the neuropsychology of memory.' In Cermak, L.S. (ed.). *Human Memory and Amnesia.* Hillsdale, NJ, Erlbaum.

Teasdale, J.D. and Fogarty, S.J. (1979). 'Differential effects of induced mood on retrieval of pleasant and unpleasant events from episodic memory.' *Journal of Abnormal Psychology,* 88, 248–57.

Thompson, C.P. (1982). 'Memory for unique personal events: the roommate study.' *Memory and Cognition,* 10, 324–32.

Thompson, C.P. and Cowan, T. (1986). 'Flashbulb memories: a nicer interpretation of a Neisser recollection.' *Cognition,* 22, 199–200.

Thompson, C.P., Skowronski, J.J. and Lee, D.J. (1988). 'Telescoping in dating naturally-occurring events.' *Memory and Cognition,* 16, 461–8.

Tulving, E. (1972). 'Episodic and semantic memory.' In Tulving, E. and Donaldson, W. (eds.). *Organization of Memory.* New York, Academic Press.

Tulving, E. (1983). *Elements of Episodic Memory.* New York, Oxford University Press.

Tulving, E. (1985). 'How many memory systems are there? *American Psychologist,* 40, 385–98.

Tulving, E. and Thomson, D.M. (1973). 'Encoding specificity and retrieval processes in episodic memory.' *Psychological Review,* 80, 353–73.

Wagenaar, W.A. (1986). 'My memory: a study of autobiographical memory over six years.' *Cognitive Psychology,* 18, 225–52.

Waldfogel, S. (1948). 'The frequency and affective character of childhood memories.' *Psychological Monographs,* 62, 1–34.

Warrington, E.K. and Weiskrantz, L. (1982). 'Amnesia: a disconnection syndrome.' *Neuropsychologia,* 16, 233–49.

Wetzler, S.E. and Sweeney, J.A. (1986). 'Childhood amnesia: an empirical demonstration.' In Rubin, D.C. (ed.). *Autobiographical Memory.* Cambridge, Cambridge University Press, 191–201.

White, R.T. (1982). 'Memory for personal events.' *Human Learning*, 1, 171–83.

White, S.H. and Pillemer, D.B. (1979). 'Childhood amnesia and the development of a socially accessible memory system.' In Kihlstrom, J.F. and Evans, F.J. (eds.). *Functional Disorders of Memory*. Hillsdale, NJ, Erlbaum, 29–73.

Whitten, W.B. and Leonard, J.M. (1981). 'Directed search through autobiographical memory.' *Memory and Cognition*, 9, 566–79.

Williams, D.M. (1978). 'The process of retrieval from very long-term memory.' *Tech. Report 75*, La Jolla, Calif., University of California, San Diego.

Williams, D.M. and Hollan, J.D. (1981). 'The process of retrieval from very long-term memory.' *Cognitive Science*, 5, 87–119.

Williams, D.M. and Santos-Williams, S.M. (1980). 'A method for exploring retrieval processes using verbal protocols.' *Attention and Performance*, VIII, Hillsdale, NJ, Erlbaum.

Williams, J.M.G. and Broadbent, K. (1986). 'Autobiographical memory in attempted suicide patients.' *Journal of Abnormal Psychology*, 95, 144–9.

Williams, J.M.G., Watts, F.N., Mcleod, C. and Mathews, A. (1988). *Cognitive Psychology and Emotional Disorders*. Chichester, John Wiley.

Winograd, E. and Killinger, W.A. (1983). 'Relating age at encoding in early childhood to adult recall: development of flashbulb memories.' *Journal of Experimental Psychology: General*, 112, 413–22.

Winthorpe, C. and Rabbit, P.M. (1988). 'Working memory capacity, IQ, age and the ability to recount autobiographical events.' In Gruneberg, M.M., Morris, P.E. and Sykes, R.N. (eds.). *Practical Aspects of Memory: Current Research and Issues*, vol. 2. Chichester, John Wiley, 175–9.

Wood, F., Ebert, V. and Kinsbourne, M. (1982). 'The episodic-semantic memory distinction and amnesia: clinical and experimental observations.' In Cermak, L.S. (ed.). *Human Memory and Amnesia*. Hillsdale, NJ, Erlbaum.

Yarmey, A.D. and Bull, M.P. (1978). 'Where were you when President Kennedy was assassinated?' *Bulletin of the Psychnomic Society*, 11, 133–5.

Zola-Morgan, S., Cohen, N.J. and Squire, L.R. (1983). 'Recall of remote episodic memory in amnesia.' *Neuropsychologia*, 21, 487–500.

· AUTHOR INDEX

• SUBJECT INDEX